W9-DDO-773

THE

REVOLUTION

IN

PSYCHIATRY

ERNEST BECKER

THE

Revolution

IN

Psychiatry

The New Understanding of Man

The Free Press of Glencoe
Collier-Macmillan Limited, London

4490

For information, address:

The Free Press of Glencoe
A Division of The Macmillan Company
The Crowell-Collier Publishing Company
60 Fifth Avenue, New York 11

Collier-Macmillan Canada, Ltd., Toronto, Canada

DESIGNED BY RONALD FARBER

Library of Congress Catalog Card Number: 64-11213

If it were proposed to confine the culture of Astronomy to Navigators alone, loud Homeric laughter would greet the proposal; yet those very laughers would see nothing irrational in confiding the culture of Biology [the science of organism and milieu] to the . . . Medical Profession. . . . But this is an evil which must spontaneously disappear before the advance of Science. . . .

G. H. LEWES (1853, p. 166)

Although powerful institutional pressures lend massive weight to the tradition of keeping psychiatric problems within the conceptual fold of medicine, the scientific challenge seems clear. The task is to redefine the problem of mental illness so that it may be encompassed under the general category of the science of man.

THOMAS SZASZ (1961, p. 297)

ACKNOWLEDGMENTS

The ideas in this book are the product of a long history and of many minds, and my indebtedness will be obvious from the many references cited. I wish personally to thank Professor Stanley Diamond, and Drs. Martin Hoffman, Ronald Leifer, and Thomas Szasz for indispensable critical readings of the manuscript, as well as for continuing, stimulating exchanges on the questions it raises. Naturally, everyone but myself is absolved from responsibility for the final work.

To the society which will value man.
And which, consequently, will institute *a fully critical education*
as a dominant human value.
In this society psychiatry will be an agent of social change,
rather than a shelter from social confusion.

PREFACE

THE IMPETUS to this work is the growing sense of frustration in the human sciences, which has been weighing on us for several decades. It stems largely from our failure to put the various disciplines into some kind of meaningful unity. Disciplinary fragmentation and often simpleminded but feverish fact-gathering are no longer merely inconveniences or obstacles: they are a positive menace to a science of man. We are in effect burying man with our disciplinary proliferation, because we have failed to get a clear, whole perspective on him. The problem is as old as the rise of modern science. By the end of the nineteenth century its dimensions were so stifling that Lester Ward was moved to his inspired attack. Today the science of man is virtually paralyzed by it—we seem to have run the full limit. As I see it there is only one way we can hope to make any headway: by rejoining the rich current of the human sciences that flowed at the beginning of this century, and by offering bold and comprehensive theories and syntheses.

Accordingly, in a previous book, *The Birth and Death of Meaning: A Perspective in Psychiatry and Anthropology,* I made a first attempt to meet the problem of disciplinary fragmentation by proposing a radical recentering of the human sciences. This recentering would take man's sense of self-value as the proper invariant point of reference around which the various disciplines should revolve their efforts and subject matters. As I presented this basic framework it remains largely suggestive, because I did not explain comprehensively how the sense of self-value is sustained in action, nor consequently how it is undermined when action bogs down. Most of the present work attempts to explain just this, over a broad range of behaviors—shame, guilt, jealousy, schizophrenia, depression, love, sadism, and so on. The two independent books, then, are logically complementary: the first sketches an abstract framework for a science of man, and the second provides body for that framework by spelling out several dimensions of individual action. The *single principle* which gives the framework theoretical viability is *the principle of self-esteem maintenance* by the developing organism (Becker, 1962). Having plotted this principle over a broad range of diverse types of actions we can make *deductions* from it. This means that we can proceed to build a mature hypothetico-deductive science.

I do not claim completeness for this approach, or intend to present a "system"; nor do I make any claim to originality. In the history of the human sciences such a man-centered orientation has been proposed several times—Lester Ward's effort remains the model. But what *is* new about the present situation is that only now do we have enough knowledge to begin to forge a broadly inclusive and logically consistent science of man around such an orientation. Thus we can at last see our way out of the disciplinary morass to significant achievements as well as new imaginings and fact-findings. In short, we can finally do what has so far proved wishful, and we can gather the full fruit—a fruit for which generations of conscientious workers in the several disciplines have waited so patiently—namely, a compelling rational basis for moral action.

Admittedly, there are many questions and problems raised by the framework I propose and by the challenge of a man-centered science. They will demand the best efforts, skills, and courage of a variety of talents, working separately in our universities, and in common wherever possible. But the problems should not obscure the fact that the time is now more opportune and ripe than ever to put a man-centered science on a sound, interdisciplinary footing. There no longer seem to be any good scientific reasons for hanging back from exploring these possibilities.

ERNEST BECKER

Contents

INTRODUCTION

LIKE MOST REVOLUTIONS, this one had a quiet start. It has been brewing for over fifty years—perhaps closer to a hundred. It is hardly possible to get a clear perspective at this time because we are right in the middle of its history. Names and dates suggest themselves; they rise up before one's attention as somehow very significant, but the picture is far from clear. Many currents flow together, and the names are legion. The oldest current is the nineteenth-century revolt against positivism, mechanism, and a science that would exclude man and human values: Renouvier, Marx, Lotze, Windelband, Dilthey, Rickert, Bergson—a host of names comes to mind. This is a current that is gathering momentum in the modern existentialist movement with its familiar names: Jaspers, Heidegger, Sartre in philosophy; Binswanger, Buytendijk, Minkowski, Bachelard, Straus, Rollo May, and many others in existential psychiatry.

Joined to this current is the more familiar Freudian revolt against taking reason for granted in human affairs; and then there is the well-known neo-Freudian subrevolt, led by Adler, Fromm, Karen Horney, Harry Stack Sullivan, which sought to broaden his theories. There are curious cross-currents in all this confusion: for example, the image of an ailing William James, in 1909, shaking Freud's hand and opining that the future of psychology rested with him and his theories. But now we are finding that the pre-Freudian tradition has a broadness and sweep that is exactly what we need and have lost. And we are finding one thing above all, a curious paradox: Freud, father-figure of the psychoanalytic uprising, has somehow slipped into the camp of the counterrevolutionaries. At least he looks this way to those who are struggling with the dead weight of the past at this point

1

in history. In the future he will surely attain to his fullest revolutionary stature, but this is not our concern now.

Now things are too muddled and fluid to assign merits. Through the confusion one figure, however, seems to be growing in prominence. For over sixty years John Dewey patiently held out for a broad view of man and society that is now becoming more urgent. In his philosophy are united all the currents in the revolution, and in the future one may be able to say that he marked the epoch. Phenomenology, or the immersion of man in nature and the relationships between organisms and objects; the prominent place of unreason in human affairs; the need for a science of man in society; the primary accent on human values, with science as a tool—it is all there. Dewey's views were so broad that they lacked incisiveness. His writings are so vast and plodding that students do not know where to begin. His categories are neither attention-catching nor sensational. Certainly "doing" and "undergoing," "transaction," and "fusion," are no match for "Oedipus complex," "penis envy," "Id," and "latent homosexuality." But they are more explanatory; they sum up far more of the authentic human drama.

What is the revolution in psychiatry if it can include all these currents? It is the invasion of psychiatry by philosophy and the social sciences. The target in this revolution is the narrow medical view of human ills. The aim of the upheaval is to present a broad behavioral view of human malfunction, and to subordinate firmly the persuasive but inadequate and inverted physio-chemical approach. The medical model offers only a reductionist approach; it cannot serve a true preventive program, even though it has proved useful in ameliorating symptoms. The point of attack in this revolution is on the psychiatric syndromes themselves, which must be re-examined and redefined. The outcome of the revolution, if one reads the signs correctly, should be to accomplish a reconstitution of psychiatry as we now know it; to merge it into a broad, human science so that the study of human malfunction can be placed firmly in a combined science of man in society, to which an enlightened social psychiatry will be a contributing discipline.

This task seems formidable in the face of the dead weight of institutional pressures. But a century of history is already on its side, and recently new impetus has come from within medical psychiatry itself. In re-analyzing the paradigm psychiatric syndrome—hysteria—as a failure in human communication, in cultural behavior, rather than as a mysterious medical failure in "psychosomatic" performance, psychoanalyst-psychiatrist Thomas Szasz (1961) also pointed the way to a reassessment of all so-called "mental illnesses" as broadly culturally behavioral, rather than narrowly medical, phenomena.

It remains, however, to see whether a comprehensive, fully behavioral view of the two most important and baffling psychiatric syndromes, schizophrenia and depression, can be developed. This is the task to which this book is largely devoted. The view of the syndromes presented here draws on fifty years of development in the human sciences. Although it gives a picture of human behavior that includes Freud, it draws also on sociology, anthropology, social psychology, and psychology, as well as existentialism and phenomenology. I have drawn most heavily on the psychology and philosophy of John Dewey. Indeed, Dewey's views on human nature and man's conduct are so prominent in the book that it might almost be subtitled "A Deweyan Theory of Mental Illness." I do not mean by this to implicate Dewey in the views presented here, or to borrow credence for them from his closely reasoned philosophy, although if the theories detailed here do not fare too badly under major criticism, they will stand in support of Dewey's views on education, social criticism, the problem of rational man in democratic society. Furthermore, they substantiate Dewey's transactional philosophy, as it continues the current of pragmatism begun by Peirce and James: we see that by definition "mental illness" refers to action that bogs down, or that is constricted within an extremely narrow range—and this constriction occurs even though thought may continue furiously.

As we examine this thorny, sensitive problem area in human striving we give behavioral support to a basic pragmatist thesis: that mind subserves total organismic striving, that in this universe action is primary.

Thus, the revolution in psychiatry does not reflect narrow sectarian interests. It ranges as broadly as human problems range. The benefit of any revolution is that it places ideas to the fore. It creates partisans, diehards, radicals, new doctrines, and new versions of old doctrines. But everyone and every thought emerges more clearly etched. The sharp light of rational scrutiny is brought to play on a drama that is normally largely whispered in the wings—much to man's woe. Everyone must come foward, speak his piece, and be judged on the merits of his ideas in their relationship to the needs of the time. Nothing is more remorseless or beneficial than this kind of judgment.

As for the plan of the book: The theory of schizophrenia appeared previously as a brief paper in the *Archives of General Psychiatry*; Chapter IV appeared as a paper in *The Journal of Nervous and Mental Disease*. Both theories are considerably reworked, improved, and expanded; especially the theory of schizophrenia, the original of which was a mere sketch for the present comprehensive treatment in three chapters. The rest of the chapters appear for the first time. Chapters I to III are devoted to a transactional theory of schizophrenia, in which it is treated in behavioral language. Chapter I is a general discussion of the problem of human action, devoted to various aspects of a behavioral view of human meaning and experience. This chapter is the most technical part of the book, and after it is read the rest should follow with ease. The discussion of schizophrenia proper (Chapters II and III) is postponed until this view has been detailed. The whole special problem of schizophrenia, then, becomes a review of the general problem of human experience, as it is exacerbated in some individuals. These three chapters contain the basic theoretical orientation. Chapter IV is a brief but comprehensive theory of depression, which complements the preceding chapters and carries their ideas further. Chapters V and

VI present an integral and economical approach to personality functioning, developed in a thoroughgoing philosophical and psychological framework of object relationships. Chapter V contains a critical overview of Freudian and other personality theory and presents a concise understanding of the human personality. Chapter VI continues Chapter V by exploring the post-Freudian view of personality phenomena such as anxiety and emotion, and offers a new clarification of the refractory concepts of shame and guilt. Chapter VII pinpoints the argument of the entire book by viewing the syndromes as coerced means-ends performance. A further case against the possibility of a "scientific psychology" is presented along with a discussion of the problem of identity and of the reach of culture into the human personality. Chapter VIII carries us beyond psychiatry, to a review of how man constructs a human world by means of aesthetics and love. In this way, the chapter sums up the cultural constraints on human reason and well-being from still another point of view; and thus it also sums up the need for a fully social and post-medical approach to the problem of human action.

Taken as a whole, then, the book presents behavioral theories of the two major "mental illnesses." At the same time, it attempts a detailed clarification of major concepts dealing with human action, including a concise view of personality functioning. Hopefully, the work unites in one framework insights from a variety of disciplines and contributes to closing the gap between the social and psychological sciences by attempting a broad statement of the principles of human action. The thread of continuity throughout the work is the reporting of the major mid-twentieth century revolution specifically in the relationship of psychiatry to the human sciences.

The Legacy of Words and Definitions

Scientists, like revolutionaries, are constricted by the old regime. The views that one reacts against determine, in part, the form and content of the reaction. This is an especially difficult problem where one is hoping to take the psychiatric diagnostic categories out of the narrow jurisdiction of medicine, and make them part of a broad, human science. What to do with such words as "schizophrenia," "depression," "psychopathy," "mania," that run through the following pages? They are so heavily overlaid with a tradition of social opprobrium, of narrow medical usage, that we retain them in our formulations at our own peril. I attempt, in the following pages, to redefine these words so that the behaviors they reflect will lose the connotation and constriction of medical "syndrome" labels. By the very retention of these categories from "the old regime," however, I may seem at times to be giving substantiation to traditional psychiatric diagnosis.

This is not my aim, although the effect may be unavoidable. It is well to be clear at the very beginning that these words are used only as pointers; in the present stage of knowledge and history it would be impossible to communicate without them. As they are used here they mean quite different things than they do in medical psychiatry; they permit us to conceptualize ways of being in the world, ways of reacting to experience, to which no medical valuation is attached. It is also well to state at the very outset that my own position in regard to some of the behaviors detailed here is not neutral, but my valuation is not a narrowly medical one: it stems rather from a perspective of social criticism, which indeed is part of the revolution. Thus, as we see in Chapter VII, "normal" does not mean "not ill"— it means "not stupid."

Schizophrenia represents a special difficulty in terms of new and old definitions, and in terms of valuations. As we outline it, in Chapters I to III, it is synonymous with the broad problems of human existence. I use the word "schizophrenia" here to cover a whole continuum. Thus, it includes usage in two interchangeable senses which are overlapping and may be confusing. In the first sense it is nearly synonymous with *Homo sapiens*, since everyone shares the schizophrenic's problems to some extent. In a second sense, I use it to describe individuals at the most acute end of the schizophrenic continuum, those who suffer more than ordinarily from the attempt to be human. Even though schizophrenia becomes crippling in its extreme forms, one has only to glance down a list of historical figures to see how creative even seriously "schizoid" individuals have been. "Schizoid" is perhaps a better word than schizophrenic, but it also has a pejorative valuation. There is no way to dodge the issue. Schizophrenia refers to variations on the distinctively human mode, *with all that this entails*: namely, the immense enrichment of human life precisely because of and by means of human variation. Certainly if history had eliminated, or changed, individuals from among those we now call "schizophrenic," mankind would be immeasurably poorer in art, science, and religion than it is now; our world would be unrecognizable. Karl Mannheim, addressing himself to this very problem, wondered whether society would indeed be able to get along without utilizing the historical contributions of its introverted members (1953, p. 300).

Our task here is to contribute to an understanding of what these medical labels really mean in a behavioral sense. It is always up to society to decide what kinds of individuals and what kind of contributions it will propagate and value. Perhaps when we will have clearly understood the kinds of individuals to which the "syndrome" labels apply, these labels will no longer be useful. It is this task to which this book is devoted. Perhaps too, all considered, it is really addressed to the newer generation.

The human mind is not a goal. Nature has started the bird's brain after already putting potentially the human on its way.

(1955, p. 253)

I

Schizophrenia

PRELIMINARY: THE NATURE OF HUMAN

EXPERIENCE AND MEANING

IT IS JUST OVER a hundred years since schizophrenia was recognized as a "disease," and over fifty since it was given its name. The history of this hundred years (as I read it) contains the ready explanation for our long puzzlement over its nature. It is the history of the ascendance of medical psychiatry, of the complete annexation of mental malfunctioning as a medical prerogative. Nineteenth-century diagnosticians redoubled efforts to keep man under medical wraps and dress his behavioral disorders in Greco-Latin cant. Thus the science that knew least about total symbolic man and most about the animal body fully established its sacrosanct

9

domain. We are coming to know now that it had no business there.

In 1860, those who could have shed light on the malfunction of the symbolic animal had not yet arrived and developed their anthropological, sociological, and psychological ideas. Only toward the end of the nineteenth century did Darwinism become fully assimilated, and only then did it become possible to understand the development of the human organism in evolution and in culture. Baldwin, James, Dewey, McDougall, George Mead, and a host of others had enough to do in systematizing their ideas about human uniqueness; it could hardly be expected that they would lay claim to the domain staked out by Kraepelin, Bleuler, Charcot, Freud, Jung, Adler, and other medical psychologists. The result of this lopsided jurisdictional development was that human malfunction has continued to be treated largely in nineteenth-century disease categories up to the present day.

The theoretical picture of schizophrenia that I am going to introduce in the following pages is thus one that might have been elaborated much earlier. In fact it was, in part, and by such unlikely "psychiatrists" as Bergson and Dewey—but not specifically in reference to any "mental illness." Only the existentialists and phenomenologists seem to have grasped very early the purport of philosophy and psychology to a thorough understanding of psychiatric problems. We will see that it is not without significance that James ended as a philosopher, and that Jaspers drifted from psychiatry to philosophy after completing his monumental *General Psychopathology*. It is even more significant, in fact, that Dewey's philosophy tended toward a thoroughgoing social criticism. Thus the major thinkers of the twentieth century tried to grapple with the full problem of the uniqueness of man's nature in society, while most of the minor medical practitioners bent themselves studiously to look for chemical and other malfunction of the brain. True, Freud, Jung, and especially Adler, focused very early on the source of human difficulties in early social relations. But as we read the historical record now, it seems that their efforts were hobbled by their medical affiliations: ultimately, their broadest generalizations served only to give weight to the medical claims of legitimate jurisdiction over the whole of man's functioning. It was as if to clinch the idea that anything worth knowing about man could be studied by a qualified physician in his office. Only lately have the baffled mind healers turned back to the philosophers for better understanding: Fromm to Marx, Sullivan to George Mead, Binswanger to Heidegger. Thus it is only now that it seems possible to achieve some understanding of the general nature of schizophrenia.

The Problem of Human Action

All organisms are born to act. If we know nothing else about them we at least know this. In the lower forms nature provides a built-in response-readiness, and the organism comes instinctively equipped to handle a sector of the world. Each animal, as Jacob von Uexküll (1957) saw, addresses itself to its own peculiar behavioral world. But nature seems to have treated humans shabbily: only man arrives on the scene with almost no guiding instincts. Devoid of innate mechanisms by which to design a realm of experience, man had to carve out his own. This story has been amply told by ancient and modern philosophers, and we have come to understand man as the uniquely symbolic animal. Man constructs a symbol-world that not only points to things in nature but also provides a rich fund of experience in itself. By means of symbols man has created an outer world richer than that of any other animal. It is saturated with objects that command attention. This symbol-world also forms a reservoir of meaning that can be mined in private—a psychological world of significance that nourishes man when the external world lets him down.

The internal symbol-world serves to clear the external world for action. The symbol designates regularities in the environment and labels organisms according to their qualities; it renders the world predictable and safe for the human actor by informing him of what he can expect from everything around him. Safe, predictable action is the *sine qua non* of survival for any organism; for man it is especially necessary. Anthropologists have determined that every culture must provide this kind of action-world for its members. Each culture must provide answers to what we can call "The Four Common Human Problems." Only when they have been answered can the human animal navigate with comfortable predictability in an otherwise chaotic world:

1. What kind of reactions is one to expect from volatile human-objects?

2. What are the supports and limitations of my powers?

3. In what sequential schema is my action to be embedded?

4. How can I best orient my action to safety and to maximum satisfaction? (cf. Florence Kluckhohn [1950]).

A close scrutiny of these four problems reveals that they all refer to predictability, safety, and satisfaction. They are all concerned with picking out objects in the environment and signaling something about them to the observer. Also, they relate these objects to the actor's powers. In effect, they enable the actor to tell something about events *before* they occur. By signaling the probable consequences of events, these events acquire meaning. An event or an object is "meaningful" when we can predict its effect on us. Meaning is the elaboration of a wide network of dependable relationships and expectancies. It is a framework in which projected action is always possible. The creation of meaning, then, is the creation of action-possibilities, earned by being able to predict the consequences of action.

This is the behaviorist view of meaning elaborated by James Mark Baldwin, Dewey, and George Mead. Meanings do not come into life "ready-made" as it were. Meanings, contrary to the Jungian mythology, are not born with man. Meaning is

created in organismic action as problematic situations are overcome and reduced to predictable habit. Meaning is built up as
a function of reactivity. Bird-watching, for example, is meaningful only because the observer is presented with the *sight* of a
beautiful bird, to which he can *react*, and which he registers
in *a framework* of "birds seen and to be seen." Meaning, for the
organism, reduces itself to a simple sequence: "see, place, and
move forward." Baldwin, after Alexius Meinong, distinguished
between objects which merely "subsist," such as numbers, qualities, propositions; and those physical objects which really "exist"
(1906, pp. 239-241). However, if we take the stance of the active
organism in reference to its objects, we could blur this distinction,
and say that even physical objects merely subsist, until firm behavioral patterns are developed toward them. That is, even physical objects subsist until we actively convert them into existences.
A safe-cracker, for example, may see indubitable meaning in what
barely registers in our perception as a blank space of wall. Underneath it, for him, is an object that permits a whole series of
behaviors.

It is this framework of expectation and prediction that constitutes "mind." From a behavioral point of view, mind on any
organismic level is *the total field of meanings*. In the lower
animals, these meanings are not verbal; they exist only in behavior. In man, they are elaborated into a total field of conscious cause-and-effect; a network of symbolic ramifications which
we are pleased to call conscious mind. Meanings are already in
nature in the form of objects which can be responded to. The
symbol serves merely to make meaning acutely conscious. Thus,
by means of the symbol, predictable consequences of action are
stored up in memory for ready use. Symbols have only to be
scanned by memory, and they hold up to attention the consequences of lived action. The gain in ability to predict is thus
immeasurably richened by accumulated experiences that can be
readily recalled.

Man is the "highest" animal because he has the largest

repertory of behavior. What we call "individuation" can be conceived as a process of growth in the store of dependable and flexible responses. As soon as we develop an apt response, we reduce a problematic situation to an habitual one. The individual, attempting to predict what will happen in a problematic situation, searches himself for potential responses by means of which it can be overcome. He calls up past experiences, combines and recombines in imagination solutions which once worked, and so devises a particular behavioral response. As problematic situations are overcome and reduced to habit the world is *converted* into a meaningful behavioral environment. Objects which heretofore merely *subsisted* are fashioned into objects which *exist* for attention and behavior. An amorphous world of raw events in flux, a world of immediate and unrefined sensation, is reduced to a clear focus: objects are arranged, placed, become more lucid. Sensations become refined as they are referred to things and connected among themselves. Man creates an object world by placing himself behaviorally in it. And he can do this only by fashioning dependable responses to once-mysterious random events.

Now we have a direct and basic definition of meaning and are in a position to understand something crucial about the answers to our four common human problems: "answers" to these problems cannot be imparted merely verbally; they must also be *lived.* They must be fashioned largely *in behavior;* only in this way do they become a secure part of the total experience of the acting individual.

But all this is not apparent to man. We forget easily how painfully we learn. The symbolic animal has one big blindspot: he imagines that he "teaches" his offspring to navigate in the world, that people in society "learn" from the precepts of one another. Being symbolic he imagines that people are fashioned by symbols, that it suffices to stuff their heads in order to render them human and wise. In one sense, of course, this is indisputable: symbols are social, they are learned from others. But to talk about "symbolic learning" is a misleading generalization, because it obscures the true *process* of becoming human: the behavioral process. It is only in this way that the organism can place itself securely in the object world. People are fashioned like all other animals—by behavior. Symbols enter in only to facilitate and enrich the process. The symbol channels and guides behavior, creates a focus on an object, doubles, triples, and multiplies immeasurably the facets of objects for our attention and action. A "hard thing" becomes a "rock." But not merely a rock; it becomes "quartz," possesses "crystals," and so on. There is no limit to where symbols will guide our eyes. But despite this tutoring and deepening, it is the organism that uses the symbol, that must tend away from or toward the object signaled. The organism tends, moves, recoils; the symbol is merely a counter. Behavior, movement, energy-conversion are primary. Symbols are gadflies that edge the organism on, but it is the organism that edges. Man has been so well aided by symbols in his help-less exposure to nature that it seems as though *organisms* exist in a *symbolic* world; that somehow they are subservient to it. But symbols share in an organismic world; the symbol is a part of flesh-and-blood behavior: "Dead men tell no tales."

Why this insistence on the behavioral primacy of the physical organism? In introducing a nonmedical approach to the problem of schizophrenia one would perhaps have expected the opposite: namely, a stress on the importance of symbols in the constitution of the self. This has its important place, and we will discuss it in Ch. II. But paradoxically, it is precisely the total organismic nature of behavior that has been neglected in the medical approach to schizophrenia. The medical accent has been on part-functions, on physiochemistry for the most part. It fell largely to philosophers to elaborate the nature of the total organismic response to experience. And it is by considering this total organismic response that we will gain entree into an understanding of schizophrenia, an entree that we could never gain through the study of part-functions or micro-phenomena. Understandably, perhaps, psychiatric medicine shied away from cogitations on the total organismic nature of behavior because this does not permit localization of function for analysis. It serves only to create a broad, general picture and indicates no focus for ameliorative intervention. It is important to note this because a good deal of the narrowness of the medical approach to human malfunction is due to the problem of attributing causes. Causality, as we know, is not a simple matter in nature: objects and events hang together in complex interrelationships, and if we try to isolate one specific relationship we must leave out a lot of other important influences. This is the well-known difference between simple causality and a coherent field-theory approach to phenomena. But for the purposes of human action, causality always has to be simplified. We attribute cause partly depending on where *we can intervene* in any system. What we call "cause" reflects our *intention* to act, and *the powers* we dispose of. Take, as an example, a TV screen that goes hazy when a certain light bulb becomes loosened in a nearby lamp. If we want (intend) only to clear the screen and it suffices, say, to turn the bulb to do this, we could say that the bulb "caused" the interruption. This hardly does justice to the complex environmental and electromagnetic situation that might be involved, but it does enable us to remedy the situation and to note the "cause." Now, suppose we wanted (intended) to move out of the neighborhood; using poor reception as one of the reasons, we might then say that the cause of the poor reception was the subway train, which loosened the bulb; we should then have to move to a new neighborhood. Or, further, suppose we wanted (intended) to leave entirely and move to some other country. Then we might say that the reception in this city was poor because of all the interferences. Our attribution of cause is partly a function of our intent and powers. The greater our powers and the more comprehensive our intentions, the less narrow need be our attribution of cause. (Of course, if we don't intend to act or intervene at all, we can throw out the notion of causality entirely, as have some modern researchers in social science. Then, Buddha-like, we can contemplate the nature of things in all their glorious complexity.) (Cf. G. W. Allport, 1952, p. 384, n. 3.)

All this is relevent to medical psychiatry. The psychiatrist has had to seek cause *in* the patient, because he had nothing else to work with. He could not attack the whole family, much less the whole of society. Therefore he looked for chemical imbalance, brain damage, poor socialization. But the broadening of psychiatry into social psychiatry is now widening the area of search for causes. When the problem of behavioral malfunction is given over to all the human sciences, the search for causes will finally take place in the broadest possible interrelated area, and we will at last do justice to our subject matter. We will see man as a moving, growing process in society and history.

Theoretical understanding, then—to return from our digression—does not immediately lead to a prescription for therapeutic action. And for those who are tasked to relieve human suffering, to set malfunctional situations aright, understanding alone has little appeal. With the philosopher, of course, it is quite the contrary; he relishes the privacy of his study and the snug fit of his creative armchair. And since our task here is to sketch a theoretical understanding, let us turn to him.

The Problem of Total Organismic Experience

One of Bergson's major contributions to the fund of human ideas was to see thought as derivative of total organismic action. Under the influence of Darwinism, late nineteenth-century philosophy took the mind down from its previously privileged stature, and included it within nature. Mind could no longer be thought of as separate from body: mind served body; and since the main preoccupation of organisms is the negotiation of action, mind was seen to subserve action. For some reason we are strangely reluctant to accept this view. Fifty years after Bergson, R. W. Sperry complained that we still fail to view mental activities in their relation to motor behavior (1952, p. 296). It would be difficult to construe the reason for this. We may imagine that it is due partly to the continuing emphasis on microscopic research. It seems that we will not gain an understanding of man until we cogitate within the broadest possible framework needed to describe his action. This means not only that mind is a function of behavior, it means much more. We saw above that growth and development of the organism takes place by shaping reactive behavior to a well-defined object world. In other words, the world that exists *outside* the organism, and the experience *within* the organism, are complementary aspects of one transactional behavioral process. We usually do not *see* an object unless we are prepared to respond to it in some way. (One has only to recall his first experiences with a microscope, how he may have failed to see anything definite until he was told *what* to look for.)

Preparativeness to respond depends largely on developed neuromuscular patterns. Sperry has phrased this succinctly; perception involves the use of a neural process—a potentially behavioral process: "In so far as an organism perceives a given object, it is prepared to respond with reference to it. This preparation-to-respond is absent in an organism that has failed to perceive. In the case of the triangle, a person who perceives it, is ready to point to it, to outline it with his finger, to show its location and orientation in space, to pick it up, describe it, etc."

He continues, affirming that meanings can exist on a preverbal level; they are a function of behavior: "Animals lacking the verbal and symbolic capacities of man illustrate the principle more simply. The perceiving animal is able to avoid or to approach the triangle, to run under it or up one edge of it, to leap to a corner of it or to pick it up in its mouth by one of the points, etc. The presence or absence of adaptive reaction potentialities of this sort, ready to discharge into motor patterns, makes the difference between perceiving and not perceiving. . . .

That the preparation for response *is* the perception is suggested by further considerations . . ." (1952, pp. 297-301). Thus, in order for an object to exist on any level, *in order for it even to be perceived* as a precise object, the organism must be able to call up a response to it. This view, by the way, is not at variance with psychoanalytic theory, which assigns considerable importance to the kind of objects the patient relates to. That is, either "whole" objects or "part" objects. When we say that a patient relates to people only as "part-objects" we mean precisely that he is able to call up only a limited range of behaviors with reference to them. Thus, to relate to a woman as though she were only a vagina in which to prove one's masculinity means that this is the only self-satisfying behavior which one really knows toward women. The schizophrenic, who relates to people only on the basis of their sex, is not showing a hypersexuality so much as a poverty in behavioral range: he reduces the object to that aspect with which he can cope. Many individuals begin marriage with a mere sexual partner only to discover later that they have learned to relate to a whole person. They discover more of the object as they develop a broader spectrum of behavior toward it. Thus, sexual behavior is not always "preferred" behavior so much as it is at times "desperate" behavior—the individual seeks some kind of avenue of approach to the object. One's whole life is an education in broadening his range of behaviors to objects.

Bergson, who very early linked mind to behavior, understood well the behavioral nature of perception and memory. He noted that our whole intellectual life rests upon sensory-motor functions accumulated through experience (1959, pp. 169-170). The past is stored up in the organism. In his treatise on memory, Bergson, like Ribot earlier (1895), conceived of this storage as taking place in two very different forms: (1) as motor mechanisms, and (2) as personal memory-images. Motor mechanisms, Bergson thought, represent the "truer way" of nature in the storage of memories: motor mechanisms bring memories to bear on the present in the form of total organismic action. Memory-images are more autonomous, more divorced from present action, more inclined "to go their own way." The memory-image merely "represents" past. The motor-memory "*acts* the past" in the present (pp. 65 ff.). Thus, Bergson concluded that motor-memories are memories *par excellence*.

Dewey, perhaps influenced by Bergson, or Ribot, made total organismic experience a central tenet of his philosophy. Dewey's words might well have been Bergson's: "An inexpert huntsman has buck fever when he suddenly comes upon the game he has been pursuing. He does not have effective lines of motor response ready and waiting. His tendencies to action therefore conflict and get in the way of one another, and the result is confusion, a whirl and blur. The old hand at the game may be emotionally stirred also. But he works off his emotion by directing his response along channels prepared in advance: steady holding of eye and hand, sighting of rifle, etc." (1934, p. 97).

These statements by two major twentieth-century philosophers are some thirty years apart. Today, still another thirty years since Dewey wrote the above, little has been achieved in refining these observations. We have only the vaguest, most general notions on how experience is built into the organism. In fact, the passage of time seems to have accomplished the opposite: instead of more refinement we are proceeding to consecutively grosser conceptualizations of the process of organismic modification by experience. The early "memory trace," for example, tended to denote a process whereby precise memories were "stored" in cells in the cortex. The influence of the old mind-body dichotomy is evident here. When this dichotomy was superseded by a view of the total functional organism, "memory trace" came to refer more broadly to the registration of experience (somehow) in the nervous system of the animal.

In the 1920's, Sir Henry Head put forth the idea of "schemata," which seemed at first to make more precise the registration of experience. But Head made it plain that he did not intend "schemata" to refer to a localized, persistent modification of structure. The schemata were to be envisaged as physiological dispositions of the organism. Even more, they could be considered as a *continued physiological process* (Oldfield and Zangwill, 1941-1942, 1942-1943). For the research scientist, this represents very little change from the previous vagueness. Oldfield and Zangwill, in their excellent review of Head's idea of schemata, are uncomfortable over not being able to envisage the formation, continued existence, and functioning of something as important as the schemata (1942-1943). The construct seems too vague to aid scientific conceptualization, it seems in need of more precise definition. But this is only part of the dilemma. The famous psychologist Sir Frederic Bartlett finds the term "schema" at once both too definite and too vague: "It suggests some persistent, but fragmentary, 'form of arrangement,' and it does not indicate what is very essential to the whole notion, that the organized mass results of past changes of position and posture are actively *doing* something all the time; are, so to speak, carried along with us, complete, though developing, from moment to moment" (Oldfield and Zangwill, 1942-1943, p. 116).

In his own thinking, Bartlett retains the term "schema" for want of a better one, but he defines it in his own way: "An active organization of past reactions, or of past experience, which must always be supposed to be operating in any well-adapted organic response" (1954, p. 201). Thus, for Bartlett, past responses of the organism operate as a "unitary mass."

For those interested in precision, this still represents no progress. It is evident that with a view of the schema as a "unitary mass," it is possible to equate schema with the total organism, even with all the cells and processes. Indeed, Mary L. Northway complains that Bartlett's usage employs the schema in several senses: "The schema is at times thought of as comparable to the forces exerted by social custom on behavior, at times as a form which is like that both of a biological standard and of a social pattern, and at times as the content of memory and the apperceptive mass into which new material is received, even as new physiological impulses are registered against the stored effects of previous ones. The confusion which results makes systematic appraisal difficult and experimental development vague. The term itself must be clarified and defined" (1939-1940, pp. 322-323).[1]

Dewey's View of Organismic Experience

All this is instructive. It conveys the striking fact that in over sixty years of cogitation on the manner in which the organism is modified by experience, and in turn brings experience to bear in the present, we have not progressed beyond Ribot's and Bergson's "body-memory." In the present state of knowledge we are still forced to conceptualize in the grossest terms. We have no precise idea about the exact process by which the organism builds itself into a rich and effective acting unit. But the results are there for all to see: We do know that some organisms are "richer," more sensitive, better coordinated than others (cf. Ittelson and Kutash, 1961).

Dewey attempted to explain this some forty years ago, and put forth two categories which we can still find serviceable, in view of the paucity of our knowledge. He defined experience in terms of two major phases: "doing" and "undergoing" (1958).[2] Each organism acts and registers experience. The organism is both a locus of causality and a locus of perception. Every animal that exists in nature, then, possesses, in varying degree, the ability to act and the capacity to experience. Since meaning grows up in action, in the developing and registering of sensitivities to objects, each organism contains a store of meanings (i.e., a capacity to predict the consequences of action to a given range of objects). Each organism becomes, to use a term favored by Baldwin, W. M. Urban, and Dewey, a "funded" reservoir of meanings. There is nothing mysterious or unscientific about this usage. It is equivalent to talking about any of the variations of "neuromuscular set"; and, as we have seen, we need have no qualms about precision or accuracy of definition. The organism as a "funded reservoir of meanings" conveys as much as we now know about total organismic experience.

Using this simple scheme of doing-undergoing and funded experience, Dewey was able to contend that organisms vary in richness, depending on the particular history of each. This variation is not simply a matter of "more" or "less" experience. It is somehow a matter of a more or less proper "balance" between doing and undergoing. The organism that continually finds gratification without delay, frustration, or set-back moves ahead without sufficient registering of experience. It doesn't relate its experience to an assessment of its own powers. This is equivalent to saying that the ego grows by meeting and overcoming obstacles; it tests its powers and learns to overcome obstacles by contriving solutions to painful (but not overwhelming) set-backs. If action is too facile, too fluid, the organism fails to develop several important attributes: It does not learn the capacity to delay action; it becomes deficient in a self-reflective registering of experience; it loses the capacity to refer experiences to properly tested powers; it loses, in sum, a sagacious self-consciousness. For the human animal this loss is critical, since his primary trait is a consciousness of "I" and a self-reflective placing of himself in the world. Circumspect delay and weighing of action is the foundation of conscience.

Too much undergoing, on the other hand, without sufficient experience of the exercise of one's powers, results in other kinds of deficiency. The organism must have a leverage, a purchase with which to regulate experience. Otherwise it is helplessly flooded with sensation. The organism brings order into a chaotic mass of sensation only by exercising its own active powers. Meaning is won by behavior, not merely by registering experience. Meaning "tends to be lacking where incoming sensory impressions, perceptions, ideas, impulses, and tendencies are in confused and disorganized relationships. It is gained wherever these relationships resolve themselves, by any means of analysis, synthesis, rhythmical patterning, perceiving, imaging, symbolical formulation, rationalization, or other activity, into organized and harmonized units, schemes, or systematized wholes" (Pickford, 1950, p. 250). The overly passive organism, failing to exercise its own powers, does not gain the wedge of dependable control. It loses, in fact, some of the power of man's chief tool: namely, the ability to abstract.

The Nature of Abstraction

All animals use abstraction implicitly. The human animal carries it to an extreme refinement. To abstract is to refer an object to one's own intended use. We pick out some aspect of the object that enables us to consider it in the light of our designs. We have learned a special quality of it, through our experience with it. We overlook the manifold other potential qualities of the thing, and consider only how we may act toward it. We group it with a whole class of objects which it resembles in some way: *but the way the object resembles the class depends on how we can use it.* Any proper "sittable-into-thing" becomes a "chair," and we take no time to examine the uniqueness of a particular "sittable-into-thing." We are interested only in its "sittable-into-ness." On the other hand, the artist, like Van Gogh, finds other meanings in a chair; he will dwell upon conveying the existential uniqueness of a particularly striking or personally significant chair: *This* chair. For a dealer in antiques a chair is more than a chair because he can do something else with it, and so on. Otherwise a chair is a chair.

Baldwin went to the heart of the matter and saw that true abstraction is not so much a conceptual singling out of a particular use-aspect of a thing, but rather progress that the *organ-*

ism has made in being able to *adjust* to the thing in a certain way. Baldwin saw that an abstract concept was less a mental picture than it was *an expectation*. "It is the possibility of a *reaction* which will answer equally for a great many particular experiences" (1895, pp. 329-330). Or, in Bergson's words, abstraction "is a similarity felt and lived . . . a similarity which is automatically acted" (1959, p. 154). The universal, by common agreement, "is found in the behaviour of the creature" (Wolters, 1933-1934, p. 135).

We can see where this leaves the organism whose development has been lopsidedly in favor of undergoing at the expense of doing: it will live in a poorer world. Poorer, precisely because inhibitions in its actions will skew the quality of its perceptions. We perceive objects according to our ability to act on them; they come to *exist* for us, rather than merely *subsist*, on the basis of our powers to include them in our action schema. Not only will the organism which lacks experiences accumulated through the exercise of its powers tend to be swamped by relatively undifferentiated sensation; its world will be less well discriminated, poor in clarity and quality. Poorest of all, of course, is the organism itself, which does not feel its place in a world of things. Lacking objects the organism therefore lacks life meaning.

Here is a crucial result of different approaches to experience. "Doing" organisms and "undergoing" organisms live in different kinds of worlds, with different kinds and numbers of objects. We have here a fundamental way of distinguishing human worlds. As an example of the variation of objects in clarity and discrimination, take the striking blonde in a freshman English class. For the boy in the class who has never had any active experience with girls, she would look different than she does to one who has. For the beginner her face would be a blur of beauty that he would match uncritically to a favorite fantasy-image; not having known other beautiful girls closely, he would be unable to compare in detail features of her physiognomy. To approach her would present a major behavioral problem: What to say, how to stand, how to look—his awkwardness and lack of coordination would be painful. Lacking practiced behavior toward young women, and lacking experience of gratifications from them, he would see girls as he has been told and otherwise learned they look. The girl would merely subsist in his environment as a partly constituted object.

The process of constituting her a fully experienced object could be long and difficult. The freshman would have to say the proper things in order to discover that he could thereby control her responses. She would lose some of her awesomeness as she became controllable by gestures emanating from himself. By making a date and proceeding, say, to the culturally prescribed schedule of holding hands, kissing, and necking, on subsequent dates, the girl-object would increasingly come to exist. The freshman's lived experiences with her would provide him with a fund of motor-readinesses that makes for a new quality of perception: perception as readiness to act; perception underpinned by known expectations; perception that contains a subconsciousness of one's own behavioral repertory. The girl he would see on entering the class at the end of the term would differ markedly as an experienced object from the one who was there at the beginning. She would be a point in space toward which he would tend with a certain sureness, with a practiced efficiency. His whole "seating" in this part of the world would differ in quality. The classroom area would take on a solidity and concreteness: it would become a new behavioral space referable to the sure exercise of his known powers. In this sense, from the point of view of the acting subject, it is fair to say that the locus of the object lies to a considerable extent in his behavior, as well as in the external world. Strictly speaking, it is neither "in" the subject, nor "out there." It is constituted in the transaction. If we insist on "locating" the object—the full external object—we should have to locate it in the *relationship* between acting subject and object. Thus, in the following diagram, we could say that "X" is the locus:

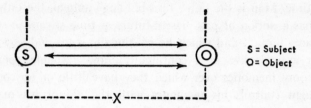

Perception of objects, in sum, is not entirely a matter of what the external world offers; we do not only see and recognize objects, but we bring our entire past to bear in the process. The organism stores up its own modifications, and thereby expands and deepens the content of experience (Dewey, 1934, p. 24). The organism carries with it the richness with which it will apprehend objects.[3]

Action, then, is a process of self-creation. Appreciation of this fact led Goethe to observe that a man is nothing other than the sum total of his acts. It led Dewey to a similar apt observation: "To say emphatically of a particular person that he has soul or a great soul is not to utter a platitude, applicable equally to all human beings. It expresses the conviction that the man or woman in question has in marked degree qualities of sensitive, rich and coordinated participation in all the situations of life" (1958, p. 294).

The Creation of Behavioral Time

In its creation of objects and meaning the organism funds experience and takes control of the external world. While we do not know "where" the organism funds, or precisely what, we can trace the broad outlines of man's enrichment through experience.

The human animal lives in a symbolic world of its own creation. A peculiar characteristic of this world, in comparison to all lower animals, is that it contains a sense of precisely measured time. Man is the only "time-binding" animal, the only one who has a notion of past-present-future, a time stream in which he places himself and which he continually scans and appraises. Lower animals live in a continuous "now," troubled perhaps by sensory memories over which they have little or no control. But man controls his memories with the aid of his massive central nervous system. When the cerebral cortex became a central exchange for the regulation and delay of behavior, the stage for creating a consciousness of precise time was set. The organism could consciously delay response to a stimulus, and present in awareness several alternatives chosen from memory; in this way a controlled time stream came into being. To delay response and call up past solutions for present and future action represents the ultimate of organismic mastery. Man, through memory and delayed response, rose above subjection to the buffetings of ever-new, ever-immediate challenges. Memory sketched out a past, anticipation filled in a future. Man projected his experiences into a time world that gave him an aloofness denied to other animals.

One of Bergson's great contributions, we noted, was to abolish the mind-body dichotomy by showing that thought subserves the acting organism. Another lasting contribution was his conceptualization and analysis of time. Bergson saw that the organism's primary sense of time was a consciousness of "pure duration." This subjective time is a consciousness of being; the organism experiences its own continued existence. Pulsating life has a sense of continued presence in a flow of events. The flow of events takes place in the external world of space; but the primary experience of time is an inner sense.

The other kind of time, clearly different from subjective time, is the objective, physical, homogeneous, or measured time. It is the time that it takes events to happen in the external world, a sequential time. It may be measured by phases of the moon, flooding of the Nile, or complex clocks. But the measured intervals must be regular, they must allow us to put some kind of predictive order into the external world of events. Man patiently studies chaotic nature for harmonies by which to regulate his strivings. If time were to flow without check-points, the result would be a slavery to the random event. This is the world to which the lower animals are condemned.

The fixing of time, then, becomes part of the organism's experience. We might conceive of a generic term to describe this process, and call it behavioral time. Behavioral time would describe the creative merger of inner and outer worlds—the process of integrating measured time-spans into the organism. As the organism behaves with the help of a conceptual time scheme the internal world of subjective time is amalgamated with an external yardstick: memories are placed and controlled and expectations are fixed.

Bergson thought that the measured external space and external time were not properties of things. Neither were they absolutely necessary to our knowing things. But they did serve beautifully as an abstract expression by means of which the organism obtained a purchase for its action (1959, p. 207). By building into all our past and future actions a perspective of measured time, we allow ourselves the much-cherished predictability. The world would subsist without measured time, but it would hardly come to exist for comfortable manipulation; neither could the organism stretch its self-consciousness to remembered dates, places, and things.

Behavioral time, in other words, is part of our creation of objects and meaning. By means of behavioral time we can delineate expectancies in sequential order. Every time we call up a proper response to an object, and can predict its effect on us, we create a time perspective. The conversion of problematic situations into objects is thus also a conversion of problematic situations into time perspectives. When we find out that action A, leads to result N, through stages B, C, D, we get a new view of A, and a new feeling toward it (Frank, 1938-1939). We can then no longer view action A without girding ourselves to experience the sequence B, C, D, which we know will now lead to N. All this we expect to happen within a specified time lapse. The freshman in our previous example, who constituted the blonde in his class as a full external object, did so by building in a certain time perspective. His future approach to other girls will now *contain a consciousness of this perspective.* He will know that after uttering a greeting, A, events B, C, D will have to transpire before arriving at goal N. B may be, say, the second date, which may have to take place after a respectable delay of one week. C will be the third date, at which time a certain range of behaviors known as petting may be brought into play—providing the girl allowed herself to be kissed at sequence B. Goal N, representing, say, the hallowed "pinning," will be sensed from a perspective of properly elapsed time and action. The sequence A to N will exist in the freshman's behavior, sensed and ready to be brought to bear when the appropriate object is perceived. The creation of behavioral time is thus inseparable from the constitution of full external objects. It is a process of coinciding pure inner time with certain objective expectancies. This weaving together of pure subjectivity and measured objectivity gives the organism a handle by which to predict the course of events in relation to its own intended actions. Self-powers are tallied against the exigencies of sequences to be experienced.[4]

We can see, then, that learning is the accrual of behavioral time. With each learning sequence we extend past remembered time into the present and future (Moulyn, 1947, 1952). Every act of learning is the integration of felt present with some objective past and future correlates. Until we have learned to predict the result of an action we are at the mercy of the present. The instant of learning is the harnessing of future eventualities. As we learn we accumulate funded experience of time perspective in which the organism tends toward the predicted event. But this tending-toward takes place on a felt continuum of measured expectations.[5] The result of learning is that behavioral time perspectives seem to give the organism a gyroscopic integrity; it achieves its own bridging balance between present and future. Thus time becomes part of the "schema" or "set." Each individual becomes an amalgam of time perspectives: a math-problem-solving time; a professional-success time; a seduction-sequence time; a money-accruing time; and so on. With behavioral time the organism builds a span between itself and the world, a span that varies in richness and intricacy according to the particular lived experience of the individual. By linking past-present-future with a broad range of objects the human animal permits himself a confidence and assurance denied to any other. He moves forward securely into a known world.

Space, too, is of two kinds: a habitual action space, circumscribed by the individual's body movements; and an abstract, measured, conceptual space: the kind we draw on a map, or conceive as the shape and bounds of the cosmos. Many primitives have built the action space of their home territories solidly into their every movement. They will infallibly follow out coves and inlets over frozen expanses, but would be unable to chart these things abstractly on a map (Hallowell, 1955, Ch. 9; Cassirer, 1953, pp. 67 ff.). Lived, action space is built into the organism by behavior; distance spanned by habit becomes part of organismic expectancy and rhythm. Conceptual space too becomes part of our cognitive world; but even though we have the road map we are strangers until we have traveled the road.

The Problem of Integration

The creation of measured time and measured space is a peculiarly human attribute by means of which man fits himself more securely into the world than other animals. The creation of objects through behavior is something every animal does. But the development of abstract categories of space and time, in the center of which the individual places himself consciously, is unique in nature. By means of these abstractions man refers himself to intervals and distances which he may never really experience with his total organism. To imagine oneself ceasing to be reborn, for example, after two Kalpa of reincarnations, is to cover conceptually a space-time interval beyond the experiential powers of a single lifetime. Yet this calculation can and does enter into present acts. It can, for a Hindu, become vital to his feeling of safety and well being in the present *to know that he will not* be reincarnated at some specified future time. A sinful present act, to an organism heavy with beliefs about the future, can throw a whole lifetime out of joint by its ominous overtones. In other words, man pays for the advantage of his conceptual space-time world by having it weigh constantly on the present.

Evolution made the development of a symbolic world possible for certain of the higher primates: It gradually increased the period of postnatal dependence of young on their mothers; slowing down in maturation seems to have allowed the brain to grow. In *Homo sapiens* a large brain combined with the gift of language to permit the animal to do something truly unique: each individual learned that he was an "I" with expectations and responsibilities in a world of other "I's." Language, self-reference, responsibility, and values were learned in the long period of postnatal dependence. As the brain grew while the body remained helpless, the individual came to see himself as an object, he could turn in and reflect upon himself. Unlike the cat, instead of merely "being" a body, the symbolic animal finds that he "has" a body. The body becomes a means of placing the symbolic self in the world.

It is this symbolic self that takes command of the world by versatile fabrication of names. Man creates his own world, in large part, and makes it a more comfortable home than the chaotic, raw, event-world of nature. But the comfort of his psychological world, and the advantages of self-reflexivity, are paid for with a heavy price. The infant's long period of helpless dependence fills him with one great anxiety: the anxiety of object-loss, the fear of losing the succoring maternal object.[6] The process of child socialization is one in which this anxiety is (hopefully) gently employed to educate the child into the cultural symbol world. In the interests of keeping his object, the child accepts the gradual regime of disciplinary frustrations necessary to make him an independent cultural actor.

The end result of this training is to constitute an individual with an acute sense of "I," and with notions of proper or improper action. The individual comes to feel warm about his own identity when he acts properly; he tends to feel anxious when he acts improperly or in some mode for which clear-cut prescriptions may be lacking. The child's early fear of object-loss has been skillfully transmuted by his training into the adult's fear of wrong action. The individual's basic sense of primary comfort and warm self-value comes to be inseparable from prescriptions for action that he has learned. Thus we can understand that past, as well as intended, action in man's symbol world always hangs heavy in the present. And, present action becomes a haunting past or an ominous future. To violate a cultural canon may result in a slow roasting of the self-conscious "I" in the hell of eternity.

All this means that for the human animal predictability does not bring peace. Freedom from the tyranny of the present moment is bought with a heavy consciousness of past errors and fear of future repercussions of present errors. The individual loses forever the possibility of securely settling down in the world, even though he has carved it out beautifully for his own use. A consciousness of measured time gives a consciousness of a beginning and an end. Knowledge of imminent death provides an undercurrent to one's highest satisfactions.

We can see how inadequate the idea of "homeostasis" is when applied to human, symbolic behavior. The tidy picture of equilibrium (Stagner, 1951) presented by this concept has no place here. It may suffice as a rough summing up of merely organic processes, as Cannon used it. In his view, the organic processes maintain a level of homeostasis that frees the cognitive individual to act. But this seems to set up a dichotomy between organismic equilibrium and the total conceptual adjustment that man seems to seek. G. L. Freeman rightly objects to what seems implied in Cannon's view, namely, that the body frees the "mind" to act (Freeman, 1948, p. 286). But Freeman goes on to make a correction which leads to a greater error than Cannon's implication (cf. Toch and Hastorf, 1955, pp. 83-84). He says that "all creative efforts of man are fundamentally associated with the maintenance of essential steady states of fluid matrix of the body" (p. 140). To see all human striving as attempts to maintain body equilibrium is simply to continue the reductionist fallacy on a somewhat higher level of total organismic functioning. Truly human motivation cannot be explained by such a view. The fact is that man will *sacrifice his body* to maintain intact *the logical structure* of his *symbolic meaning* framework: the Hindu widow who committed suttee on a stranger's pyre because she imagined this fate to have been preordained in a previous lifetime, attests to this (Hallowell, 1955, pp. 108 ff.). On a level of symbolic meaning, physical values are surpassed.

On crude levels of organismic functioning the integration of organism and environment seems easily acquired. Each organism exists in a certain state of tension, a minus situation which it attempts constantly to overcome. No sooner is food ingested, waste excreted, satisfaction momentarily achieved, than the tension begins again to rise, and equilibrium to slip away. Both Bergson (1959, pp. 15 ff.) and Dewey (1934, Ch. 1) saw that the problem of integration increases sharply as animals progress up the scale. For the simple organism, possessing no distance receptors, tension lies directly between the contact surface and the interior of the organism. With the development of more complex receptors—sight, hearing—the scope of the animal's action is enlarged, and so also is the problem of satisfaction. From mere perception by contact, organisms progressed to a point where they were subject to influences from great distances. Man can see stars which existed hundreds of light years ago. With the perception of distance, gratification is deferred. Satisfaction in the "now" acquires the flavor of rarity. As Bartlett observed (1954), man is blessed with the best distance receptor of all— memory. But this is not an unqualified blessing. The weight of a Kalpa of reincarnations, as we noted, can now hang on an unfulfilled present. A mental patient's memory of anal rape suffered at the age of five invades with sickly undertones each present moment of an otherwise successful life. Each day man draws up a profit-and-loss statement of life's symbolic achievements weighed against a valued image of himself. There can be only momentary and fleeting balance of the scale. A disparate symbol weighted with an unpleasant memory can upset the most intricately equilibrated structure of meaning.

The creation of a rich and dependable object world; the building-in of secure sequences of behavioral time; the comfortable mastery of space; firm links between the acting organism and the external world; all of these add up to solid answers to our four common human problems. "What shall I do? What may I hope? What can I know? What *is* man?" Kant had his own famous version of the dilemma of human action. There seems but one way to reduce man to a livable quietude: by "behaving" the answers in some kind of direct engagement in life. But even in the happiest of circumstances only the moron can enjoy peace. The fullest organismic experience and the most total organismic integration is only a fraction of human fulfillment. Since this is so, we shall be able better to understand the experiences—in the following pages—of less fortunate individuals. We have to see the full complexity and precariousness of human action before we can understand its aberrations.

Notes

1. It is not necessary for scientific constructs to be well defined (although it may be desirable for specific purposes). This demand is a heritage of reductionist research. The fact is that we do not yet have clarification and definition of the schema. Instead, we have been given other terms. Among a wide variety of researchers each has his favorite: Nina Bull uses the term "attitude" (1951, 1955, 1957); David Shakow uses "set" and "segmental set" or "part-set" (1962). H. Helson uses "pooling"; he understands that the organism pools all past and present sensory experiences and establishes an "adaptation-level" or average of its experience (1951, p. 381). G. L. Freeman uses "set" in a global way: it would refer to a complete "repatterning of the internal milieu, including restructurization of glandular controls" (1948, p. 286). A variation is "hypothesis-set," a readiness to perceive and experience which is "confirmed" by an external object. (On the question of precise definition, cf. Ch. III, n. 10.)

2. Schiller very early gave an excellent portrayal of the "receptive" and the "determining" faculties (1954, p. 69); the doing-undergoing conception dates back much more than forty years. Others also used these categories: Bergson, in *Time and Free Will* (1910b), had spoken of "intensity of feeling" and "intensity of effort"; William James had contrasted the "sensitive" type with the "motor" type (Perry, 1935, Vol. 2, p. 272); and Baldwin, too, spoke about "motor attitudes" versus "receptor experiences" (1895, pp. 325 ff.). Baldwin directly anticipated the view of schizophrenia that we will set forth: he saw that mistaken and confused treatment of things, by the child—often called "vague generalization"—is due to *fewer motor attitudes than receptive experiences* (1906, p. 154, n.).

3. Here we should mention a recent criticism of Dewey's doing-undergoing categories by Justus Buchler (1955, pp. 138 ff.). He criticizes Dewey's view that an excess of receptivity may crowd out action, and that, on the other hand, an excess of doing may reduce receptivity. I am not sure that I understand his objection to Dewey, but I do disagree with his conclusion that one man ". . . is not less or more of an assimilative or manipulative being than any other, but a being that in part assimilates different things. . . ." Our whole discussion should show this to be erroneous.

4. Psychological time, then, is part of our primary experience.

Physical or measured time is predictive time that becomes part of our learned experience. We value learning and prediction so much that we tend to slight present experience. One result is that we think external, measured time—an abstraction gained by measuring space—is *the real* time. Another result is that we live more in future, expected time than in present, experienced time. Take, as a striking example, a star we can see, but know is now dead, calculating that it burned out several hundred light years ago. *Even though we now see it, we deny that it is there,* insisting that it is dead. We are affirming, with this insistence, not the fact that we do not "see" the star—but rather, that if we *went to* the star, it would not be there. Hence, the predictive, action value of measured, objective time takes precedence over direct, immediate experience. It seems that man must value the predictive over the present, by the nature of things. Prediction guarantees the life process by enabling future experience. Present experience assures nothing beyond the fact that it can be immediately snuffed out.

5. See Moulyn (1952) here for an excellent illustration of traveling along a road with a road map.

6. Bowlby calls this the "Primary Anxiety"—the basic separation anxiety that is akin to the anxiety thought to be seen in the lower primates (1961, p. 267). It is interesting, in view of our discussion of Freud, James, and Dewey in these pages, that Bowlby places himself in agreement with James's early (1890) and simple observation on primary separation anxiety: "The great source of terror in infancy is solitude" (Bowlby, 1961, p. 266). In this formulation, primary separation anxiety would be distinct from later learning and gratifications. (See also the discussion of anxiety in Ch. VI.)

Dear to us are those who love us, ...
but dearer are those who reject us as
unworthy, for they add another life;
they build a heaven before us whereof
we had not dreamed, and thereby
supply to us new powers out of the
recesses of the spirit, and urge us to
new and unattempted performances.

RALPH WALDO EMERSON
(quoted in Cooley, 1909, p. 320)

II

Schizophrenia

(1) A FULLY TRANSACTIONAL VIEW

WE HAVE SEEN at some length how important it is for the organism to become a rich residue of funded experience. Answers to fundamental questions of being in the world have to be fashioned in behavior (if the organism is to behave in an external object-world). We saw too that no matter how basic this fashioning is, man remains prey to the indeterminacy of his intricate symbol-world. Man acts simultaneously in two worlds, in other words, in an external object-world and an internal symbol-world. Ideally, these worlds are fused, the one supporting the other. Thought finds its primary function in the facilitation of action. But inevitably these worlds "drift

apart." Frustrations in the object-world drive one to seek satisfaction in a fantasy-world. Deprivations in the present lead one
to await satisfaction in a hoped-for future, or lead one to
reminisce in an imaginary, reconstructed past. The dream mode,
like the cinema, brings fantasied fulfillment in a shallowly lived
present. The shortcomings of our world are remedied in fancy
allowing one to transpose the body of his wife into that of his
favorite movie star.

The Problem of the Symbolic Self

These differences between the imaginary and the real worlds
are undoubtedly at the core of the age-old distinction between
mind and matter. We "know" there is a separation. Man's symbol-world and his organic body may be phenomenally fused into
an acting unity; but the symbol-world tends to assert a logical
integrity and autonomy. Symbolic pleasures range further and
wider than organismic ones, they seem to possess a qualitative
uniqueness. Mind and body may not be rooted as different
phenomena, but they express a fact about experience: It tends
to be contained in two disparate modes.

The process begins very early. In fact, its germ is contained
in the slow postnatal development of the higher primates that
we noted earlier. The symbolic self develops a consciousness of
its body as somewhat strange and alien to it. The animal body
comes upon the child's awareness *after* he is already on the way
to becoming a social, symbolic self. In psychoanalytic terms this
process is summed up by saying that the body becomes an object
for the attention of the ego (Szasz, 1957b).[1] The dichotomy is
usually aided by the parent who, seeking to discourage undis-
ciplined physiological functioning, affirms the alienation of the
body to the symbolic self. The child, in order to be loved as a
symbolic identity, as "My Jimmy," learns that the body is a
source of danger to his own feeling of warmth about himself. His

sense of self-esteem tends to be tripped-up by areas of body functioning. Furthermore, as Adler insisted, the child's natural inferiority in a world of powerful adults is something he must overcome. A major means at his disposal is to plunge into the symbol world that is greedily offered for his use. Where physiological relationships are discouraged, and body processes abhorred, the symbol-world provides ready refuge. Not only refuge, but a source of positive rewards from the loved objects, for a display of verbal and intellectual dexterity. The whole humanization process thus enforces a sensed dichotomy (Becker, 1962, Ch. 6).

Let us take a closer look at some of the problems of the symbolic self. This should allow us to pull together roughly most of the ideas so far sketched. We enter here upon a complex area, and cannot expect to see any exact picture. The most that can be done is to trace some broad outlines, to expand upon some obscure hints. In brief, we can get some clear ideas about this major problem area of human functioning, but we cannot reduce it to perfect understanding at the present time. Perhaps for this reason science has been reluctant to treat it: insights that titillate the imagination and the curiosity, or that imply much more than they say, are not the stuff that sound research is made of. But this is the way our phenomena present themselves to us, in the present state of knowledge. The challenge may be scientifically imposing, but we cannot retreat from it into reductionist physio-chemical research (cf. Kety, 1959).

The symbolic self or the self-conscious ego is a real phenomenon. Each individual goes forth into the world with feelings attached to himself as an identifiable person. The self-system, as Sullivan aptly called it, possesses a logical integrity of its own, even though it is "housed" in an organismic body. A word of praise from someone deeply respected can inflate the self-system to bursting proportions, while the body remains the same size. A "swell (swollen) head" is an apt metaphor. The self-system includes in its symbolic inventory all one's possessions: person-objects as well as automobiles, rifles, and bank-vault deposits. One's Cadillac can be more necessary to the self-system's intactness than can one's arm: "I'd give my right arm to own that" comes close to expressing a major truth about man: anything the self identifies with strongly and feelingly, becomes necessary to one's well being. The work of Head and Schilder on the body-schema or body-image, and the ideas of the phenomenologists and existentialists on the body as a "situation," leave no doubt about these remarks.

A word of censure, on the other hand, can undermine the most flourishing self-system. To "deflate the ego" is another apt phrase: a symbolic failure—say, to win a coveted academic prize—acts like a psychic puncture: while the body remains the same size, one's sense of self collapses in a heap. The wish to see the ground open and swallow one in a moment of acute embarrassment again brushes close to reflecting real desires. Primitives have been known *to die* of shame. The self, wounded, saps real life energy. This proves best, perhaps, that although the self-system and the body feed on different nourishment—symbols vs. organic food—they are irrevocably part of one active life. To undermine symbolically one's sense of value is to cripple a total organismic life. But this should not be surprising: since the self is constructed of symbols, of mere word sounds, it can be destroyed by a mere word sound. Since everything that makes man human is contained in his symbolic self, his whole human existence depends on symbolic satisfactions. With the lower animals, on the other hand, we can suppose that the sense of well being depends entirely on how the body is functioning. *The tragedy and grandeur of symbolic man is that his sense of worth is irrevocably inseparable from his symbolic constructions.*

This process begins as the child tries to keep the parents' love by performing according to their desires. He keeps his own sense of warm self-value by fashioning this value in the parents' symbolic currency. He has no alternative if he is to keep the parental love and support. Thus he loses forever the animal ability to regulate his own well being. Even Mephistopheles gave Faust a better bargain than that which parents and society give the child.

Again we must be struck by the difficulties that symbolic man has in negotiating satisfaction in this world. We noted just now how easily self-worlds and body-worlds tend to drift apart. And now we see that the undermining of the self-world alone can cripple or kill the body-world—as fluctuations on a ticker tape caused strong men to leap from tall buildings in 1929. Thus man has a kind of "natural deficit" in negotiating action in nature, a price he pays for being able to name and manipulate things. The deficit and the strength are two sides of the same coin. On the negative side, symbolic indeterminacy and raw exposure to total undermining by sounds and images; on the positive side, the ability to point, place, class, manipulate with sure mastery.

At this point we can return to a problem raised at the very beginning of our inquiry: what gives some individuals a more rich, more complex existence—what makes some "great souls?" We saw that organisms experience in two ways: by doing and by undergoing. We concluded, with Dewey, that an excess of doing tended to empty experience of its content; that an excess of undergoing tended to undermine power. Some "balance" was needed between doing and undergoing: the organism had both to do and to undergo, in some proportionate fashion. The "great soul" seems to be one who has achieved both a richness of experience and a flexibility in action: an apt proportion of the receptivity to undergo and the power to manipulate.

Now it will be obvious, if we but scan our own acquaintances, that there are few "great souls." The timeless monumentality of a Goethe attests to this. Doing and undergoing by their very nature leave room for the widest differences in proportion. The fact is that people vary in capacity to live in a richly experienced world. Not only has man been given an unequal two-sided coin with which to transact life, but each individual comes differently equipped to savor experience. If man pays by nature *for his ability* to manipulate, what about those who pay further *by their inability* to manipulate? What about those to whom doing has never been an easy skill—*who suffer by nature from the self-body dichotomy and who suffer by parental mistraining from lack of organizing powers?*

A close look at the result of this twofold deficit reveals something striking: the lack of power to manipulate results in a relatively empty organism—a "poorly funded" one. Too much receptivity, inability to organize experience and perceptions, leads to an empty organism. And, an organism that is poorly funded tends to exacerbate the self-body dichotomy. A fatal circularity is set up which accentuates the human fate. The result is a paradox: *a person who is more "human" in his self-body dichotomy than are others,*[2] but who, in this very ultra-humanity, is less than human because he cannot initiate action. The human symbolic self is already grotesque—ask any cynical adolescent. But some symbolic selves are more grotesque than others; that is, some have to make ingenious efforts in fantasy in order to fill themselves with experience. Man nourishes his sense of value on his fund of satisfying experiences. But when these experiences do not derive from lived human situations, the sense of value is unreal and otherworldly. The self is grotesque to the degree in which it is contrived; in which it does not rest on real powers gained in real world situations. People who typify this personal dilemma within a natural human dilemma we group roughly under the appellation "schizophrenic." But the "split" is not in *their* thinking; it is in *ours*. We have no word for describing those who are at the same time naturally more-than-human and individually less-than-human.

The Naturally More-Than-Human and the Individually Less-Than-Human

The tapestry of our discussion—the four common human problems—provide indicators for action. But they provide one thing more: When an individual has answered them by behaving them, he provides himself with the one thing most necessary to man. Each individual, in every culture, must feel himself to be a locus of primary value in a world of meaning (Hallowell, 1955). To fail to feel this is to be individually less-than-human. But we seem to have run into a contradiction. We said that in order to feel valuable, one must answer the questions. To answer the questions means to live them, and act them; but one cannot live them or act them unless he feels himself valuable. This circularity, however, is not in our thinking; it is in the nature of the problem. Actually, what happens is that the mother, through nourishing, fondling, and admiring the child, imparts to him his early sense of self-value. This is the initial charge. Thus propelled, he begins to behave the answers to the four common problems. Behaving them and living them, he reinforces his sense of primary self-value. Given the maternal start, then, the circularity is self-reinforcing.

Cultural meaning cannot be "imparted"; it must be achieved in this circular fashion, thus the individual becomes human *and* cultural at one and the same time. Meaning has to be built up day by day, built into the organism, by overcoming problematic situations. Objects and meaning are "created." Early peer contacts, in baseball, playing "hooky," the myriad events of childhood that we term "inconsequential"—these are all a process of converting the world into dependable experiential objects; an environment is created for the individual as he fashions a range of responses to it. Life can only become behaviorally meaningful as this creation and fashioning takes place. Other individuals in interpersonal situations become meaningful objects only as one learns to fashion dependable and organized behavioral responses to them. By means of this acting process, the individual is "indoctrinated" in his culture, in the only way he can be: by being obliged to take part in the meaning that it offers in the continuing hierarchy of problematic situations. Thus the individual not only builds experience into himself, he also builds *himself* into the experiential world of a particular culture. The detached dreamer and nonparticipant is more apt to lack a built-in sense of purpose.

As the youth learns the rules of the cultural staging by living them, as he practices the proper roles, ceremonials and performance parts, he develops a critical sense. This critical sense becomes part of a sure standard for judging the conduct of others. As a self-assured judge of others, one is less vulnerable himself. Furthermore, the building-in of standards sharpens one's visual acuity to further details of action and performance. In the very process of judging the conduct of others, of calibrating their deficiencies against one's own—in the attempt to overcome interpersonal problems—the individual creates measuring scales. These scales permit further refinement of meaning by committing perception to greater symbolic acuity. Critical scrutiny of ideas in problematic performance, in other words, inculcates a more realistic and more binding sense of values. We saw earlier how much *perception* of an object depended on being able to *call up a response* to the object. The nonperformer, in certain situations, condemns himself to be a nonperceiver. The youthful scrimmager sees indubitable meaning and personal commitment in a ball landing three inches from a first-down marker. During all this his schizophrenic peer sideline spectator may only hear noise, the thud of bodies, and see a breathless floating object called a "ball." Only the schizophrenic, with his circumscribed range of gross responses to a threatening world from which he excludes himself, never inches out more secure meaning by perceptual engagement in the details of the experientially and existentially given.

The Crippling of the Power to Act

The schizophrenic seems to have been hobbled at the very beginning by not being given the "maternal start" necessary to initiate the self-reinforcing circularity of manipulation → meaning → self-value. Unless the child is constituted as a locus of primary value, he cannot get the circuit moving. This is not the place to review the growingly vast and well-known literature on early mother-child relationships in schizophrenia. Rather, I am concerned with accentuating a different side of the problem, the long-range developmental aspects of behavior in life situations. I need only mention that failure to love and value the child sets up a primary deficit. The child has no way of knowing that he is valuable unless he observes someone who thinks so. This is very plain. Demonstration of love is proof of love.

Somewhat less plain, and more in the current of our discussion here, is the opposite extreme: the child can be undermined too by considerable maternal attention and love. The natural dependency of the young primate is here accentuated by the mother; the child is forced to become exceptionally dependent. It is this forfeiting of the very ability to act independently that cripples his powers of "doing," and makes him predominantly an "undergoing" organism. One cannot feel self-value unless one becomes a locus of manipulatory causality: "I am doing; therefore, I am" (Goldfarb, 1961, p. 26). It is not enough that one is *told* or shown that he is loved. He must sense his powers in order to feel valuable within himself. The child who gets few rewards for independent behavior and little training in coping with problems unaided by the mother, is almost a sure candidate for psychosis. He suffers from the "silver cord syndrome" (McCord, Porta, McCord, 1962, pp. 70-71).

All animals surround their young with care, and train them for rapid, self-sufficient action and independence from the parents. Only the human animal can fail to give his young proper care,[3] and only he can fail to train them in the exercise and development of manipulatory powers. Humans are not prone to push their "fledglings" out of the nest to force them to fly. Rather, they are apt to bed them suffocatingly into the down. Again, from another point of view, schizophrenia is *par excellence* a human malfunction. The process of unnatural dependence of the child on his mother's powers is aided by something additional. The long period of dependency in the higher primates combines, as we noted, with the slow development of the brain to unusual size. This long period of interaction with another animal of its kind, by a child endowed with a hypersensitive nervous system, results in a process called "identification." In effect, what seems to happen is that the child "becomes" the parent before he is himself. Anecdotes abound on how children discipline themselves by taking the parents' attitude. A period of "de-identification" and detachment from the maternal object becomes necessary in the child's struggle for independence. Psychotherapy reveals scores of cases in which patients cannot conceive of their body belonging to them. The body is the parent's object, and the child reacts to it as the parent does (Anna Freud, 1952, p. 79; Greenson, 1954; Szasz, 1957b, 1960). Excessive dependence may force him to a point of total unawareness of his own body needs—even to ignorance of his own sensations and need for food (Hilde Bruch, 1962). He may forget to eat, or not even know that he wants to eat. Thus, the inability to develop executive, manipulatory functions falsifies one's whole situation in the world. Not only is the body somewhat alien to the self in certain of its functions; it can even be totally alien to a symbolic self that has identified with the succoring parent. Either a lack of basic well being or too much trust can be crippling to the individual.

It is worth mentioning two further ways in which the individual can fail to develop a sense of his own powers. One is conveyed by the now-familiar idea of the "double-bind" (Bateson, *et al.*, 1956). Instead of being given one message, the child is given two or several messages at the same time: "I am punishing you because I love you," etc. Conduct cannot be predicated with certainty; situations come to be surrounded with ambiguous overtones. Crippled from the start is the child's capacity to determine what other people are really like, and what he can expect from them. Crippled too is a sure knowledge of how he is to act in order to satisfy them, or to control their acts in some way. Hence, problems, one, three, and four of the four common problems receive ambiguous answers from the very start; anxiety is aroused in interpersonal situations and straightforward action is undermined.

A final mode of crippling action is what Laing aptly calls the "mystification" process (Laing, unpublished paper). Mystification, which is related to the double-bind but is not identical to it, confuses the child about *who actually did* initiate some action. The child, for example, tells the mother that he has masturbated. To which she says "*My* boy didn't do that." The net effect of this is to convey the message: "You say you did that (or thought that, etc.), but really you *did not*." You are not, in other words, an unambiguous locus of causality. This mystification need not result only from such parental decisiveness—it can result also from the opposite, from "parental perplexity" (Goldfarb, 1961, p. 30) which infects the child. The parent may be frequently paralyzed, indecisive, and bewildered in the face of common experiences, and transmit this to the extremely sensitive child.

Once an undercurrent of fundamental insecurity about one's powers is established, the way is clear for elaborating it into a basic mode of existence. The human tendency to a dichotomy of self and body finds itself stretched here to unusual proportions. Laing has traced brilliantly the difference between what he calls the "embodied" and the "unembodied" person (1960). This is actually a modern elaboration of a basic idea put forth eighty years ago by Ribot (1895, pp. 90, 105). Here is what Laing says at some length:

People who lack a fundamental security . . . do not seem to have a sense of that basic unity which can abide through the most intense conflicts with oneself, but seem rather to have come to experience themselves as primarily split into a mind and a body. Usually they feel most closely identified with the "mind" . . . . Here we have a basic difference in the self's position in life. We would almost have, if the embodiment or unembodiment were ever complete in either direction, two different ways of being human. . . . The embodied person has a sense of being flesh and blood and bones, of being biologically alive and real: he knows himself to be substantial. To the extent that he is thoroughly "in" his body, he is likely to have a sense of personal continuity in time. He will experience himself as subject to the dangers that threaten his body, the dangers of attack, mutilation, disease, decay, and death. He is implicated in bodily desire, and the gratifications and frustrations of the body. The individual thus has as his starting-point an experience of his body as a base from which he can be a person with other human beings . . . he has a starting-point integral in this respect at least. Such a starting-point will be the precondition for a different hierarchy of possibilities from those open to the person who experiences himself in terms of a self-body dualism (1960, pp. 67-71).

The unembodied person, on the other hand, does not feel that his body is a base of operations for the self. Either it belongs to the parent by right of manipulation, prohibition and monopoly; or it belongs to anyone but oneself by forfeit—by failure to learn to use one's powers. Thus the existentialists speak of an "emptying or impoverishment" of the body, in which the self becomes "free" while the body becomes "unfree" or self-estranged (Binswanger, 1958b). It is a process of depletion of the self.[4]

The "unembodied" person is forced into a mode of existence that has decided disadvantages. He loses from the start a sure self-referential framework into which to fund experiences, and from which to look out upon the world. "Weak ego," "poorly established body image," "inadequate body schema," all of these terms apply to this mode of existence. A strong self-concept, more or less firmly rooted in the body, seems a precondition for subsequent accumulation of a rich store of self-related experiences. With no framework to serve as a "steadying flywheel" (Spiegel, 1959, p. 97) a negative circular process is set up: low feeling of value ⟶ sense of depletion of self ⟶ inadequate funding of experience ➔ failure to sense the growth of self-powers, and so on around.[5]

Bergson, also, as we saw earlier, adumbrated over 60 years ago the importance of a "body-memory." He saw the necessity of some kind of "agreement" between firmly rooted body memory, and fleeting image-memory. Some time before Dewey he offered his version of the constitution of a great soul: One in whom body-memory and recall-memory are nicely merged and balanced. "Is it not by the constancy of this agreement, by the precision with which these two complementary memories insert themselves each into the other, that we recognize a 'well-balanced' mind, that is to say, in fact, a man nicely adapted to life?" (1959, p. 146). Bergson understood, in other words, that the whole body had to move to respond to reality, in order for reality to be fully experienced.

But what if the body is not felt to be under one's own aegis? What if one is emptied from it, if it is a source of vulnerability rather than firm orientation? The answer is obvious: the person who tends to be unembodied will tend to be less organized in experiencing interpersonal realities. In this area he will show "stupidity." The *sense* of the external world depends on one's ability to bring to bear his full *senses*.

I use the word "stupidity" advisedly. If meaning is built up through behavior and only through behavior we must, as we saw, accept Dewey's definition of mind: Mind is the total field of operative meanings. Mind is the total field of knowledge of cause-and-effect sequences, sequences that refer to activity. Where one does not have an area of dependable meaning he lacks mind. In interpersonal transactions the schizophrenic thus lacks a mind, or an area of mind. His total field of operative meanings has little or no reference to expectations from person-objects.

Nor does having the proper words, going through the verbal motions, constitute full meaning. Words must reflect total funded meaning. The word sound must join an organismic residue of experience.[6] The gap between word meaning and lived meaning is easily captured by listening to a schizophrenic adolescent recount his biography. Dewey, continuing in the same vein as Bergson (above), stressed that word meanings like "friend" or "enemy" had to stand for something *that was also present in* the organism (1958, pp. 291 ff.). The word had to *make sense*, as well as merely to "signify." Sounds coming from the voice box have to be allied through the nervous mechanism, *with the quality of the lived event* (pp. 291 ff.). Thereby we *feel* what "friend" or "enemy" means in reference to a particular person; we do not merely push the sound out of our voice box. The quality of our lived, funded experience gives body to the symbolic sound. Of course, we can "understand" a word meaning without necessarily having lived through the particular qualitative situation to which it refers. Our total, coherent framework of self-consistent cultural symbolism takes care of this. We know what a unicorn would look like without ever seeing one. We put enough words and images together to constitute it. But subsequent unicorns would no longer be mere word-sound unicorns if we had had some experience with one. If we lack a firm, lived behavioral pattern toward an object, the word meaning is shallow at best. Dewey goes on to give an excellent illustration, by pointing out that "Socrates is mortal" says very little—"S is M will do just as well," to those studying logic out of textbooks. But to those disciples of Socrates who had just heard the news of his condemnation to death, "Socrates is mortal" fuses the total organism. Full connection of mere word sound with total organismic experience is made. It is this same immediate presence of the full sense of a word which occurs in poetry (pp. 291-293). In each individual there will be a difference in the range of experiences that find intimate alliance with words. This may be a clue to one aspect of the puzzling phenomenon of "schizophrenic language." When words no longer refer to potential organismic action, or to any felt organismic involvement, they lose their quality as true language. Dewey's observation is apt: he calls this split between word sound and organismic quality a "shortcircuiting." "When shortcircuiting through language is carried as far as limitation to this [linguistic] apparatus, words are mere counters automatically used, and language disappears" (1958, p. 292). The schizophrenic who is unaware that his language makes no sense seems to have shortcircuited all organismic involvement in sensed meanings.

If mind were composed of mere words, all individuals would have the possibility of being alike—it would suffice to approximate vocabularies. But when we understand mind as the alliance of symbolic with organismic sense, we can see that true mind has to have been lived. Now we affirm again that mere words cannot impart answers to our four common human problems.

To go back to our hypothetical freshman who pays court to the attractive blonde in his English class: It is probable that *Playboy* magazine had provided him with a sufficient vocabulary and imagery of what girls "are like" (if his red-blooded American interests were along these lines). But it is obvious that with all the words in the world he could have no idea of what *a girl* is like, constituted as a total organismic behavioral object. Only his own dependable response pattern, integrating word-counter and total physiological sense, can convey the real meaning of "girl." It seems to be something like this that helps explain certain schizophrenic awkwardnesses: words are not fused to organismic meanings. For example, Anton Boisen, in his courageously frank autobiography (1960), cites his fantastic "love affair" with Alice. Now it is obvious to anyone who reads this that he had little behavioral idea of what a woman was like; whereas he had a highly rarified fantasy picture of a "true love." It is fair to speculate that the word "woman" had little or no real relationship to any secure range of behavioral responses that his organism could call up. Hence when he received a distressing letter from Alice, one of his reactions was an ejaculation (p. 57, n. 1). There seems to have been no organic behavioral correspondence to a culturally appropriate stimulus. "Woman," "me," "love," "body," "failure"— all probably blurred and jumbled together.

Of course, Boisen attributed this utter awkwardness and incommensurateness to his own uncontrolled "evil." The schizophrenic is caught up in his own "stupidity"; he reacts inappropriately and interprets the inappropriate reaction incorrectly. It is little wonder that religion, with its own coherent logic, offers a ready explanatory way out of interpersonal ineptitude and imagined wickedness.

The schizophrenic's inability to experience emotion seems to be another aspect of this problem. There is a difference between mental verbal attitude and total motor attitude. Nina Bull goes so far as to say "no mental attitude without preceding motor attitude" (1951). But the problem seems not that simple. Word sounds can give a mental attitude that may be unrelated, as we saw, to organismic experiences. The symbolic animal seems able to strike a symbolic attitude, which, however, can be unrelated to anything he feels. This is the difference stressed by Magda Arnold—the difference between mere sense perception and emotion. "To perceive or apprehend something means that I know what it is like as a thing, apart from any effect on me. To like or dislike it means that I know it not only objectively, as it is apart from me, but also that I estimate its relation to me, that I appraise it as desirable or undesirable, valuable or harmful for me, so that I am drawn toward it or repelled by it" (1960, Vol. 1, p. 171).

It may be that the word "schizophrenia" is after all apt here: there seems to exist a real possibility of a split between mere apprehension and true experience of meaning. Emotional participation in life is the process of reworking meanings in a total organismic experiential sense. It is a total participation. Where there are no funded organismic meanings to rework, there will be little experience of emotion. Schizophrenic "flatness" strikes us as grotesque for a very good reason: symbolic dexterity divorced from a lived experience of the sense of the words is eerie: it is ultrahuman in a world where there are no gods, where everything that moves and makes itself felt is embodied in flesh.

Fantasy-Objects versus Real Objects

The achievement of ultrahumanity comes about by a process of withdrawing from the human world—a process begun by early withdrawal of the self from the body. Ineptitude in the use of one's powers leads to ineptitude in the world of people. One withdraws from his dealings with unpredictable and anxiety-arousing person-objects, and turns instead to safe and dependable manipulations of symbol-objects. This is something we all do to some extent. Symbol-meanings may not draw on our total organismic experience, but they do have an appeal all their own: they can be hung together in esthetically satisfying fashion: if we succeed in giving our symbol-world some credible cause-and-effect consistency in itself, it presents us with a beautiful structure. This holds for logic, mathematics, or chess endings. Dealing in symbol-meanings means to trace out the ramifications of symbol-events and forfeit a sure knowledge of action-events. Only in self-conscious scientific experiment are the two forged together. In our private lives we are not so rigorous. Our symbol-world and the real world can meet, in fact, at very few points.

The schizophrenic tends to sacrifice one to the other. Thomas Szasz noted this, and pointed out that the impersonal object quality of abstract symbol systems like mathematics are especially valuable for schizoid personalities who seek some kind of objects—something to hold the attention, something that will reflect back an appraisal of the self: "Object-contact may be sought and obtained by means of abstract symbol-systems while at the same time a distance may be maintained between self and object. It is virtually impossible to have a relationship and yet maintain such distance with concrete external objects (people). The fascination with and value of abstractions—whether as 'addiction' to books or as religious or scienitific systems—lies precisely in this" (1961, pp. 145-147).

The result of this option is that it separates the individual further from involvement with his own body. In fact, one curious feature of symbol-systems is that they seem to *call* for the elimination of immediate physiological sense, if they are to be pursued for their own sake. Dewey noted this feature of symbol-systems: mathematics, for example, is by definition an artificial inhibition of immediate issue in conduct. The symbol-system suspends action so that the symbols can be fabricated within themselves. Consummation in the real world of felt, external experience is distracting (1958, pp. 291 ff.). Preoccupation with symbols closes off action in a larger field for the express purpose of elaborating symbolic meanings esthetically within a narrow range. In this process, the body is not only not involved, but it becomes, as Dewey noted (1916, pp. 163-178), "an intruder." The perception of artificial symbolic meanings is best pursued by divorcing bodily activity. (C. S. Peirce noted that he involuntarily held his breath while thinking [Perry, 1935, Vol. 1, p. 432].) To opt for experience in the artificial symbol-world serves, then, to further "disembodiment." In World War I Harvey Cushing noted the effects of spinal transection on human psychology. Cutting off the external world by eliminating afferents from the sacral segments "turned all men into philosophers, even when they had widely diverse personalities and educational and cultural levels" (Kubie, 1961, p. 220).

Not only is the individual separated from his body, by opting for experience in the symbol-world, but he is also separated further from the possibility of acting without anxiety in the real world. It cannot be overstressed that the primary function of knowledge is to facilitate behavior. We plunge into the symbol-world normally only to find some solution to blocked action. Once we find it we apply it to an external problematic situation. Knowledge, as George Mead noted (1936, pp. 350-351), does not belong "to the world of spirit by itself." But the schizophrenic tends more and more to limit it there.[7] He learns the consequences of symbol-events rather than the results of action-events. His knowledge becomes unpragmatic; it tends to confine its function only to the world of the symbol. The symbol-world, we noted, contains its own meanings: logical and esthetic coherence of ideas. Symbol-objects are valid objects of revery, as much as person-objects are valid objects of conduct. But, as Dewey observed (1958, p. 342), symbol-objects "are not as *good* objects" with respect to the direction of subsequent action. What we learn from them, in short, is hardly as dependable as what we learn from the "world of hard knocks." Everyman his own scientist: we have to bring our satisfying symbolic theories to the test of action, to be painfully disproved in the real world. One hard fact is worth a dozen beautifully embroidered symbols if one's intention is to act. In this sense, the schizophrenic never has a firm grasp on "truth." He unblocks all his action in symbols, in theory. He never gets down to the hard unblocking of interpersonal problematic action. "Internal unblocking" is only a partial test of truth—and a partial test is very tenuous. A grip on private meanings is really a firm grasp of ether.

Living in the world of fancy becomes pervasive and exclusive. Besides preferring symbol-objects to person-objects, one comes to shrink from the *very form* of the real. Sartre conveys this nicely: ". . . we must understand what a preference for the imaginary signifies. It is not at all a matter of preferring one sort of object to another. . . . It is not only this or that image that is chosen, but the imaginary state with everything it implies; it is not only an escape from the content of the real (poverty, frustrated love, failure of one's enterprise, etc.), but from the form of the real itself, its character of *presence*, the sort of response it demands of us, the adaptation of our actions to the object, the inexhaustibility of perception, independence, the very way our feelings have of developing themselves" (1961, pp. 210–211). The result of this is that to act in fantasy instead of reality is to *become unreal oneself* (Laing, 1960, p. 90).

One reason for this is that fantasy-action separates one even further from a true appraisal of his powers. The lack of power to act in the real world closes off a chief source of self-knowledge. Fantasy-objects never correct us. Sartre notes that a chief characteristic of imaginary action is that it can have no consequences other than those we wish it to have (1961, pp. 209 ff.). Fantasy-images are poor images, they never surprise us. One can steal a kiss from one's fantasy movie heroine with never a fear of being slapped or hailed into court. Fantasy-images are submissive and compliant. If we strike our fantasied enemy, notes Sartre, no blood will flow, or only the amount that we wish (pp. 209 ff.). Unreal events stop when we stop dreaming them. Hence it is a fundamental error to talk about a "rich fantasy life"—as we do in psychiatric hospitals. Fantasy-images are shallow, disconnected, unsurprising. They are *safe*, but not rich.

Only the real external object surpasses us, leads us on, delights us, confuses, and withholds even as it reveals. In the fantasy-world our powers grow to extreme proportions: there is nothing we cannot do or understand. But in the world of real objects our powers are tested, opposed, our understanding challenged, led on (Wild, 1959-1960). The real object is the source of the only truth we can know, even though we each dress it in somewhat different garb. The fantasy-object permits us to live in falsehood, it supports our paranoia, our sense of injustice, our perception of ugliness and evil where we want to see ugliness and evil. But we cannot see our imagined world reflected in *a real face*, if we *can look* at it. Real external objects purify us, they let out the foul gas of our murky images. Sartre phrases this distinction well:

Thus we can distinguish two irreducible classes of feeling from the very fact of the extraordinary difference that separates the object as an image from the real object: real feelings and *imaginary* feelings. By this latter adjective we do not mean that the feelings themselves are unreal, but that they appear only before unreal objects and that the appearance of the real object is enough to put them to flight at once, just as the sun dispels the darkness of the night. We may attack an enemy in thought, only to find ourselves actually helpless when confronted with his real presence. . . . What has happened?

Nothing, except that the enemy now really exists. A while ago, the feeling alone gave the meaning of the image. The unreal was there only to permit the hatred to objectify itself. Now the present over-flows the feelings completely and the hatred remains in suspense, foiled. This is not what it hated; it is not adapted to that man of flesh and bone, very alive, new, unpredictable. What it hates is but a phantom tailored exactly to its measure. . . . It does not recognize this new creature that opposes it" (1961, pp. 209 ff.).[8]

The unexpected uniqueness, "thingness" and splendor of the real world thus puts the fantasy-images to shame. But the schizophrenic turns less and less to external things. The very fact that the real world dispels makes it unsafe, loaded with anxiety. "Better to reign in hell than serve in heaven." The fantasy-world may not be rich and surprising, but it contains its own quiet charm: the sheer limitlessness of possibility of satisfaction; the effortless manipulation of its symbols and images; the utter impossibility of being contradicted.

People can be roughly divided, then, into those who tend toward living in the external world of person-objects, and those who tend to live in the internal world of fantasy-objects. But let us be on our guard against making these two modes into a real dichotomy. We all live in *both* worlds to some extent. We are showing here, merely, that the proportions vary, and that the person we call "schizoid" or "schizophrenic" is one who tends to live on the internal side of the continuum. This tendency can of course be carried to extreme proportions of inwardness. The whole history of human culture is a history of the inter-action of both worlds: the bringing to bear of man's fantasy-world on the hard world of nature, the interaction of one in the other. The symbol-world, taken in manageable doses, pays dividends in the real world. $E = mc^2$ had to be esthetically and logically satisfying in fantasy before it led to the harnessing of nuclear energy. The symbolic systematizer is by definition the one who finds the real world of things somewhat less satisfying than what he can conjure up in his mind. And whether his symbolic constructions have any relation to reality or not, they always spur people on.

The image-maker has, from the beginning of civilization, tried to fabricate his own answers—or his own version—to the four common human problems. Dissatisfaction with other people's answers, not being able to do as they do, is a stimulus to a private reworking of symbolic meanings. And as soon as one proposes his own new version, others are stimulated thereby. Paul Radin put forth a theory of religion which holds that the maladjusted shaman in primitive culture creates a believable religion by trying to make sense out of his own partly controlled fantasies (1957). From the beginning, it seems, man's fictional world was elaborated by those who weren't satisfied merely to act. But the shaman was fortunate in one sense: he was positively socially rewarded for his very antisocial queerness. He could get back a satisfactory picture of his identity even though he dug deep within and brought up supernatural nonsense that had no relation to reality. Answers to the four common problems have always been at a premium, and man will entertain any implausible offering—from water spirits to virgin births.

The Problem of Identity

Shamanism, however, no longer has a market. With the exception of Holy Roller and snake-handling cults, man has on the whole become more sophisticated and rational. The result is that those with luxuriant fantasy lives no longer have available social roles. Also, there is another side to the coin. In a society where supernatural fantasy and trance states are valued, the maladjusted individual can have no idea that he is "queer." He may be an unwilling tool of the spirits, a tortured mouthpiece of the gods; he may wish he didn't have his grotesque inner life, and he may try to avoid the call to shamanhood—a call usually signaled by hallucinations—he may, in sum, shrink away from this social role, and wish he were not "singled out" for it. But he need not think himself "queer" in the sense we use the word—as "ill" and in need of medical attention.

In our society we alert everyone to scrutinize themselves for potential queerness. We encourage them to espy the slightest indications that they may be "different" from others. For the most part, it is "unsafe" to like Bach; and a high school girl to whom chemistry was fun and A's came easily, told all her chums that she got C's and hated the subject. With this cultural background, when individuals stumble in the hard business of life, when they try to appraise their manifold problems with the limited means our education gives them, we encourage them to "look within" for the possible fault. The final rub takes place when they enter our psychiatric hospitals and admit, under gentle urging, that they had reached a point where they feared "losing their mind."

In truth, the person who feels "different" from others, who has not been able to get along smoothly in the interpersonal cultural world, has to pretend to be living in the world with the others. Evidently this becomes increasingly difficult to the extent that one lives in a fantasy-world. A sense of felt indentity becomes difficult to maintain. We must remember this: The basic identity question is "Who am I?" This question is partly answered by being put to someone else—the individual alone cannot supply the answers. Society tells the symbolic animal who he is, and the process starts with the very first inculcation of social symbols *from another* social animal. The whole human growth process is one of finding out who one is partly by means of the reflected appraisal of others. Sociological theory has made this abundantly clear. One finds out who he is by performing parts in socially designated roles—butcher, baker, laundryman, chief. The individual says to himself "I am this because this is what I am to others." Initially, at least, there is no other way to know or say this. With fortunate child training, the individual may learn very firmly that he is such and such a person, destined to live such and such a life, according to certain fixed rules. In psychoanalytic terms we say that he has internalized a strong superego. He may need to rely less, as he grows up, on reflected appraisals by others. His rigidity is compensated for by a certain freedom from social capriciousness.

But the schizophrenic above all never learns this. We have seen that there are only two ways to establish the individual as a firm ground of value, which would start him off early with some identity security: In the first place, an abundant showering with love, so that the child feels he is indeed someone of value.[9] In the second, practice in the exercise of one's powers, so that one comes to know that he is the locus of them (Erich Fromm's basic definition of identity). Thus we have the extremely painful, paradoxical situation of the schizophrenic: He is most dependent on continuously reflected appraisals of his identity because he never learned sure behavior patterns in childhood—and, at the same time, he is *least able to earn* a positive appraisal in interpersonal performance, because he lacks sure behavior. He can't get what he needs most (identity), because in order to be able to get it, he already has to have it (interpersonal performance skills). This is just another version, phrased in terms of identity, of the circular nature of answers to the four common problems, that we noted earlier. As Searles aptly remarked (1961a), the schizophrenic needs to find something in himself that contributes to the growth and enrichment of his fellow man. He needs, in other words, a social role, which is by definition a performance part for the creation of interpersonal mana in which all can share (Becker, 1962, Ch. 8). But one cannot find something in himself that has never been inculcated in the first place, or developed through experience.

The literature on the problem of identity is so vast, and Erikson's work (1950) so eloquent, that there is no point even in summing it up here. Rather I would like to elaborate on some neglected emphases that highlight the theoretical picture being developed here: the primacy of action, the need for some kind of objects, the importance of total organismic sense of words; and the tendency to dichotomy in fabricating life-meaning, that is, using both external person-objects and internal symbol-objects.

Vocabularies of Motivation

One of the important currents of the post-Freudian epoch in the human sciences is the changing view of motivation. Freud, firmly in the tradition of Schopenhauer and post-Darwinian philosophy, saw human action as the result of inner urges to expression; these urges were considered prior to and stronger than the civilizing influences of society. Freud saw man's "real" motives as baffled by social training, always seething under the symbolic veneer imparted by society. We know now that this view of human motivation is at best hypothetical; no scientific proof has been adduced for Freudian instinct theory. In fact, with the drift of psychoanalysis itself toward a full ego psychology, more and more evidence is being accumulated for the opposite: for the predominantly social character of human motives. This is no news to the sociologists; many of them revolted quite early against instinct-based theories of human nature. When George Mead elaborated his ideas on the social behavioral genesis of mind, a complete sociological approach to motivation was made possible. In a sense, the human sciences had come of age, and were prepared to deal with their subject matter on its own terms. The matter is as plain as day. The terms of a symbolic animal are symbols learned from others in the slow period of early child development. By the time the humanization training is over, all physiological processes have been conditioned to cultural satisfactions.

The human animal behaves in terms of consequences it has learned to anticipate, and these consequences are usually sketched out in some kinds of words. People "act in terms of anticipation of *named* consequences" (Mills, 1940). In other words, when we can judge the consequences of action that takes place in society, we take possession of social motives. And the only way for a symbolic animal to clearly assay a situation is to be able to frame it in words. When we put enough word-motives together, we have answers to the four common human problems; we have, in sum, a complex fabric of meaning that is adequate ground for satisfying action.

One could object here that much human action takes place in a more or less automatic, nonverbal mode. This, of course, is true. It indicates that the process of developing certain habits is largely one of forgetting to label verbally all the elements of the situation, as one masters the action. One begins learning to drive, for example, by repeating "Now I will shift, now I will release the clutch," etc. In this kind of learning, the word-indicators for conduct eventually disappear as the process is reduced to automaticity. The same applies to much of early childhood training. But here a truly preverbal and nonverbal motivational element enters in. In his attempt to keep his loved objects, and earn even more love, the child develops a behavioral style which his objects approve. He is undergoing a training process of more or less automatic reactions. He is unaware, of course, of his conditioning, and is not able to frame alternatives in words at this early time—nor even to suspect that alternatives exist. Nor is he able to frame in words the kinds of feelings he senses from others toward himself, which are so important in constituting his own feelings toward himself. It is this early training that constitutes the "unconscious" part of motivation: the partly automatic behavioral style to which the child has committed his self-esteem. But, still contrary to the Freudian thesis, these subverbal and preverbal motives (perceptions) *are not presocial.* They are learned *in social interaction,* and are not born into the world with the child. For this reason, when the early learning situation is later verbally reconstructed in therapy, early perceptions can be unlearned. "Transference" is another name for this early, unaware perception-action mode.

As the individual grows, he learns a vocabulary of motives appropriate to each experiential situation. Motives become more explicit than they were in the early learning period. As the child learns a number of various performances in different roles— starting, say, with "cops and robbers," and "cowboys and Indians" —he learns the proper vocabulary accompanying the roles, and thus the correct motivation. The symbolic self, it must be stressed, is a role actor; and it is only by means of exercising powers in the motivational vocabulary of the role that the individual comes to discover himself. That is, he discovers himself in the meaningful action of the social performance part. This answers the "Who am I?" of identity.

The identity problem for the schizophrenic is compounded in a number of subtle ways. Since he is interpersonally inept, questions that he poses in regard to his own identity tend to be answered in terms of internal fantasy-reveries and private symbolic elaborations. Since the schizophrenic takes little part in culturally meaningful interpersonal action, he tends to become "stupid" in shared interpersonal vocabulary.[10] He fails to develop cultural nuances, the "wise" vulgarity that puts people at ease. The schizophrenic is often socially humorless because he cannot operate on several levels of message (Szasz, 1961, pp. 151-152).[11] The situation seems to be threatening enough, without confounding it with nuances. The catharsis of humor is doubly denied to the schizophrenic: Humor releases cultural tensions that all share. But this means that one must share in two things: both the shared meanings *and* the shared tensions. The schizophrenic lacks the shared meanings, and his own private tensions and anxieties are unknown to others.

Again, the self-reinforcing process: Failure to get a satisfactory reflection from one's acts drives one further away from using external objects as meanings. If one is shallow in external-object meanings, one cannot possibly constitute a self via interpersonal actions. There is no place to begin. Thus, the schizophrenic never fashions a secure answer to problem one of the four common human problems. As Harry Stack Sullivan observed, he never knows what the next person will be like, and never suspects that he can be pleasant. James Mark Baldwin beautifully describes the socially anxious person:

> To people who are thus constituted, the social relation is, purely from an organic point of view, the most exhausting, nerve-trying relation which one can well imagine. It is quite impossible to keep up even the most trivial social contact, such as travelling with an acquaintance, sitting or walking with a friend, etc., without soon getting in a condition of such nervous strain that, unless one breaks the relation occasionally to be alone, even the "yes" and "no" of conversation becomes a task of tasks. . . .This "sense of other persons" may break up all mental processes. The present writer cannot think the same thoughts, nor follow the same plan of action, nor control the muscles with the same sufficiency, nor concentrate the attention with the same directness, nor, in fact, do any blessed thing as well, when this sense of the presence of others is upon him (1899, pp. 204-205).[12]

This social anxiety leads one to rely more and more on the construction of a self in fantasy. The social act shows the schizophrenic in all his helpless ineptitude. Therefore, ". . . he must at all costs never be what his act is. If he were what his act was, then he would be helpless and at the mercy of any passer-by" (Laing, 1960, p. 93).

Now, we must pause to emphasize how disastrous it is to thus renounce engagement in one's acts. It is a process which is pervasively and relentlessly undermining, and in the end must take the heaviest possible toll. Why is this so? Simply because one cannot *develop into an individual except by choosing,* and by becoming responsible for the choice. To refuse to choose, to refuse to be held accountable for the choice, is not merely a matter of transgressing verbal commands or shirking on ethics. By renouncing the individuation that results from responsible choice, one *abdicates from the life process itself*—from organismic differentiation as it exists in nature, and as it is continued with the aid of symbols on the human level. (We could say, of course, that the schizophrenic is differentiated and individualized, but in a peculiar way: his self is elaborated *vis-à-vis* his body. It is this that seems to prove hazardous to the functioning of the total organism.)

In the end, the individual has an identity that must be accepted by him "on his word alone" as it were. And this is impossible. For the human animal security of meaning can only be achieved by enlisting tangible person-objects in our identity cause. However thoroughly man functions as a symbolic animal, the reality of tangible objects remains the greatest source of conviction. It is not for nothing that the first love affair of the identity-hungry adolescent is more a matter of finding someone who can *listen* rather than someone who can be held on to.

If all this were not enough to consititute a good schizophrenic, the matter is complicated even further. Epidemiological studies of schizophrenic disorders in modern society have proceeded under the impetus of a good hunch: there is something about industrial, complex society that exacerbates the problem. Early studies postulated the harmful effects of "social isolation" and "disorganization" in large cities (Dunham, 1959; Faris, 1944; Slotkin, 1942). These would influence the family and patterns of child rearing, as well as contribute to adult isolation. But perhaps more to the point, as far as the average individual is concerned, is the fact that identity confusions seem to be aided by the vast number of roles in complex society. There are any number of possible answers to the "Who am I?" question.

If the schizophrenic has been unable to learn a proper vocabulary of motives to go with a few relatively simple social roles, he will be even less able to adapt easily to the extremely nuanced performance in many ambiguous types of role behavior. In primitive society, for example, roles are relatively integrated. On a hypothetical primitive level a woman may be associated with the motives represented, say, by the words "wife," "children," "family obligation," and so on. But society sustains her in all these identities, and the unity of her personality is assured.

In modern, commercial industrial society, on the other hand, a woman's designations may be more subtle, she becomes a possibility of "romantic love," "career," "wealth," "clever children with good heredity," "winter house in Key West," "appreciation of Bach in common," and almost infinitely more. In itself this would not be confusing, but society does not sustain her in the unity and integrity of all these performances. Without this kind of support, social performance becomes mechanical, and the individual gets lost in the artificiality of her roles. Thus, a woman may be *only* a "house in Cannes" (see Diamond, 1963). In addition to this, there are the motives learned in early interaction with the parents, *which are not adequately symbolized*, but which also tug and stir uneasily on the borders of attention. In other words, as the prescriptions for the performance part become more nuanced and varied, the motivational facilitation of action becomes more ambiguous and confused. We say that modern man is confused by plural choices; this is undoubtedly true. But his straightforward conduct is even more undermined by the complex amalgam of motivation—by the richness of prescriptions with which he can facilitate *any single* situation in order to dress it in meaning and to keep self-conscious action moving forward.

When a variety of nuanced symbolism can surround any situational context, there is cause for confusion. It leads us to sense an antithesis between "appearance" and "reality." Clarity of perspective becomes submerged by the richness of the view. For example, one may not use the same vocabulary of motives in talking about marriage, say, to his wife, as he may in talking about it to a friend—or even (perhaps) to his mother. The result of this is that he may come to question "the real me." A marriage choice that could be wholehearted comes to be confused by the variety of meanings which can motivate the choice. The individual tends to get lost in vocabularies and subvocabularies. The confusion of "inner" and "outer" motive is only an apparent one. The individual tends merely to see himself in the perspective of manifold possibilities of self-justification. His action-choice no longer unambiguously absorbs and sustains his full identity.

It is this that contributes to the fallacious assumption that the schizophrenic, especially, has some "strange intuition" about the motives of others (Stanton and Schwartz, 1954, p. 200). When the schizophrenic ignores the explicit meaning of a statement and focuses on the inferred meaning, it stimulates a like movement in his interlocutor—especially if this interlocutor is a self-scrutinizing, "counter-transference-conscious" psychiatrist. The interlocutor, in other words, scans himself for alternative vocabularies of motivation, which are reasons for acting that are not in his immediate awareness. The point is that he may find several other vocabularies that fit the situation, and so he attributes some strange intuition to the schizophrenic. (This is also why we find skeptics at once so clever and so annoying: they cause us to burrow for alternate vocabularies and so appear "wise" as they cause discomfort.) As for the schizophrenic, this much must be said: if even the psychiatrist tends to be confused by alternate vocabularies of motivation, we can readily grant that someone with a weak identity will be even more confused about which is the "real me" who is speaking and acting.

There is, of course, a reverse side to the coin. And this aids the schizophrenic to commit the cardinal blunder that leads to self-destruction: the renouncing of commitment to his acts. When many vocabularies surround any single contextual situation, the actor can automatically "step away" from any firm engagement in it. By this means he enables himself a certain psychological distance and disengagement, which may seem to be equivalent to mastery and freedom.[13] But even this vicarious "omnipotence" is bound to be confusing. It edges one further into a fantasied reflection of identity rather than an acted one. "Real" and "apparent" facets of roles are further dichotomized and confused. Individuals come to feel totally different *about themselves*, from one moment to the next, *in the same unchanged role*. For example, if one looks at one's mistress as a drag on his career he can feel hate for her. The very next moment he may feel extreme tenderness for her, as her role as a satisfying love object comes into awareness. The seeming duplicity and "inconsistency" of the identity is not so much a question of change as it is one of shifting focus of attention covering many motives of various degrees of clarity. Our identity is predicated on the vocabulary of motives that presents itself to the attention at any given moment, and is referred to one's self-image. And these motives may not be clearly symbolized, but may urge implicitly for attention nevertheless. The harassing "inconstancy of love" is a question of the range of symbolic self-justifications available as motives for a particular performance part in which a loved object is concerned. The upshot of all this is to further expose the fallacy of the instinctive-drive theory of motives. Man doesn't stumble socially because "base" antisocial motives rise up from a private subterranean "unconscious." Rather, straightforward social action is caught up in a tangle of profuse *social* motives, in various degrees of explicitness and self-contradiction. In the human there is no fated antithesis between "inner needs" and social precepts. Social precepts become inner needs, and social confusion, therefore, becomes a sense of bafflement from within.

Thus the schizophrenic clutches to a private vocabulary of fantasy-motives which constitutes his supposed "real self." The major problem in constituting a real self is to give it duration. This cannot take place if the self is subjected to the indeterminacy of social intercourse. If one act can undermine a self, and one social role fragment it, then it can have no duration except in fantasy. But let me stress that this applies not to the schizophrenic only. This is the anxiety of every social actor: "I am nothing if each situation can construct me anew." Sartre saw this clearly as the explanation for the basic anxiety of the gambler who swears off (1953, pp. 18-19). His anguish, as he is tempted to play again despite his pledge, is not one of "social resolution" versus "base motives." Rather, it is, as Sartre saw, the fact that the individual *knows* that the situation takes primacy over a fantasy-pledge. That is, the situation as *engaging act* takes primacy over the identity as *symbolic construction*. The identity is a constructed fiction—the life action in a situation is alone real.

The creation of the identity, as Erikson showed, is an artistic task, and it is never finished precisely because each situation puts the creation in jeopardy. Every action adds to the identity, causes it to be rearranged in some way. In order to keep his feeling of value, and create a credible answer to "Who am I?," the individual has to create an identity that is more durable than that reflected by any single situation. He cannot accept as sufficient justification a momentary aggrandizement that is always varying with each new situation. Hence the anxiety of the gambler as Sartre explained it. Man thrives on a credo of how life "should be." Nature, on the other hand, seems blissfully unconcerned with anything except keeping action moving forward, proceeding from one situation to the next. But man is tasked with the creation of a durational symbolic self. Thus every individual is obliged to create the cause-and-effect myth of his own past. But each new situation joggles our creation, causes us to rework it somewhat. The discontinuity of situational motive and self-image is probably what Goethe referred to when he talked about man's need to forgive himself each night, to absolve himself so that he can begin again anew. Man, in other words, absolves himself of motivational inconstancy by creating an illusory duration which is the primary grounding for meaning.

The schizophrenic, in fantasy, achieves a durational "real self" most readily by using a vocabulary of religious or otherworldly motives. The "real self" is thereby rendered independent of external experience: most religious motives have little to do with life as most people live it. This frees the individual from the changing vocabularies of a continually different performance present. It gives him a secure self in an eternity of duration. Answers to the four common human problems are thereby cheaply purchased at a bargain counter, so to speak. They are not painstakingly, daily fabricated in the encounter of self and inter-personal world.

Religion also helps by providing a coherent and esthetic fabric of meanings of its own. These meanings may help the schizophrenic to explain and cover up his alienation from his body, and from the control and coordination of its activities.[14] They also help to explain and justify the massive guilt of the schizophrenic. Never having been given a sense of primary value, and never having been able to earn one by social performance, he feels guilty *just for existing*. Laing cites a patient who had been so denigrated by his father, that he subsequently felt guilty *"at seeming to be anything worth while to others"* (1960, p. 141). We know that guilt results mostly from action contemplated or undertaken in the face of prohibition or other constriction.[15] An extreme of inactivity in the face of massive constriction results in the schizophrenic's "identity guilt." To feel guilty just for being would be unexplainable, were it not for the fact that religion provides answers for this very thing.

With all this we can see how an individual who begins life already somewhat "disembodied" continues to further alienate himself from any sense of his own powers. The fantasied self never gains underpinning. The problems of identity in role behavior in a complex society pile up on those of early failure to negotiate self-value and integral functioning. The schizophrenic seems to be inexorably caught in a formula for human failure; a formula for a complete breakdown in functioning, in which the grotesque fantasy-world crowds out all possibility of action and conscious control; a formula that leads to progressive withdrawal, from social to personal deterioration.[16]

How are the workings of this formula to be explained? Laing, in his stimulating and searching theoretical study (1960), sees the problem in terms of a basic dichotomy of the embodied and the unembodied self. He traces out in theoretical detail the vicis-situdes of the progressively disembodied self; the increasing loss of control over one's body, which leads to a belief that others have power over it and are manipulating it; there are further confusions which result from a drifting of the self into "true self" and ."false self" fragments—in sum, Laing draws a very credible theoretical portrait traced out in phenomenological terms. The loss of the world and the subsequent loss of the self conceivably can take place along these lines and in these terms.

But this theoretical view would be hard to defend against critical attack, primarily because it would be difficult to adduce empirical evidence to support it. The phenomenological and existential theorists have assumed a herculean task in the present state of knowledge; consequently, they are easy to attack, easy to dismiss as fabricators of their own fantasy. The attempt to capture the process and inner meanings of the extreme schizophrenic disorganization has (to some) the unavoidable flavor of crystal-ball gazing; there is no sure way to get inside another's mind. The question we can ask is simply this: Why must this kind of interpretation bear the brunt of theory? It seems to me that the phenomenologists have attempted too much in a too limited area by concentrating on explaining the end state of schizophrenic disorganization. And on the other hand they have not attempted enough by not fully exploring how the individual got that way. It may be that we can explain the precise nature of the florid symptomatology of the schizophrenic end state. So much the better. But it is not enough in the first place, because it cannot by itself lead to a full explanation of the syndrome. And, in the second place, there is no need to insist on rigorous explanation of the dynamics of the end state as basic substantiation for a theory. The scientist is not tasked to explain the unusual in itself. Rather, he needs only to describe the usual, and to indicate that the unusual lies somewhere on the end of the continuum; we explain the extraordinary as an extreme case of the ordinary.

We know that to a self-reflexive, symbolic animal, the body becomes an object differentiated from the ego. We know too that the individual needs a feeling of primary value, and the experience of the exercise of his powers. We know further that when he does not have them, he tends to withdraw into his own fantasy-world. In extreme degrees, continued long enough, this seems to accomplish something similar to that noted in sensory deprivation experiments: that is, default of stimulation by external objects leads to a loss of the external world (Bexton, Heron, and Scott, 1954; Bliss, et al., 1959; Hebb, 1958; Heron, 1957; Solomon, et al., 1961). Periods of being cut off from the external world deprive the individual of the ability and the desire to cope with it (Hebb, 1949). In sum, schizophrenia affirms the supreme uniqueness of the human animal: Of all animals, he alone possesses a nervous system and distance receptors like vision and memory, of a superb degree of complexity. Of all animals, in other words, he is the best equipped for action in the external world. But his supreme uniqueness lies not only in this. Of all animals, paradoxically, he is at the same time alone in *being able to stop external action completely, and to keep activity going in controlled inner thought processes alone.* Thus the same mechanism that enables him to find an external world more rich than any other animal, permits him to lose the capacity to act in it.

"Total" Identity versus "Social" Identity [17]

The theorist does not need to offer much more than this understanding.[18] We need only understand that the florid end state, the breakdown, can result from exaggerations of a way of being in the world, from a certain life-style.[19] Now, this leads us to an important consideration: *Breakdowns do occur among inward individuals, who seem nevertheless to have achieved an unusual social-role success.* Often these people break down at the point of highest achievement, when there seems least reason for it. What are we to make of this? Schreber, Nietzsche, Max Weber, a host of great names comes to mind. If successful performance in social role gives a sense of valued identity, is there not some contradiction here? There is no way to answer this question except by thorough firsthand study of the individual case. The history of the individual's progressive development would have to be traced. However, some important light on these breakdowns seems to be shed by a theoretical dichotomy we stressed earlier: Bergson's and Dewey's distinction between total organismic sense and mere word-sound stimulus. It may be that half a lifetime spent relatively empty of organismic meanings, relatively disembodied, cannot be securely made up for by later role-reflected word-images; it may be that early deficiencies in self-value and funded experience represent a continuously precarious foundation upon which to build adult symbolic achievements (cf. Ribot, 1895, pp. 90, 105, 121). In certain fundamental areas of the personality the individual has failed to amass firm, behavioral experience. The adult role identities would have a quality of being "un-anchored"—to use a gross metaphor. The human animal doubts naturally and believes irrationally. A deep inner conviction of basic lack of worth is hard to build on. "You can not do it. You can not do it"—nags a deep-seated voice. Max Weber, later in life, was faced again with the issue of reflecting a paternal image: he seems to have preferred to give way to a fatal illness rather than risk plunging into another depressive withdrawal (Hughes, 1961).

The highest social achievements may only serve to make one feel more and more hounded by a sense of deep unworthiness. And, conversely, they can balloon one's fantasy-identity to gigantic uncontrollable proportions. Witness Wilhelm Reich. In his work on identity, Erikson provides an insight which seems to apply here: If one tries to renounce his past, then he really comes to feel bound by it. Try to bury it under an avalanche of achievement, and it smothers your most coveted prize. In matters of identity, Goethe's maxim holds: One has only to consider himself free, to feel himself bound; he has only to consider himself bound, to feel himself free. But there are some things that one cannot admit himself bound by: the very admission would be a surrender. It takes strength to consider oneself bound. It seems important for symbolic achievements to be rooted somehow in securely possessed and realistic self-feelings. It seems inescapable that total organismic feeling is the heart of living. We noted that primitives have died because they felt ashamed—and to feel ashamed is to feel exposed and empty. Others have died because they believed deep down that they were hexed. If to believe irrevocably and to feel wholeheartedly are enough to take a life, they are surely enough to undermine the achievements of a merely symbolic versatility. True, we are talking here about things that are hardly self-evident. But they seem to describe adequately complex processes; and we have to envisage them as possible explanations before we consent to study them.

Notes

1. For an interesting case study corroboration of the current thesis that the body is an object in the environment of the self, in schizophrenia, see Stuntz (1959).

2. This is the existential basis for hypochondriasis. It explains why only the human animal can be hypochondriacal—he is the only one who has a symbolic self "separate" from the body. Much of the symptomatology of advanced states of schizophrenia follows from this: the body is both a strange object, and a locus of meaningful activities for the attention of the self. (See section on regression in Ch. III; and Szasz 1957b, Ch. 8.) For a general theoretical discussion, see Baldwin (1906) and Sartre (1956, pp. 303-359).

3. Of course this also happens among the lower animals, but in man it is endemic.

4. Binswanger goes on to point out that this process takes place concurrently "with the still unknown schizophrenic *noxa*" (p. 342). By thus postulating an *additional* causal process for schizophrenia, he defeats his own phenomenological thesis of schizophrenia as a mode of being-in-the-world. Laing makes no such error, and

sees the schizophrenic mode of existence *as* the *noxa*. If the process can be accurately described in one language, one language suffices.

5. Thus one could also conceive schizophrenia as an early "deficiency in internal objects," as does Szasz (1957a).

6. Cf., in this context, a distinction that we draw later between "total identity" and "social identity;" cf. also some of the suggestions on mania, in Ch. IV. Recently, Michael Polanyi revives the discussion of the difference between tacit knowledge and explicit knowledge (1959). Ryle, too, makes the important distinction between "knowing how" and "knowing that" (1949). I think Ribot was one of the first to specifically draw attention to the total organismic grounding of the unified ego or personality (1895, p. 155).

7. Hence his meanings must always be partly unreal. When we unblock a problematic situation in thought, this is merely a prelude to an application of this solution to a real physical situation. The purely mental unblocking, without a physical follow-up, must withhold some of the satisfaction of unblocking, since it is not translated into action. Suppose, for example, that we do a piece of work, send it off to the press or hand it in to our boss. And then, say, we remember an error, or perhaps a better way of phrasing an idea. We make a mental note of it for later correction to be made when we get the work back. But we cannot *act directly* on the paper. Part of our satisfaction is held in limbo. Now imagine it always being held there, say, never getting the paper back to make the correction. Something of this kind may occur with the schizophrenic in his interpersonal difficulties. There is always a residue of withheld satisfaction in the merely theoretical furthering of life. The schizophrenic is like a theoretical scientist who never proceeds to experiment; hence he must always live, as we note below, in a degree of meaning unreality and incomplete satisfaction.

8. Cf. also Boverman's recommendations on the treatment of paranoiacs (1953), where he suggests breaking into their fantasy system, rather than supporting it as some therapists have done.

9. For a more lengthy discussion of performance styles by individuals strong and weak in feelings of self-value, see Becker (1962, Ch. VIII).

10. The schizophrenic, on the interpersonal scene, is much like the immigrant on the cultural scene: both have difficulty manipulating

a strange language in a situation where they want badly to be admired. The following social-psychological excerpt on an immigrant in a strange society could also be used to describe the schizophrenic in *his own* society: "In the new environment he is often without the prestigeful status he enjoyed in his country of origin and he is very much in need of recognition. If at such time he cannot express himself adequately the crisis is acute. He feels that the limits on his range of expression result in a poverty of thought and that he is not his 'old self' " (Herman, 1961, p. 160). The "country" of the schizophrenic's "origin," of his "old self," is his private fantasy-world. The "new environment" is the interpersonal encounter.

11. Lacking a sense of social humor, the schizophrenic also deprives himself of a dependable tool to use in interaction. Humor is a safe way of entree into human groups, a way of relaxing others, of covering one's own blunders. To lack humor is to lack a basic interpersonal device. For a full detailing of the subtleties of its use, see Erving Goffman (1953).

12. Baldwin adds an autobiographical footnote to this passage (p. 205). He notes that he prevents the distressing "outgo of energy" in interpersonal situations by a strong muscular effort of expanding the abdomen while taking a deep breath. This personal comment is significant for two reasons: it is an honest self-description hardly possible today, when "schizoid" has become a pejorative term denoting illness. Also, this is a description of one technique a schizoid may use to "seat himself" in the body.

13. Cf. Goffman (1961) on "role-distance." See also Becker (1962, p. 191).

14. See also the explanation of schizophrenic "hypersexuality" in the section on regression, Ch. III.

15. See discussion of shame and guilt, Ch. VI.

16. Strawson theorizes on the experiences of a disembodied spirit in the afterworld, a hypothetical description that could serve at the same time as a beautiful approximation of the extreme schizophrenic's experiences in *this* world, that is, when he feels almost completely disembodied and has renounced all commitment to his acts (1959, pp. 115-116).

17. Rogers makes a similar distinction, stressing the difference between "role self" and "real self," and citing the individual's

need to become "all of one piece" (1962, p. 29). See also Gendlin (1961) on the importance of experienced feelings as a guide to behavior and meaning.

18. Much less should he have to predict with certainty breakdown in any particular case. A. B. Hollingshead (1961) opines that we should look forward to the day when we will have theoretical models that permit us to forecast with precision: the conditions which invariably give rise to schizophrenia during the sixty-year life span of an individual. On the level of complexity of the symbolic animal, I think this kind of precise predictability is not possible or even necessary. It doesn't exist even in medicine. The most we can do is establish and seek to provide the optimum conditions for humanization, and the optimum conditions for social self-realization and identity. Once we expose the colossal failure of our civilization to value man, we will have accomplished more than mere medical predictability in the individual case. Fortunately, and paradoxically, our medically inspired research on schizophrenia is pointing precisely to such an exposé—as we shall see in Ch. VII.

19. Our whole discussion has implications too for the diagnosis of schizophrenia. If "schizophrenia" is not an illness, but rather a way of life, it should not be diagnosed on the basis of florid symptomatology alone. This is the artifact end state. The way of life may lead to the loss of one's world—and it may not. If the therapist is intent on enriching the object-world of some schizophrenics, then he ought not to wait until the end state for diagnosis. Schizophrenia can be accurately diagnosed on the basis of a long and continuing history of shallow object-relationships. This explains a good many "depressions" later in life, when the schizophrenic's shallow world has finally slipped away. It also explains the breakdown of an individual who was sheltered by a military or monastic routine, and suddenly finds himself thrown out into the world on his own meagre resources.

It is in this light that schizophrenia can best be seen as a total social value problem: How do we humanize people? With what range of objects and what kinds of meaning? What kinds of life-ways are open to them, and what kinds of creativity do these permit? And so on. (Cf. Chs. IV and VII.) For a discussion of the intimate connection between schizophrenia and Marx's concept of alienation, see E. Becker "Mills' Social Psychology and the Great Historical Convergence on the Problem of Alienation," in *The New Sociology: Essays on Social Theory and Social Values in Honor of C. Wright Mills*, Irving L. Horowitz, Editor (Oxford University Press, forthcoming).

*The world seems mad in pre-occupa-
tion with what is specific, particular,
disconnected in medicine, politics, science, industry, education. . . . To see
the organism in nature, the nervous
system in the organism, the brain in
the nervous system, the cortex in the
brain is the answer. . . . And when
thus seen they will be seen to be in,
not as marbles are in a box but as
events are in history, in a moving,
growing never finished process.*

JOHN DEWEY (1958, p. 295)

III

Schizophrenia

(2) A FULLY TRANSACTIONAL VIEW

ONE OF THE RESULTS of the Freudian
hold on the human sciences is to have created a situation
similar to the public pampering of Picasso, that is, when the
mass of men do not consider themselves capable of criticism, the
thinker has leeway to play all sorts of inverted games. This has
been especially true in the Freudian theoretical treatment of
schizophrenia. Schizophrenia has proved so baffling and defiant
to the understanding, that the theorist was allowed his own
fantasy in attempting explanations. The weakest part of psycho-

79

analytic theory—its pansexual obsession—was here applied to a point of *reductio ad absurdum*. Freud put forth his deductive formula with calm self-assurance. It went something like this: The paranoid schizophrenic is full of hate and delusions of persecution from a hostile world; the reason for this, basically (the *reductio*), is his latent homosexuality. "I love him," says the latent homosexual, "but the culture forbids me to. Therefore I must pretend to hate him. But in order to pretend to hate him, I must have a reason. Therefore, I hate him because he persecutes me." The paranoiac creates, in other words, a hostile, threatening world because of his own homosexual tendencies.

The sexual emphasis of psychoanalysis is hardly unjustified. Confusions in humanization during the Oedipal training period often come to center on the sexual zones. Historically, Freud was correct to hold to his emphasis against wide criticism. To have given way on this point would have rung the curtain down on some of the human animal's indispensable scrutiny of himself and his motives. But Adler very early saw how misplaced it was to try to explain everything theoretically in terms of early sexual desires. And Dewey offered a terse comment (1922) that holds good today: that psychoanalytic explanations in terms of sexuality are a typical example of the fallacy of confusing an artifact product with an initial cause. Dewey also commented that this kind of theory was an example of how smugly man holds on to simple reductionist explanations. Freud himself was an alarmed witness to this smugness among his own disciples. At a meeting of the psychoanalytic society he exclaimed that if psychoanalysts continue to reduce everything to the Oedipus complex psychoanalysis will be a laughing stock.

Lionel Ovesey (1955) offered a reinterpretation of homosexuality in paranoid schizophrenia; and his view confirms Dewey's first observation: Homosexuality is not a cause, but rather is to be understood as a *result* of a weak ego.[1] Doubts about sexual identity are a logical consequence of "Who am I?" confusion. Other psychoanalysts have also been dissatisfied with the sexual formulation of schizophrenia, and have attacked Freud's view vigorously. Macalpine and Hunter (1955, 1956) demolish Freud's formulations only to prove how ineluctable is the grip of his theoretical system. They put forth a view of schizophrenia as rooted not in the Oedipal stage of development, but rather in the procreation fantasies of the pregenital stage. This does point up some of the dynamics of the hypochrondriacal self-body split; but it is at best a part explanation that serves to keep the theoretical matter "in the family" so to speak.

Of all the problems of psychoanalytic theory there is one we would expect least: While pretending to *get behind* what people were saying, theoreticians actually took *too much* account of the preoccupations and descriptions by patients. (We shall see a striking example of this in the chapter on depression.) When the patient talked homosexuality, homosexuality became part of the theoretical formulation explaining the syndrome; when the patient talked procreation fantasies, then this too became a new theoretical foothold for the analyst (for Macapline and Hunter). When the patient reported soothing symbols, Jung espied man's fall from the wholeness of belief. Least reliable of all, of course, are the patient's own reconstructions of his experiences (cf. Robbins, 1957, p. 18). Boisen overlooks completely the failure of his idealized personal relationship to Alice—seemingly the one important object in his shallow interpersonal life—as a possible contribution to his breakdown. Instead he sees the whole thing in cosmic religious terms.[2] After all, the patient has been "brainwashed" by his culture like everyone else. In the nineteenth century, three times as many schizophrenic patients as now had religious preoccupations; today twice as many have sexual preoccupations (Klaf and Hamilton, 1961). Man seeks to explain, and he employs the only vocabulary he has learned. One reason for preoccupation with the sexual function is that it provides a ready focus. The symbolic animal uses sex in his private life for all kinds of self-justifications, and for all kinds of victories in interpersonal games that have nothing to do with sex. Sex is a vocabulary for those who may be very poor in words to describe their fears and cravings. In part, and for many people, sex reflects stupidity (cf. Ch. I, n. 2). For the schizophrenic, sex may be a desperate handle. When the environment is loaded with over-whelming anxiety, and one feels about to be annihilated, sensations in the sexual zone provide an oasis. As in Baldwin's use of his stomach muscles, the body becomes a locus of experiences. Thereby one declares his presence. He anchors vagueness and threat by commiting perception to a definite focus of sensation on his body (Szasz, 1957b). Furthermore, he can go on to say: "The reason I'm having so much trouble is on account of this damned sexuality, this evil curse." Boisen seems to have interpreted in these terms his wholly inept ejaculation on receiving a letter from Alice. Thus, a wordless bodiless, emptying passage through life is given some kind of direct link to the prevailing cultural mythology. To create a sexuality identity in times of stress is at least to have *an* identity. Not only does it explain whole areas of inter-personal as well as organic ineptitude, but further it provides one important thing: it links one to a prevailing religious system which offers its own confirming explanations of man's basic evil and inexorable guilt. Alternatives and expiation rituals are pro-vided. Action is thereby kept moving forward in a self-consistent scheme, and the individual provides himself with, and justifies, a way of life.

Regression

From all this we can see one thing: Human action is not straightforward and simple; it does not reduce itself to the facile labels we apply to it. The concept "regression" itself is one such label. Psychoanalysts conceive of human growth in terms of passage through maturational stages: oral, anal, phallic, genital. The idea of "regression" fits hand in glove with this theory. When an individual is not performing the way we think he should, it is an easy matter to consider that he has reversed the clock and regressed back to an earlier level of behavior. Thus Freud's theory of paranoid schizophrenia as a conflict of latent homosexuality saw the individual reliving Oedipal confusions. Macalpine and Hunter's "procreation-fantasy" theory of paranoid schizophrenia sees the individual reliving pre-Oedipal experiences. And so on. The limpid simplicity of the psychoanalytic view of man's nature finds its complement in the equally fallacious label "regression."

Certainly, regression describes something. It describes an adult who is acting childish—and in this sense the word is serviceable. My complaint is that it has obscured the development of theory on schizophrenia because it has been used in conjunction with psychoanalytic theory—with the simplistic notion that human growth is a saga of the vicissitudes of sexual energy. This has prevented us from seeing the humanization process in its full complexity. We have looked at oddities in behavior as a simple "reversal of the clock." But it should be obvious that the life process cannot go backward in time. The deterioration in schizophrenia presents a challenge to the understanding that cannot be reduced to such facile notions. Rather, it sums up the whole process of becoming human, in all its richness. By probing into this deterioration from the broad view of behavior that we have sketched here, we can at the same time sum up our presentation. Let us then examine three major aspects of regression in schizophrenia: the creation of time, the creation of abstract categories, and the creation of meaning.

Time in Regression

We saw earlier that the development of dependable behavioral responses to an object overcame a problematic action situation, and in a sense "created" the object. We saw too that it did one thing further: Every time a series of dependable responses was created to object A, a time perspective was also "built into" the organism: Object A, by definition and by behavioral constitution, implied a series of event-sequences in time. Henceforth, to see object A also meant to experience a readiness to undergo a certain progression in time. A sense of time is created in action. Thereby the individual fixes himself in a meaningful past-present-future, and can confidently find his place in a time stream. Problem three of the four common human problems, finds its answer as time perspectives are built in through action.

If we accept this view, we at once understand something fundamental about regression, namely, that the incapacity to fix time is a *behavioral poverty* and not a "part of" a temporally "regressive" process. Paul Schilder, for example, quotes a schizophrenic who cannot control his memories, cannot hold the past back, cannot envision a future: "Is there any future? Previously, I had a future, but now it shrinks more and more. The past is so obtrusive, it throws itself over me and draws me back" (1942, p. 217). Schilder observes that "it seems as if the schizophrenic, in his regression, lost the inner relation to the time experience." In other words, one definition of regression is that the ego relinquishes control of temporal perspective. But it would be just as correct to talk about an ego that has never been able to fix itself securely in time—one that lacked behavioral temporal perspectives. "Ego feeling" means a sense of continuity in time (Freeman, Cameron, and McGhie, 1958, p. 99), derived from a sense of control over objects. Meerloo correctly talks about a "schizophrenic time experience," the failure of a weak ego to order experience (1954, p. 61). Variations in ego strength, that is, seem to place time perspective in different values (cf. also Rioch, 1959). The future seems distant to a weaker ego, and the past immediate in the present. Time sense is a consciousness of relation to objects. Only thus can we understand an idealized love affair like Boisen's for Alice, which was unaffected by an *eight-year* period in which they did not meet. Normally, as we saw, we constitute a woman in a behavioral time-perspective, and she becomes a full external object. We internalize a response-readiness pattern that makes the object real by fixing it in *behavioral time*. Thus this eight-year period in Boisen's relationship has nothing determinate about it. Behaviorally, for him, a loved female object was probably literally timeless.[3]

If the ego has not accumulated any experience in behavior toward certain objects, then these objects are not securely fixed in time. This explains past traumata which are always upon us, always immediate. We have never been able to outlive them because we have never been able to develop the behavior necessary to control them, to outgrow them. As soon as we let our guard down, faces and events from the past begin popping into the present. We have only to recall how many times, walking on the streets of a strange city, and absorbed in reverie, we see suddenly a familiar face "from our home town." For an instant we forget where we are, or wonder incredulously what our Kansas village mailman is doing in Copenhagen. Only when we come out of the reverie by an effort, affirm our control over the time stream, do we realize that a faint resemblance in some face has played tricks upon us in an off-guard moment.[4] The opposite holds true for the future: it seems incredibly distant to a weak ego. This explains partly the schizophrenic inability to plan, and his consequent aimlessness. The self must be able to exert some control over the time process and over objects, in order to keep past at bay and future in harness.

It is to the credit of the phenomenologists and existentialists to have brought into theory on schizophrenia a view of time in all its complexity. Each individual "has" a different past—a different history of experience lived. But even more important, each individual *recreates* a different past, at each moment of the present. The past is constantly being reworked according to the needs of the present. Carl Becker's famous dictum "Everyman his own historian" applies not only to history: it applies as well to each individual's view of his own life. The events we pick out of the past for our own attention, the weight we give to them, the interpretation we place on them—all this depends on how we feel about the present and what we want to do about it (cf. Schilder, 1936). The neurotic, unhappy in the present, writes a gloomy history. If the future holds no hope, the past is also a quagmire of futility, of so-so events that need not have been lived (May, Angel, and Ellenberger, 1958, pp. 37-91). The future, after all, is never "achieved," never exists or comes into being except in the present. The future is only a complex of words and images, fabricated according to the intentions of the present (Schilder, 1936, p. 543). If we lack a satisfactory plan of action that we can frame in words, then there is no future dimension to our conduct. To be fully alive in the human sense, to have an artificial time dimension to one's experiences, it is necessary to create one. The individual takes his past and future in hand, and reworks and frames his life like an artist his materials. The identity, as Erikson showed, is a continuously fashioned work of art, never completed. And the identity is precisely the projection of self into past and future experiences. It is the creation of a self in a time stream. To have a weak identity is, partly, to lack manipulatory control over the time stream.

The meagre self, the weak ego, lives in a long present. One remembers something like this in the slow passage of time in childhood. The past was shallow in meaningful lived events. The future was indeterminate, unplanned, not in one's control. The future was far away, the past amorphous. The present sprawled out, heavy with sensed immediacy, with a profusion of events that crowded into experience. The child, like the schizophrenic, is an "undergoing" organism predominantly, rather than a "doing" one. For neither one has the past become, in Dewey's words, a "storehouse of resources" (1934, p. 196) which can be brought to bear on the present. Nor can the child or the schizophrenic take the present firmly in hand to create a future: the child has delegated control of his powers to his parents; the schizophrenic has never acquired this control. There is a sense, then, in which failure to have accumulated a rich store of funded experiences leaves an organism "childish." This similarity lends itself easily to the label "regression," especially when the schizophrenic's powers bog down completely. But in both cases we are speaking of *present* experiences in a *present* world. It is plain that the complexity of failure to control time-perspectives can hardly be understood in terms of "turning back the clock."

Abstraction in Regression

The same holds true for the extreme schizophrenic's notorious inability to abstract properly. This is not a question of reverting back to a "primitive" or "prelogical" mentality, or of reliving the child's early concretization. The ability to abstract, perhaps even more than the sense of time-perspectives, depends upon the power to do. Baldwin—as we saw—noted this long ago. More recently, the phenomenologists have applied it in psychiatry. J. H. van den Berg's observations go right to the point: "Our healthy space is characterized by direction, usefulness, aim and intention. The motor bus that I see standing at the stopping-place is for me at once a conveyance going from . . . to . . . , even though I don't know the names of the starting-point and the terminus. It has an intention, a direction, usefulness. That is how I see it. The flowers in the living-room I see at once as a decoration of this space, I see them at the same time as 'just opening their buds,' my seeing measures the time they will remain fresh. The catatonic no doubt . . . does not see flowers 'opening their buds,' nor a motor bus from, to. Neither does he see use or intention" (1955, p. 46). To fail to see use or intention is to declare simply that one does not feel or have any—he cannot refer *his* actions *to* objects. To see a bud opening is to "look to" its opening, to see in the still-closed bud its future opening. The ability to abstract is, then, closely related to the sense of time. It involves thinking in terms of *one's own* future action. Abstraction, as we saw, is a process whereby ". . . the organism universalizes by its own activities" (Wolters, 1933-1934, p. 142). Abstraction is not mainly conceptual, it is primarily behavioral.

This allows us to understand "concretization" in schizophrenia —the inability to see objects in terms of their class properties. The class aspect of an object is its use aspect. To concretize is merely to declare one's intention, one's use-power, bankrupt. Again, this is not a regression in time, but rather, *a change in executive capacity toward objects.*

Renée, in her autobiography, gives an excellent example of what concretization means, how it is misinterpreted by doctors, and how it is mistakenly considered a "reversion to animism." She points out that a chair became, not something to *sit* in, but an object in itself: chairs, jugs, tables, "defied" her with their "presence"—their "existence." "When, for example, I looked at a chair or a jug, I thought not of their use or function—a jug not as something to hold water and milk, a chair not as something to sit in—but as having lost their names, their functions and meanings; they became 'things' and began to take on life, to exist . . . the doctors . . . thought I saw these things as humans whom I heard speak. But it was not that. Their life consisted uniquely in that they were there, in their existence itself" (Sechehaye, 1951, pp. 34-35).

In other words, normally, the organism in its executive capacity toward objects uses abstraction as it plunges ahead in action, appropriating things as class objects for its own use. The existential quality of a thing, its "thingness," is not important, if one is going to assume an executive attitude toward it. Man's abstraction of the existential also serves to prevent action from bogging down with a preoccupation over the unique. In its uniqueness as a *particular* thing, each object is inexhaustible. Even the artist who is overwhelmed with the qualities of a *particular* chair, must abstract in order to paint it. Even Van Gogh's marvelous concretized chairs depict only a fragment of the physiognomy of each chair. Otherwise the artist would spend an eternity on one object. Renée's brief account conveys beautifully how overwhelming the object becomes when we cannot class it for use; what menacing proportions a simple thing-object can assume when the organism loses its executive capacity. We recapture some of this if we recall our first childhood exploration of a "haunted house," when we came suddenly upon a sofa in the shadows. The schizophrenic experiences it in his own house, in broad daylight.[5]

Thus, time and abstraction form a complex gestalt. The lack of use-power toward things completely reverses the man-made order of the world. Nature assumes a pristine, paleozoic quality: the organism—helplessly bound to the present—shrinks and hesitates; concrete objects, immovable, assume a menacing fullness. In the schizophrenic world, man-the-mover has not yet arrived on the scene.

The Creation of Meaning in Regression

We come to a final aspect of regression that in a sense is the most interesting. Our analysis of it follows as a consequence from the first two aspects, as well as from our whole theoretical view of the problem of human action.

The behavior of extreme schizophrenics, their delusions, fantasies, unbelievable fears, and "senseless" preoccupations have challenged our understanding. Usually, this behavior has been dismissed—again under the blanket label "regression"—as part of a reversion to a nightmarish or moronic infancy. We can see no logic in the careful storage of twine, paper, glass, and food scraps, in the vagina. Only the delusions themselves have been understood as having some purposeful, some intentional quality. Binswanger, noting the importance of studying the events that precede the delusions, comes very close to the view that I am going to present here. Only, I do not limit it as an explanation of delusions, but rather apply it as an explanation of most of the activities of the "regressed states." Binswanger says: ". . . delusions of persecution . . . represent a protection of the existence against the invasion of something inconceivably Frightful, compared with which even the secret conspiracies of enemies are more tolerable; because the enemies, unlike the incomprehensibly Frightful, can be 'taken at something' . . . by perceiving, anticipating, repelling, battling them" (1958a, pp. 208-209).

We saw already how aptly sexual anxieties serve this very purpose, how they permit the individual to reduce a global discomfort to a specific desire (sexual), to feel some kind of consequence (guilt), and thus to bring some concerted response into play: he can now repel a temptation, battle evil. Anxiety is focused on the body zones, given ready reference. Religious explanations enter in to charge mere body stimulus with a cosmic burden of meaning. The battle against anxiety in an empty world, we noted, seems to be aided immensely by making the body a focus of attention. One provides one's own stimulus. The body, instead of being an object for others, a meaningless, empty thing for everyone's use, becomes one's own object—a terrain of meaning right at one's doorstep, so to speak. All that is necessary is to find some way to get meaning out of it. Nature provides the sexual zones, society the endless ramifications of meaning.

Meaning, we saw, is merely a term for cause-and-effect sequences which command attention and lead to action, and which are logically coherent—which "make sense." In a behavioral world where the individual is powerless to act, there is little opportunity for meaning. The schizophrenic, consequently, has to show more ingenuity than the average person. And it is this very ingenuity—extending even to suicide—that appears most senseless to the observer.

Arieti (1961) reports a patient who attempted suicide 71 times. The patient, when he had recovered, gave two reasons for these attempts. The first was to relieve guilt and fulfill his duty of preventing himself from committing a crime. The patient felt so little control over his acts, that he imagined he might kill someone when his intention was only, say, to ask for a piece of bread. He tried suicide in order to forestall this utter lack of control over his own actions because he feared their potentially disastrous consequences for others. Self-extermination was, in other words, a duty.

Arieti, who comes close to adumbrating a behaviorist view of action and meaning in reporting this case, is quite rightly more fascinated with the second reason the patient gave for attempting suicide: "To commit suicide *was the only act he could perform, the only act which would go beyond the barrier of immobility. Thus, to commit suicide was to live; the only act of life left to him*" (p. 78, emphasis added).

How are we to interpret this? By now it is self-explanatory: The patient *could only act safely on his own body as object. Suicide remained the last controllable, predictable, focused activity —the last meaningful activity in life.* Furthermore it is a twofold meaning: In the first place, it is gained vicariously as intentionally avoiding the disaster of unintentionally murdering others. In the second place, and more importantly, it is meaning derived from perceptual commitment to acute, detailed action. One of the patient's suicide attempts was to tear his straight jacket to pieces and laboriously make a rope for hanging. Nothing could be more exquisitely time-consuming and more finely measured. Arieti aptly observes: "As a matter of fact, his acuity in devising methods for committing suicide seemed sharpened." The patient, in other words, drew himself into an object-world.

But only the first dozen or so attempts seemed genuinely self-destructive in intent. The remainder of the 71 seem to have been given over to a new type of meaningful activity: The patient took to swallowing objects or inflicting a small painful injury on himself. This painful stimulation of the body seems already to be a process of recovery. The patient is signaling to himself that the body is there, therefore "I am here." [6]

At the same time, this represents a recovery of intention, a regaining of controlled executive power. The first step in the patient's recovery is part of the same process. It began when he started gorging himself with food. Here was a new activity which linked him meaningfully with his environment. Significantly, the patient observed that only *at first* was hunger a factor:

"The pleasure in eating consisted partially in *grabbing* food and *putting* it into my mouth" (p. 79, emphasis added). Grabbing and putting are, of course, experiential acts by which the individual draws himself into a behavioral world, they replace the previous commitment to suicide. Hoarding is an extension of this same type of careful choosing and placing activity.

In an organic world where the primary emphasis is on action, and where each organism is differently constituted to act, the creation of meaning can become a very private and outwardly puzzling affair. But life cannot go on without some kind of activity. The most bizarre behavior of the schizophrenic is an attempt to pull himself up by his own fabrication of meaning. Dewey's observation is apropos here: "Until some acts and their consequences are discriminatingly referred to the human organism and other energies and effects are referred to other bodies, there is no leverage, no purchase, with which to regulate the course of experience" (1958, p. 13).

In a world where one's powers represent a mere flicker, action and meaning are narrowed down to the point where self-destruction can be the only possible unplugging. The individual moves forward to his own death—but at least he *moves forward*. In schizophrenia, suicidal preoccupations and attempts are "Occupational Therapy." So too are the various other obsessive preoccupations that defy all understanding. The schizophrenic, in effect, is creating *meaning-games*. He seems to be keeping symbolic action moving forward, while his organism is cut off from any executive powers toward the external world.[7] Physically powerless to act, the individual keeps his symbolic commitment to the cultural world. The commitment seems ludicrous and senseless precisely perhaps because it is an ingenious invention to sustain willful action in the narrowest possible range. Let us see some examples.

The creation of meaning-games seems present in most cases

of schizophrenia. A patient of Minkowski's seems desperately to be keeping himself in the world; his attention attaches itself to all objects, he generalizes each perception to broader relationships, but these relationships are always self-referential.

The smallest bit of thread had been purposely laid in his way; horses were in on the plot and deliberately excreted beneath his window; the cigarette smoked by a passer-by was a signal; a failure of the electricity was caused so that people would light candles and that many more "remains" would be stuffed down him. . . . His mind . . . decomposed every object that it met. The clock . . . was not just a clock but an assemblage of instruments of torture—cogs, key, hands, pendulum, etc. (1958, pp. 135 ff.).

Clifford Beers's famous report on his illness (1960) shows a similar ingenuity with regard to the creation of meaning. He reports the usual intricate reasoning over what to eat and what not to eat. His suicidal preoccupations were truly ingenious. Curiously, the preoccupations in his suicide game "cancelled each other out," so to speak, and the game was always made safe. For example, his long and feverish waiting for the moment when he could take the sharp implement and kill himself with it were finally met with success: *there* was the implement, he had come upon it suddenly and it lay on the ground facing him. When he finally had this chance to take it he quickly concluded that it had been "planted," and that he was being watched.

Beers staged a series of small dramas and one grandiose drama, including a counterspy game in which he enlisted a fellow patient. In these, each of his insignificant daily acts was connected to a broad pattern, and given abiding significance. Should he take the sugar pill or not? To take it would mean to kill the one who had been in his mind just previous to taking it, and so on. Hence, even taking a pill became an act loaded with meaning, *and under the control of one's powers*. One was not a mere pawn of the doctor, passively swallowing pills, but a locus of worldly control.

Boisen reported the same thing: "The different kinds of food all stood for something. I would eat no meat, no fruit, no pie, no sweet stuff of any sort, but lived on bread and water and beans, and very little of these. To have eaten of the other things would have brought misfortune upon my friends. But it was always a difficult matter to know what to eat and what not to eat" (1960, p. 120). After all, this creation of meaning is little different from that of the self-pampered dieter, who carries a calorie chart to each meal, weighs, calculates, and "cheats." Only the stakes are much higher. It seems that without these childish imaginings the grip on the world of larger reality would loosen altogether.

Another patient played a suicide game similar to Beers's. He thought he would kill himself by plunging his head through a glass door and then twisting his neck over the jagged glass. After waiting patiently for his opportunity to make for the door, he plunged his head through the glass. But at the last moment he decided not to twist, that his suicide would not help his family after all, as he had supposed it would. The patient seems to have been carrying action forward *ad hoc*—finding reasons for waiting for events, and giving other reasons as the events came up.

Renée's "doll-play" at the age of 18 seems to have been a similar process of the creation of meaning within a narrow behavioral range. To the observer, as to Sechehaye, this looked like "regression due to the development of the disease" (1951, p. 19). But it seems rather that Renée's sudden undertaking of solicitous care of the doll, and her continued thoughts about it and worry over it when she did not have it or could not be near it, are something else: secure object-oriented action, with no anxiety, and a felt manipulation through the exercise of one's own powers. Admittedly, the range of action and the object of action are ludicrously inappropriate to an 18-year old. But to see this as regression in time is to fail to understand the necessary efforts that the schizophrenic must make in his limited action world. All this is taking place *in* the present, is referred *to* the present. Furthermore, it represents a hold on the future, however slim and self-defeating it may be. Even suicidal preoccupations allow one to look *to* an eventuality. They are a toe-hold into the world, a form of self-reference and a type of commitment.

The attempt to create meaning in a limited world, with one's limited powers, appears justifiably ludicrous and senseless to the observer. If anything, it proves how vital answers to the four common human problems are. With them, the individual broadens his range of action and commitment to a full social world. To fail to do so is to condemn oneself to live precariously on a meagre store of meaning. The loss of a single loved object will often suffice to cause the schizophrenic extreme bewilderment over why man is here, what life is all about.[8] In order to have secure knowledge of the relationship of man to nature, one has to create and live the relationship—be behaviorally involved in it. This bears continual repetition; we can see graphically the penalty for failure. Progressively weaker powers, progressive domination by fantasy, progressive poverty in external objects—all these combine to drive the individual to a narrower, more inverted range of operations. The body becomes the last outpost for the self. Thus, to fail to secure answers to the problems of human action condemns the schizophrenic to a real behavioral stupidity. Any organism without powers and with a limited range of action can be called "stupid."

Finally, a word about the feelings of omnipotence in regression. Here too psychoanalytic theory has been guilty of unpardonable oversimplification. Omnipotence was thought to be merely a reliving of the infant's sense of unlimited narcissism, a return to the imagined powers of infancy, where it suffices to cry in order to bring milk and warmth, to crook the finger in order to summon the moon.

But to understand the experience of omnipotence in schizophrenia one must understand human behavior in all its complexity. It will not do to apply smugly a simplistic theory about self-indulgent adults who turn into clamoring children. The schizophrenic's sense of omnipotence follows logically and naturally *from his disordered experiences*. The feeling that one's powers fill the world, that one is immortal, is fed by at least three currents.

The existentialists have noted the first thing that contributes to the conviction that one is God or Christ, namely, the disorder in the time-space continuum (Ellenberger, 1958). When there is no sense of past or future, but only a timeless present, immortality is not only imagined—it is real. To lack a past or a future is to live in the "eternal now" of the animal world: the animal can sense only that he *is*. It takes a conceptual grasp of measured, objective time in order to know that one *was* and that one will *no longer* be. To lack conceptual time and behavioral time is to immobilize oneself in a sense of eternal present. Buddha-like, the schizophrenic radiates pure being.

Another aspect of the conviction that one is Napoleon or Christ, is the poverty of the object-world. Fantasy alone clamors for attention, and word-sounds assume the full brunt of meaning. Words, disembodied from any action or any organismic sense of action-commitment, become attention-monopolizing objects. The cry "I *am Caesar*" permeates the self and the world with Caesar-hood. The word Caesar creates Caesar, when the word alone exists in the world. It submerges the individual. This is similar to what takes place in the hysterical shouting of some religious cults, which serves to cut the individual off from the world and induce a trance-state.[9]

Along with this, is the pervasive sense of guilt of the schizophrenic. Not a single act that is not some kind of blunder, that does not have some responsibility to all mankind. If one imagines that the taking of a lump of sugar will kill the person who is in one's mind at that moment, one's omnipotence seems real. Where the slightest act is clothed in a generalized responsibility to the whole human community, one becomes the center of mankind. By his feelings of guilt and by his self-referential meaning-games, the schizophrenic becomes a felt center of cosmic causality.

Finally, the sense of destructiveness, of doom, of impending death, contributes to all this. The sense of destructiveness and death seems to be due partly to the lack of control over time-perspectives. The schizophrenic's sense of immortality, in some instances, and in others his sense of the impending doom of the world, both derive partly from the same temporal poverty. By this I mean that some schizophrenics seem to be poor historians in Collingwood's sense (1960, p. 26). Collingwood noted that the shorter the time-phase for a historical event the more our history will consist of "destructions, catastrophes, battle, murder, and sudden death."

The natural processes that come most easily within ordinary human observation, it may be, are predominantly of a destructive kind, like the historical events that come most easily within the knowledge of the historian who thinks of an event as something that takes a short time (1960, p. 26).

The schizophrenic carries his command of history to the ultimate reduction. The only events his helpless ego can envisage are those that are momentary, immediate, total: explosion, annihilation, sudden doom. It was Spinoza who observed that the truly free person thinks not about death but about life.

Thus, the world picture of the schizophrenic is all of a piece with the meagre sense of self, with the failure to constitute a broad and rich human world of action and meaning. Here we draw and close the full circle of our discussion of schizophrenia. "Mind"—the only solid mind any animal can possess—is built up in action. In order to be substantial, it must be basically behavioral. If it is fed in fantasy only, it is at best precarious. One thing is certain: Human meaning is not given in inborn drives; neither is it composed of mere "pictures in the brain." Human meaning is created in the distinctively human mode, by transactions with society, by living in a human world and sharing and enjoying its categories. These are the categories framed by answers to the four common human problems. And the answers, as we know so well by now, have to be fashioned in conduct in order to be dependable.

The Transactional Viewpoint

We began our discussion of schizophrenia in the first chapter by apologizing somewhat for resorting to vague, general notions with which to describe the coming-of-age of the human animal. We saw how important "funded experience" was, and yet how difficult to define and pin down. In a world "gone mad" with the particular, the fragmentary, the detailed, the minutely defined —in such a world one attempts a more commanding view at his peril. Scientific "queerness" and schizophrenic "queerness" are at opposite poles: in the present reductionist fad the scientist is considered droll if he *does not* limit his behavioral world to the smallest possible segment of meaning.

Having come to the end of this discussion there seems less reason to be apologetic for departing from the conventional approaches to schizophrenia. There seems less reason to invoke "the present state of knowledge" as an excuse for failing to be precise about minutiae. The fact is that in *any* state of knowledge we seem to be dealing with gross behavioral processes, when we deal with the relationship of the organism as a whole to nature. If someday we find chemical equivalents to these processes, so much the better. But the higher-level integration, the complete act, will still exist by a right of its own. It will still be irreducible. S. I. Franz probably had this in mind when he commented, over 50 years ago, that the attempt to localize functions in the central nervous system was a "new phrenology" (Boring, 1950, p. 685).[10] This whole problem has been argued at length, by those who are eminently more qualified than myself. I want only to mention it here as a continuing one, and stress the fact that it has been with us for a long time. It is especially relevant to our present dilemmas in medical research. We may be able to isolate characteristic substances secreted by deteriorated patients —the behaving organism, after all, functions as a unit. We may

also be able to intervene chemically to change or control deteriorated behavior—intervention in one part of the field influences
the whole field. But let us be clear once and for all that we
cannot *reconstitute a whole organism* by building up from micro-
levels when the organism has been constituted in the first place
by behaviors on macro-levels, transacted in complex situations.
We may *help* schizophrenics or depressed patients, chemically,
but we cannot *remake* them in this way. If we are interested in
a serious attack on human ineptitude, and not simple dabbling,
we cannot shirk the job of attending to man's whole behavioral
field. (In Ch. VII we shall see some of the implications of this.)
(Cf. also Buytendijk, 1959.)

It is not only poverty in knowledge, then, that leads to dissatisfaction with the attempt to trace down functions to their
lowest common denominator, it is due also to the peculiarities of
what we study. In fact, as more and more people in the human
sciences realize the peculiarity of their subject matter, the
dissatisfaction with the perennial ghost of reductionism grows.
If we realize that man creates a conceptual and a behavioral sense
of time, where are we going to find "time" in the nervous system? To what cells can we trace the built-in behavioral time-
perspectives—the response-readinesses to girl-objects, sailboats, and
star-gazing? Where could one localize the *quality of attention* to
experiential detail? To what can we reduce the total, spatial,
behavioral act? What about one's feeling for his Cadillac? The
strength of self-concept based on the achievements of his wife?
Of course all of this is rooted somehow in nerve fibers and
chemicals, in a vast amalgam of physio-chemical processes. But
locate it? Arthur Bentley caustically and correctly observes that
since the body is eighty per cent muscle, we might just as well
"locate" behavior there (1954, pp. 335-336; cf. also 1941).[11] If
we are intent on "locating" it, the muscles are as logical a place
as the nervous system. If the human animal did not live in a
cognitive space-time world, loaded with values and symbolic
motives, presumably the matter would be easier. But even ants

are as hard to understand as anthropoids. And according to aerodynamic theory the bumblebee should seemingly be unable to fly—it does not have enough wing area for body weight.

We no longer need to frame these objections to reductionism as strongly as did the more lonely voices of a generation or two ago. A good deal of this seems self-evident today, as we leave old blind-spots behind (and cultivate new ones). But Freud's reductionist, libido theory served as a mighty straight jacket on the human sciences for well over a generation. The value of existential analysis, historically, is that it helped take human action out of the rigid physicalist mold into which Freud and others had put it (Binswanger, 1958a). Human action has come to be seen largely as we have sketched it here—in terms of irreducible categories: behavioral space, behavioral time, symbolic motivation, learned values.

But existential and phenomenological analysis is itself guilty of restricting its focus. Having determined that the large, symbolic categories were important, the existentialists remain glued there. Rightly insisting on the importance of a thorough understanding of the patient's present—of his "being-in-the-world"—they have largely failed to take the necessary next step. The corrective to Freudian psychoanalysis is now a secure part of the fund of human ideas. It seems fair to say that historically existential analysis has served it function. Now we have to proceed further than simply analyzing "the world" of the patient. We have to shift our focus from the end state of the organism to its history, to how it got that way (cf. Jessor, 1959). In sum, existentialism has, by going beyond Freud, paved the way for a fully transactional approach to human conduct.

Freud, existentialism, transactionalism is not a historical progression. Existentialism antedates Freud, and transactionalism antedates modern existentialism. Currents trickle into history, get buried, emerge later with a full gush. Dewey did most to promote consistently a transactional view of human action, starting perhaps as far back as 1896.[12] Its initial impetus was as a revolt against the old associationist and mechanistic psychology, and against traditional philosophy. The transactional view sought to abolish the separation of man and nature, of organism and environment. But facile dichotomies that facilitate fragmented research die hard. Only now, after a lifetime of Dewey's work and writings—as well as that of others—is psychology looking with more favor upon the view of the organism *in* nature.[13] Briefly defined, the transactional approach attempts "The seeing together, when research requires it, of what before had been seen in separations and held severally apart" (Dewey and Bentley, 1949, p. 112). The transactional approach attempts to see the full subject matter, in all its relations, as part of one moving, interdependent process in history.

We have no room in our discussion for a detailing of the transactional approach, and no need for it: *The behavioral theory of schizophrenia sketched in these pages is a fully transactional statement of individual conduct.* We have seen how mind grows up in action, how objects are "created" by the organism's behavior: how the external object-world becomes rich as the organism becomes funded with experience. We have seen that answers to human problems are answers to questions about how to act *in* nature. And we have held up the extreme schizophrenic as a paradigm of the failure to constitute a fully human actor. Psychoanalytic theory could never alone proceed to an understanding of schizophrenia, precisely because it was unable to adopt a transactional approach. It continued the old philosophical and psychological fallacies of the separation of emotion and intellect, of will and thought. It failed to see the full partnership of individual and society, the social genesis of mind that George Mead saw so clearly. Psychoanalysts spoke correctly of the organism's need for "internal objects," for a rich store of action-dispositions. But they failed to make plain that the world of external objects has to be "created" as well—shaped in behavior.

Thus, we lost sight of growth as a *process*, as the creation of dependable, transactional patterns of reactivity-meaning, in which organism and world are inseparable.

In sum, it is schizophrenia which best shows up the fallacy of the old fragmentations. Without an external world with which to come into contact, the individual cannot be brought into being. But the acting individual also fashions out of that world a sector to which he makes appeal for his identity. To fail to carve out, behaviorally, a rich and extensive sector, is to condemn the organism to a deficiency in selfhood, to a poverty in objects and life-meaning.

A Note on Psychopathy

With due allowance for the number of different behaviors grouped under the word "psychopathy," it seems possible to say something about it here. The typical psychopath is said to lack a "superego," which is merely another way of saying that he does not sufficiently refer experiences to himself. If the schizophrenic is primarily an "undergoing" organism, the psychopath seems to lie *at the other end of the continuum*; he seems to be primarily a "doing" organism. Imbalance on the side of "doing," like imbalance on the side of "undergoing," robs the organism of the content of experience. Without resistance from the surrounding world the self would not become aware of itself; "it would have neither feeling nor interest, neither fear nor hope, neither disappointment nor elation" (Dewey, 1934, pp. 59-60), a perfect description of some types of psychopath. We would assume that consciousness of self and consciousness of objects should increase together. But this is not necessarily so (Eissler, 1952, pp. 111 ff.). In order for an object to become significant, the organism must feel its own powers involved with the object. The schizophrenic has too much self-consciousness because he has no manipulatory powers over objects. The psychopath has too little self-consciousness, precisely because his action seems to have been too readily facilitated for him.

We have already traced organismic experience in these terms. The only time the organism stops and thinks, doubles back on itself for a scanning of possible behavior, is when it meets a frustration in ongoing action. But if the frustrations are too severe the organism merely turns in uselessly upon itself. It develops an oversensitivity to the effects of experience upon it. On the other hand, if there are no frustrations the organism need not turn back upon itself for solutions to blocked action. Frustrations of "middle intensity" are ideal. With frustrations of middle intensity, the organism registers possible future consequences of the action it is contemplating. It involves itself in the future outcomes of its actions by calculating their effects on itself. *If we cannot appraise the future consequences of our acts, they lack meaning.* Thus we have said that the schizophrenic lacks meaning because he cannot be sure of any dependable outcome involving the use of his powers. The psychopath, on the other hand, because experience has been too fluid, does not relate future outcomes to his own present participation in the experience. As Dewey says, capricious behavior ignores the connections of our personal action with the energies of the environment. This kind of behavior does not acknowledge responsibility for the future consequences of present action (Dewey, 1916, pp. 163 ff.). Thus, Leon Salzman aptly notes that it is an error to imagine that the psychopath *cannot* experience guilt. Rather, he has no guilt simply because there is no reason for it in the situation as he sees it (1961, p. 183). He does not imagine that he has to give an account of himself. The psychopath, like the schizophrenic, has to have his whole organism retrained—he has to be rehumanized so that experience registers with a more proper self-referential balance.[14]

Notes

1. Psychoanalysis has offered its own corrective view: homosexuality can represent a means of repleting the depleted male self—in a direct way; whereas interpersonal transactions with females can only accomplish the reverse; and this is supremely threatening to one who already feels himself empty and unmanly.

2. Another patient offers a "Dick Tracy" theory of his illness (Anonymous, 1958). The schizophrenic, in his view, is a crook, a really guilty, insincere crook, one who is terror-stricken, and who moves sneakily through his own underworld. Again the patient proffers a theory based on how he feels and what he experiences. The theory is interesting only because it reflects how abysmally worthless the schizophrenic feels; it offers no real contribution to an understanding of schizophrenia.

3. This shows how inseparable are behavioral time and social object. But most researchers do not yet recognize this and continue to use multiple languages (Rosenbaum, MacKavey, and Grisell, 1957). Or, they continue the split between neurophysiological and psychological levels (Rodnick and Garmézy, 1957).

4. Burnham (1956) postulates that the schizophrenic actually peoples his present environment with known faces from his past *in order to* orient himself, say, in the strange atmosphere of a mental hospital. Actually this need not be wholly a controlled process of comfortable orientation at all, but rather an inability to keep the past out of the present world. Faces keep popping up, toward which no experiential time distance has been created. Thus they are always with one.

5. Others have observed the schizophrenic's inability to make use-sense out of the environment. Norman Rosenzweig adumbrates a definition of this kind of poverty in regression (1959-1960). In comparing schizophrenia to sensory deprivation, he finds a common denominator in "relevance deprivation." Sensory deprivation seems to strip the individual of the power to use measured responses to external objects. In one experimental group, responses to stimuli were exaggerated: subjects showed a desire either to withdraw from situations or charge into them; they expressed feelings of personal inadequacy. See D. O. Hebb (1949).

6. See T. S. Szasz (1957b, p. 158) on phantom pain as a "noisy claim."

7. The schizophrenic might be protecting himself by behavioral immobility, but keeps action moving by feverish symbolic creation of meaning. This view also seems to be phraseable in Pavlovian terms of protecting a "weak nervous system" by behavioral immobility (cf. Kasanin, 1932). There is a narrow but important difference between feeble coping and total catastrophic breakdown. Goldstein noted this (1939), and demonstrated that when coping reactions become impossible or useless, catastrophic breakdown results.

If the schizophrenic is really creating meaning-games as a coping device that wards off total breakdown, then we are faced with a further problem. That is, bringing the observer's definition of catastrophic breakdown in schizophrenia into line with something more substantial than the schizophrenic's puzzling performance. If the "meaning-games" thesis stands up to critical scrutiny, then it is obvious that what we are used to considering "catastrophic break-down" is, in most cases, real coping behavior.

8. Searles also notes the fear of death as a prominent anxiety in schizophrenia (1961b), consequent upon the failure to forge a secure identity. Cf. the observations on ego strength and historical events, in the reference to Collingwood, below.

9. Cf. the "Mu" cry of the Soto Zen sect (Becker, 1961, p. 131).

10. More recently, R. W. Sperry observes, in the same vein: "We should not expect to find that a single neuron or an isolated patch of neurons, or even a cortical center, could sense, feel, experience, or think anything in isolation. These psychic properties we envisage as depending upon a specific design and complexity in the vortex of neural activity, generally involving a reciprocal interplay of many parts" (1952, p. 311). Cf. also Straus's probing discussion of the fallacy of the trace-theory of memory (1962). The question of localization is part of the quest for precision, which we discussed in Chapter I in connection with Head's "schema." On this whole matter see Pasch (1958, pp. 202-211), who incisively shows that beyond a certain point in an investigation, precision obscures clarity. Clarity is gained by an understanding of the context, of things in their interrelationships, as well as by definition of details.

11. See especially his important essay on the Jamesian datum, which stresses that the *relations* between things are *just as much a particular datum* as are the things.

12. For a full statement of this position, see Dewey and Bentley (1949). This was Dewey's final definitive statement of his position.

13. Cf. for example, Bruner, et al.. (1957); Hebb (1958). See also the important paper by Schneirla and Rosenblatt (1961), stressing the transactional, behavioral nature of adjustment.

14. Parsons and Bales put forth a similar view of psychopathy in which they understand it as resulting from a "laissez faire" and indulgent mother (1955, pp. 255-256). In fact, a part of Parsons's scheme (see especially Ch. IV) is essentially a theory of adjustment to objects in terms of different degrees and types of doing and undergoing. For example, he says that a "negative sanction" stimulates a "narcissistic object-cathexis"; whereas a positive sanction "tends to draw cathexis to the external rewarding object" (p. 248). I take this to mean that a frustration of ongoing action causes the organism to register the experience on itself; whereas a facilitation of action orients experience more in terms of the object. Parsons also insists on the need for a "balanced input" of stimulation, and talks about an "equilibrium level" (p. 248).

This is hardly the place to evaluate Parsons's broad and rich scheme, and I do no more than mention its similarity (in some respects) to Dewey's (see also Parsons and Shils, 1952; for a much earlier statement of what amounts to the schizophrenic-psychopathic continuum, see Schiller, 1954, p. 70). However, Parsons needlessly complicates the picture of the registration of experience on the organism. In the first place, there seems no benefit gained from carrying over clumsy, physicalist psychoanalytic terms like "narcissistic object-cathexes." Granted, this conveys the idea that an object has both an "inner pole" and an "outer pole"—that it grows up *as a behavior pattern* in transaction with the external world. But it seems easier to say this directly, and to call the early superego the "inner pole" of the object or of the social motives, as we do in Chapter IV below. In the second place, Parsons's full use of precise classification and schematic diagramming of personality development merely serves to introduce a false precision into what is basically a highly flexible process. For example, he attempts to link personality characteristics firmly to the sequential stages of the Oedipal transition. This results in a scheme nearly as reductionist and rigid as the psychoanalytic one. Durkheim is largely sacrificed to Freud, as the self is deterministically reduced to early learning. Finally, Parsons attempts a formulation of the neuroses and psychoses, also in terms of the Oedipal passage. This works all right for psychopathy, principally because Parsons seems to accentuate a behavioral treatment of this personality type (1955, p. 256, n. 33). But in his phrasings of the other syndrome types, this simple scheme does not work. For example, polar formulation of the etiology of the manic and the depressive types (p. 256) would mean that the manic-depressive *would combine two extremely contradictory kinds* of early mothering. In sum, retention of the rigid Freudian developmental scheme and addiction to sharp classification leads to a simlar reductionism in explaining the psychoses. As we will see in the following chapters, the human personality is harder to pin down. Which means, I think, that science will have to shift its focus: it will master the phenomenon of man not so much by precise analysis, as by aiming to further man's potential (cf. especially Chs. IV and VII below). This is not a scientific surrender but a sophisticated coming-to-grips with the peculiar qualities of the human subject matter.

Whatever liberates our spirit without
giving us mastery over ourselves is
destructive.

GOETHE (1829)

IV

Depression

A COMPREHENSIVE THEORY

SCHIZOPHRENIA SUMS UP MAN'S com-
ing of age in society. In order to understand it we have had
to trace a lengthy picture of the process of becoming human.
Depression is much more simple. Unlike the schizophrenic, the
depressed person has not failed to learn secure answers to the four
common human problems. His dilemma, if anything, is somewhat of a paradox: he has learned these answers *only too well*.
He has built himself so firmly into his cultural world that he is
imprisoned in his own narrow behavioral mold.

If the theory on schizophrenia has been hampered by an
ingrown psychoanalysis and nearly stifled by the medical affiliations of psychiatry, what are we to say about depression?
"Incredible" is the only word that comes to mind—absolutely
incredible. The only thing to which the theory of depression—
largely a psychoanalytic one—can be reasonably compared, is to

the Eskimo explanation of *piblokto*. How else can we make sense out of the classification of "wet" and "dry" depression—depending on the amount of the patient's saliva? How else can we consider subdivisions like "shame depression," "guilt depression," and "depletion depression"? How else can we justify the magical use of electroshock, an idea inspired from slaughterhouses (Szasz, unpublished paper)—the sometimes therapeutic effects of which no one understands?

The psychoanalytic theory of depression, let it be admitted, has a certain alchemical beauty. The patient is designed on the model of a hydraulic machine, with certain outlets, and pipes which double back. There are control faucets and other "emergency dyscontrol" valves.[1] The center of the machine is a tank, with a reinforced, galvanized false bottom: It is here that the patient stores a hard core of "coercive rage." The various pipes, channels and outlets, and those that double back into the tank, transport this rage, as well as guilt, and "guilty-fear," in different directions. The depressed patient is considered to be a poorly socialized child—not fully adult. He retains, it is thought, unnatural dependencies, as well as strong aggressions created in his early years. All this is stored up in the tank. The apparatus is activated when the "overgrown child" meets a severe frustration —usually loss of a loved object, or some strong threat to his own satisfactions. It is then that he strives to make an adaptation. To avoid sketching the complex workings of the hydraulic machine, it is sufficient to note that the adaptation does not work. The various instinctive energies go off in all directions, and the patient is finally undermined by one that turns back, that can find no outlet. Thus, the primary cause of breakdown in depression is thought to be self-directed aggression. The patient bogs down into a pitiful self-accusation, whiningly protesting his worthlessness, his evil, his need to be punished. He seethes with hate, self-pity, stunted rage, and childish dependency. But this amalgam is not solvent in the tank, with the result that the mechanism can trickle to a stop. The depressed person can abandon all activity, let himself slide into the surrender of death.

For the most part, this model represents the advanced theoretical cogitations of the psychiatric profession on a perplexing human phenomenon. This much must be said: It is not easy to comprehend why anyone would opt out of life. It is understandable that we would be quick to look for some basic genetic taint, some stunted early development, that would mark such an individual off from others. But the matter is not quite so simple: The fact is that a good proportion of depressed patients have led mature and responsible lives; some have achieved notable success, financial and personal. We distort our vision if we use the above theory to explain why these people become abysmally depressed.

It is amazing that human action could have been so consistently and thoroughly conceived in instinctual and compartmentalized terms. It is to the credit of some psychoanalysts that they themselves have begun to break out of their own inherited theories, and to range more broadly for an explanation of depression.[2] This is part of the natural development of ego psychology. As the view of man as a cultural animal shaped by learning takes over from the older instinctive explanations, the way is clear for a full theoretical revolution. If the ego is the basis for action, and if a warm feeling of self-value must pervade one's acts, then it is only a step to focusing on the really crucial dynamic of a breakdown in action, namely, the undermining of the individual's sense of self-value. Sap the individual's sense of self-righteousness and he is drained of his life-predication. This is the all-pervasive "slipping-away," the unspeakably, unbelievably "Frightful"—to use an apt word of Binswanger's.

Adler very early saw the importance of self-esteem in depression.[3] More recently, Bibring (1953) signalled a truly radical break with the older theory in psychoanalysis, by postulating that an undermining of self-esteem was the primary focus in depression, that it was principally to be understood as an ego-phenomenon, and only secondarily as a consequence of self-directed aggression.

It would be impossible to overestimate the significance of this shift in emphasis. In spite of Bibring's own protestations to the contrary, theories about the role of orality and aggression are now as outmoded as the hydraulic-tank model. If self-esteem is the primary focus of depression, then it is evident that cognition plays a larger role in its dynamics than does physiology. An ego-based theory of depression broadens the area of explanation from a purely "intra-psychic battlefield" to the entire range of social phenomena. Since the ego is rooted in social reality, since self-esteem is composed of *social* symbols and *social* motives, depression becomes a direct function of a cognitively apprehended symbolic world. Nothing less than a full sweep of cultural activity is brought into consideration in the single case of depression.

Little wonder, then, that more recently a crucial sociological dimension was added to the theory of depression—again from within psychoanalysis (Szasz, 1961, pp. 280-291). In the classical formulation of depressive, mourning and melancholic states, Freud had presented psychoanalysis with a model (1917). He postulated that since the ego grows by developing responses to and identifications with objects, the loss of an object was a threat to the ego. This, Freud reasoned, was the basic dynamic of mourning and melancholic states. The loss of an object in the real world meant a corresponding depletion in the ego; to relinquish a loved object was to subject oneself to a sometimes massive trauma. Freud theorized beautifully on the rather elaborate procedures that society sets up to ease this relinquishing of objects: the funeral rites, mourning rituals, and so on. There is nothing fundamentally wrong with Freud's view of depression [4]—it explains a good deal. Its principal drawback is that it is used to explain too much.

Szasz's objection to the traditional view of depression is precisely its insistence on the *predominant* importance of object-loss in unleashing dependency cravings and hostility. He proposes to emend this by stressing that the loss of "game" is fully as significant in depression as is the loss of object. "Game," in this context, is a series of norms or rules for significant action. And for the symbolic animal, there is nothing "playful" about significance. Szasz says:

> . . . persons need not only human objects but also norms or rules—or, more generally—games that are worth playing! [And he observes at greater length:] It is a matter of everyday observation that men suffer grievously when they can find no games worth playing, even though their object world might remain more or less intact. To account for this and similar events, it is necessary to consider the relationship of the ego or self to games. Otherwise, one is forced to reduce all manner of personal suffering to consideration of object relationships. . . . Conversely, since loss of a real or external object implies the loss of a player from the game—unless a substitute who fits exactly can be found—such loss inevitably results in at least some changes in the game. It is thus evident that the words "player" and "game" describe interdependent variables making up dynamic steady states—for example, persons, families, societies, and so forth (1961, p. 282).

With this broadening out of traditional object-loss theory, there is no longer any valid pretense for keeping the phenomenon of depression within medicine. Psychoanalysis is fully linked here with social science. Since, as Szasz insists, objects and games are inseparably joined, self and society must be seen as a single phenomenon. People "create" objects by acting according to social rules. They "create" themselves as they create objects. Social rules and objects provide man with a staged drama of significance which is the theatre of his action. Man discovers himself by making appeal for his identity to the society in which he performs. To lose an object, then, is to lose someone to whom one has made appeal for self-validation. To lose a game is to lose a performance part in which identity is fabricated and sustained.

We noted in Chapter I that answering the four common human problems gave the actor the one thing he needed most:

the sentiment that he was an object of primary value in a world of meaning (Hallowell, 1955). Data from anthropology support this fundamental place of self-esteem in human action. It seems that nowhere on this once-vast globe has man been able to act unless he had a basic sentiment of self-value. Unless the individual feels worthwhile, and unless his action is considered worthwhile, life grinds to a halt. Whole cultures have begun to expire in this way: Melanesians, Marquesans, reservation Indians, and, for a time after 1929, the world of Wall Street.

The Fundamental Importance of Meaning

Self-value, then, and objects, are inseparable from a drama of life-significance. To lose self-esteem, to lose a "game," and to lose an object, are inseparable aspects of the loss of meaning. Meaning, we saw, is not something that springs up from within man, something born into life that unfolds like a lotus. Meaning is not embedded in some obscure "inner human nature," not something that is destined to be developed by successively "higher forms of life." There is, in short, nothing vitalistic or mysteriously emergent implied in the idea of meaning. Meaning is the elaboration of an increasingly intricate ground plan of broad relationships and ramifications. It is the establishment of dependable cause-and-effect sequences which permit ego-mastery and action. Meaning is at the heart of life because it is inseparable from dependable, satisfying action. Man embroiders his cause-and-effect action sequences with an intricate symbolism: flags, commandments, lace underwear, and secret-codes. The result is that particular kinds and sequences of action take on a life-and-death flavor. The dependable becomes the indispensable; the satisfying becomes the necessary. Man's symbolic life is an imbibing of meaning and a relentless creation of it. This symbolic elaboration of meaning is *Homo sapiens*' "home brew," so to speak, brought by him onto the evolutionary scene and manufactured solely for his use and delight. By means of it, man intoxicates himself into the illusion that his particular meaning-fabric, his culture's concoction of symbols and action, is god-given and timeless. In his imagination, man fuses symbols and action into a cohesion that has atomic tenacity.

Let us review here briefly how this comes about. Initially, meaning does not need language. We stressed that it exists in behavior. For energy-converting organisms, action is primary. Forward-momentum is enough to build meaning, and possibilities for forward-momentum exist in nature, in the animal's instinctive behavioral *umwelt*, in the world cut out for his perception and attention. Instinctive action gives experience which, in turn, provides meaning simply because it commands attention and leads to *further* action. But for the symbolic animal a complication enters: language replaces instinctive readiness. Man grows up naming objects for his attention and use. Language makes action broader and richer for the symbolic animal. But something curious occurs in this process: Language comes to be learned as a means of acting without anxiety. Each of the infant's acts comes to be dressed in words that are provided by his loved objects. As a child, lacking a word, he lacks a safe action. Action and word-prescriptions become inseparable, because they join in permitting anxiety-free conduct. Growing into adulthood, the individual has built his habits into a self-consistent scheme. To lack a word is then to lack a meaningful action: the simplest act has to take on meaning, has to point to something beyond itself, exist in a wider referential context. We become paralyzed to act unless there is a verbal prescription for the new situation.[5] Even our perceptions come to be built into a rigid framework. Man loses progressively the capacity to "act in nature," as he verbally creates his own action world. Words give man the motivation to act, and words justify the act. Life-meaning for man comes to be predominantly an edifice of words and word-sounds.

Now, the upshot of all this is crucial for our subsequent discussion of meaning-loss. It is simply this: When action bogs down —for any animal—meaning dies. For man, it suffices that verbal or purely symbolic action bogs down in order for meaning to die.[6] Having refined meaning with symbols, he is hopelessly dependent on the coherence of the symbolic meaning-framework. He is a slave to his own delicate handiwork. In other words, if the individual can keep verbal referents going in a self-consistent scheme, action remains possible and life retains its meaning. If he cannot, if the integrity of the symbolic meaning-framework is undermined, external action grinds to a halt. Let us see how this works in depression.

Guilt-Language

Part of the reason for the grotesque nature of early psycho-analytic explanations of depression was the original grotesqueness of a major feature of the syndrome: the delusional self-accusations. That an individual would so malign himself without apparent cause seemed explainable only by postulating that he was intent on reducing himself to nothing—that his control over some deep-seated aggressiveness had gone awry, and that this hate was now turned "against himself." This kind of interpretation is a blunder that we noted earlier in connection with the schizophrenic's imagined "sexuality": the patient's preoccupations are accepted at almost face value as part of an explanation of his condition. Thus, while pretending to "get behind" what is going on, the theorist actually is taken in by appearances. Perhaps this is inevitable in a complex young science. Perhaps too, as James noted, it is difficult to back away and look clearly at data in which one is heavily invested, which strike at the core of one's own human susceptibilities.

The whole matter now has to be recast. Instead of asking "Why does the patient feel so humiliatingly guilty?" the question should be: "What is the patient trying to accomplish *with this particular language?"* Two things, obviously, which everyone is always trying to accomplish, albeit with different means. They bear repeating: (1) The patient is trying to keep his identity self-consistent. (2) The patient is trying to entertain and elaborate the meanings of things. He is, in short, attempting to keep action going in the only way the human animal can. Depressive self-accusation is an attempted unplugging of action in the face of the Frightful, of the possibility that one's whole world will slip away.[7]

Take, as a direct example, a situation recently observed in Ghana by the anthropologist and psychiatrist M. J. Field (1960). Before Field's study, it used to be thought that depression was rare among the "simpler" peoples, and this for several reasons. For one thing, traditional societies enjoyed firmly institutionalized rituals and practices that provided dependable and ready "catharsis" for object-loss. Society united in working off anxieties attendant on the departure of one of its members; the bereaved person was supported by everyone in his grief. In sum, he lost an object only to gain—at least temporarily—a whole social performance world.

For another thing, it was thought that the absence of a Christian tradition of sinfulness lessened the accumulation of guilt so prominent in the depressive syndrome. And perhaps still another reason offered for the supposed rarity of depression in traditional society was the lingering myth that only industrial man was heroically subject to the psychic burdens of a complex, technological civilization.

But contrary to all this accumulated mythology, Field's study of rural Ghana shows that depression can be quite common in any disintegrating, individualistically anarchistic, or unreflective society. Depressed women in considerable number travel to Ashanti religious shrines, and there hurl accusations of vile witchcraft against themselves. They present a guilt-laden syndrome quite like that of our culture. The explanation is not far to seek and, as Field postulates, depression and witchcraft have probably had a long historical connection.[8] The self-accusation of witchcraft seems to provide the perfect justification for failure and worthlessness. In the case of the Ashanti woman the picture seems quite clear. She raises large families with extreme care, is an excellent house-keeper and businesswoman as well. There is enough significant activity in her life to provide ample self-justification. But often the fruit of her labor is lavished by the husband on a younger bride, when the wife grows old.

This cruel turnabout is tolerated by the culture, and evidently it is a principal cause of anxiety on the part of aging wives. But the wife seems to have little say in the matter. How is she to justify this utter subversion of life-meaning? A life-plot that had consistency, integrity, and full social support is suddenly undermined. Fortunately, the culture itself provides a ready rationalization. Verbalizations are ready-made with which to construct a framework of meaning and justification; the continuity of the staged drama of one's life-experience need not be broken: the woman can simply acknowledge that *all along* she has been a witch. Thus the circle is closed: "I have become useless because I have always been evil. I deserve this fate. I deserve to be hated."

Field's observations on depression and self-accusation of witchcraft in Ghana can be safely generalized to depressive self-accusation in *any* culture. The individual gropes for a language with which to supply a meaning to his life-plot when all other props for meaning are pulled away. The alternative to this—namely, the realization that perhaps life *has no meaning*—is much more difficult to come by.[9] This apprehension is given to very few. It is even easier to speculate that *all* life may be in vain, than to admit that *one's* life has been. It may seem paradoxical that even in the extreme case of opting out of life, a meaning must be supplied: "Let me die *because* I am worthless." But this is no paradox. It is merely a continuation of the inescapable burden of fashioning a coherent identity to the very end.

The ego, after all, as we saw at some length in Chapters I to III, strives to create a continuity of integrated experience. As

Erikson's work so eloquently shows, the identity is a painstakingly fashioned work of art. It is symbolically constructed, and continually refashioned, never complete. In this sense, the individual can be compared to a movie director who is saddled with a lifetime job of staging a plot, the outcome of which he never knows. Indeed, he never knows what will happen in the *very next* scene, but he must strive to give the whole thing credibility and self-consistency. This he can only accomplish by reworking the previous material as new events joggle his creation. When one gets down to the last twenty years of this life drama, it becomes more and more difficult to justify abrupt changes in continuity: there is too much preceding plot for it to be remanipulated with ease. Whole portions cannot be reinterpreted with credibility, much less restaged. Hence, if the continuity is radically undermined the individual grasps at whatever straws his ingenuity can muster. No movie director would accept such an assignment, yet each individual is burdened with this ultimately and perilously creative task. This makes understandable the remark that an individual cannot know if his life has been satisfactory until the moment before he expires. It is symbolically reappraisable until the very last second. The proverbial drowning man whose life passes in review is merely exercising the last impulsion of the reclaiming artist.

When sharp changes take place in one's object world, the identity problem becomes severe: One's whole performance is in jeopardy. The identity has to be maintained even though an object which validated it is no longer available or a series of actions on which it was predicated is no longer possible or satisfying. In a desperate attempt at rearrangement, a proper framework of words is sought, which will sustain both the accustomed identity and the habitual action. Self-esteem, symbolic integrity of the identity and the life-plot, and the possibilities for continued action must all be provided for. This is no mean job, and the burden of it all is on *the proper word formula*. In the face of a frustrating problematic situation the individual has recourse to thought. The situation is juggled around, dissected, spread out, reworked, recombined—in fantasy—until a prescription for forward-momentum is hit upon. Basically, the individual has two alternatives: justify somehow a continuation of action in the old, habitual framework; or scrap the old action, habits, meanings entirely, and try to build a new framework of meaning. Obviously, this latter alternative cannot present itself as an immediate behavioral possibility; it means the abandonment of one's accustomed world, the suspension literally in a void, a plunge into the massive unknown, into the gaping chasm of anxiety.[10] Self-accusation, then, can be understood as a meaningful behavioral prescription within a *closed* behavioral world.

We know there is nothing straightforward about a rationalization. But it has taken us some time to realize that neither is there anything direct and explicit about most communication. Language grows up as a way of gently coercing others, of getting them to satisfy our needs. Primarily too, language grows up as a way of allaying anxiety, especially the anxiety of object-loss, separation, abandonment. Sullivan defined the self-system as a series of "linguistic tricks" by means of which we keep our world satisfying. But in each culture people communicate different things: the range of knowledge differs, and the kinds of things people become anxious about differ. Thus, stupidity and anxiety form a sieve through which explicit communications are filtered. Meanings tend to dwell under the surface, to explode in angry gestures, to linger in facial expressions, to be contained in an emphasis or a word arrangement that has nothing to do with the dictionary sense of the words. It almost seems as if "symbolic animal" is a misnomer: People are so inept at understanding and communicating their desires; the important problematic aspects of interpersonal situations are rarely made explicit. The reason is not far to seek: The individual doesn't know the performance style into which he has been trained; he doesn't know why he feels anxious at certain eventualities; he doesn't know why he is trying to get the other person to do *just this* particular thing. In sum, most people, not knowing what has made them what they are, or made them want what they want, amble through life using hieroglyphics in a jet-age.

Jurgen Ruesch (1948) thought that the really mature person should be able to express symbolically all his desired meanings, including physiological urges. It remained for Thomas Szasz (1961) to show that when the individual does not control meanings symbolically, we call him "mentally ill." He showed that the prototype syndrome on which modern psychiatry was nourished reflected a failure in communication. Hysteria is, in effect, stupidity. It bespeaks a failure to control symbolically the problematic aspects in a blocked action situation.[11] Each culture and each family unit places a burden of ingenuity on each individual they shape. Every individual has to keep action moving under sometimes severe vocabulary limitations. The rub is, that when the individual shows himself truly ingenious, we usually label him "mentally ill." [12] Thus it is with the hysteric who uses "body-language"; as well as with the depressed person who uses "guilt-language." Depressive self-accusation, in sum, amounts to a *search for a vocabulary of meaning* in the face of an overwhelmingly frustrating situation. It is a form of language substitute, a type of stupidity by someone poor in words.

Since psychiatrists as a whole do not understand what the patient is doing with this language, they often make his situation worse. They imagine that the "burden of guilt" would be relieved if he could release his "pent up anger" (remember the hydraulic-machine model). Hence, the psychiatrist explores with the patient valid reasons for hating his objects, hoping thereby to "bring up" the anger. This *may* result in bringing some critical clarity onto the situation. On the other hand, it may dissipate the guilt language, *which is the primary unplugging.* It may also fixate the patient onto his past, which is the one thing that is irrevocably lost, *because the present is so hopeless.* One patient complained that five years of talking with psychiatrists had made her illness worse precisely because it led to increased rumination about the past (Schwartz, 1961). If the psychiatrist is going to undermine the very creative efforts of the patient, then he should also take the next logical step, namely, help the patient break out of his constricted object range, and create a new life. "But the psychiatrist is not God." Let us, then, realize this and begin to act on the basis of it. In view of all the damage that can be done in psychiatric consultations, perhaps after all the electroshock machine is the lesser of evils at the present time. By temporarily blotting out the patient's memory it allows him to discover the world anew (cf. Kelly, 1955, Vol. 2, pp. 905-908).

Jealousy-Language

We are coming to understand that the language-thesis holds true for some forms of jealousy. Take the woman in our culture who helps her husband through college, but has to give up her own adumbrated career in order to do it. Subsequently she may find that her husband, increasingly successful, spends less and less time at home, takes her less into his confidence. She finds herself growing old, her children married, her husband distant and independent. She is in roughly the same position as the Ashanti woman, except that she has no witchcraft tradition to fall back on for ready rationalization of her sense of utter uselessness and worthlessness. However, the culture provides her with another language for protesting the gradual undermining of her self-esteem and identity, namely, the possibility that her husband is "cheating on her." To be adulterous is to fail to uphold one's part of the marriage bargain. This is obviously *the closest she can come* to adumbrating that he is "cheating *her*," since the culture *does not give voice* to the idea that the frustrated career wife of a successful businessman *should* feel cheated when she has been well provided for. She may go to any length to imagine adulterous affairs of her husband, even in her own home while she sleeps upstairs. She senses that her world has been undermined and that she is being "defiled" literally at her very doorstep. But it is noteworthy that in these cases the woman rarely attempts to surprise "the lovers," even though ample opportunity presents itself. It is as though one fears undermining a rationalization that so perfectly sustains meaning. If the jealousy-language were to fail, one would be struck dumb.

Jealousy has manifold uses, as many investigators have determined. It can be a "defense mechanism" to cover one's own insecurities (Langfeldt, 1951). It can unplug action and bolster self-value in any number of ways (Shepherd, 1961). Minkowski, aware of the multiform uses to which jealousy can be put, made a distinction between jealousy based on the love relationship, and that based on other aspects of the interpersonal situation (1929). It is precisely this jealousy "inauthentique" that arises to unplug an intolerable situation when communication breaks down. Tigelaar gets right to the heart of the matter: "This so-called jealousy seems to rise only from the bare personality, from the personality which is excluded from normal communication, especially owing to a fundamental change" (1956, p. 538). Inauthentic jealousy, in other words, like the body-language of the hysteric and the guilt-language of the depressed, is a pure creation of ingenuity in a hopelessly blocked situation. By means of jealousy-language the individual *draws himself* into a situation that excludes him; he creates a bond of self-reference, spans a serious and threatening breach in his world.

We are very far here from Freud's insight into the jealousy accusations of a 53-year-old woman patient (1920, pp. 213-218). One has only to read this case closely to see the possibility of a picture quite different from the one Freud imagined. He thought that the woman's delusional accusations of unfaithfulness, directed to her husband, were a mere cover for her own unconscious desires to commit infidelity with a younger man. But it seems obvious that, on the contrary, the woman's whole situation in the world was involved: her children grown up and married; her husband deciding to continue operating his factory instead of retiring and joining her at home. The young career girl with whom she imagined her husband having an affair had defied social convention, and had entered a man's world. She took business training rather than the domestic service customary to her class. Now she had a position at the factory as *a social equal* of the men, and was "even addressed as 'Miss.' "

One cannot make out, in Freud's account, any evidence for the woman's infatuation with her son-in-law—the desired infidelity that Freud claims he detected. Indeed, he says it was "unconscious." In a short two-hours of interviews with Freud, the woman had let fall only "certain remarks" which led Freud to his interpretation. Now, it is possible that this woman sensed the attractiveness of this young man, and assayed her own possible appeal to him, as women are wont to do. Perhaps this was the hint that Freud seized upon in the interview. It is possible too that at 53 she sensed the decline of her only (cultural) value to men—her physical charm. Whereupon she had only to compare herself to the girl at the factory who had chosen other means of performing in the male world. Thus, the wife, by accusing her husband of infidelity, may have been expressing a threat to her self, as well as giving oblique voice to the idea that the culture had cheated her. Now she was no longer attractive to men, *nor* could she ever have any active place in her husband's world. He had *chosen* not to retire, but instead to remain at the factory. She had no choice. As I read this woman's jealousy-language, it is a protest against cultural injustice: The world belonged to men, and to certain courageous women who opted for a career in that world.

It is typical both of psychoanalytic theory and of Freud personally, to have reduced this whole complex matter to a mere "unconsicous" urge to fornication. Freud, as he demonstrated in his own life, in his actions toward his own wife (Fromm, 1959), could not have understood a female protest against inequality and a threat to self-value in a man's world. An inchoate female cry against helplessness and potential meaninglessness is thus reduced to a ubiquitous sexual motive. Reducing everything to supposed instincts keeps the cultural world ethical and right. A real understanding of the complex human situation is sacrificed to the smug interpretations of an encapsulated theory—and to the morality of a Victorian world.

Ranges of Objects and Meaning

It is pardonable for the theorist to make the error of narrowness when he is attempting to understand what is behind stupidity-languages. Stupidity-languages do make the person using them seem childish, whining, and somehow culpable in himself. The person provides a sorry spectacle when he tries to keep his world from caving in upon him with only the limited means at the disposal of his ingenuity. Thus it is logical to look for selfish motives in those who show themselves cognitively limited and childish. Perhaps this is another reason why theory has so long been hampered.

But people are not fated to *remain* childish, they are *kept* childish by parents and by culture. We train them to live in a certain kind of world, and to accept it dumbly. The culture, in other words, creates certain kinds of bondage from which people cannot be released without threatening others. Can a wife be released from a marriage contract when her husband begins neglecting her? Can she begin life anew at 40 when she has not previously provided herself with the wherewithal? Can a factory-operator's wife suddenly join him at 53, untrained as she is, and basically unwanted in a man's world? Anthropology has provided us with the knowledge that there are any number of possible arrangements for human action, and that they all work—for better or for worse.[13] We have discovered that the word "natural" does not apply to human relationships: these are all learned. When we say that an individual's world "crumbles" we don't mean that his "natural" world crumbles—but rather that his cultural world does. If he had been taught to operate in another kind of world, it would perhaps not have crumbled. The Ashanti could have drawn up rules forbidding the taking of another wife, and the witchcraft depression syndrome would certainly be much reduced.

We saw that theorists have considered object-loss to be the principal cause for depression, and have overlooked the importance of "games" and meaning. One reason for this error of emphasis is that some cultures provide only a narrow range of objects and games. The result is that the object and the limited meaning come to be inseparable. That is to say, the more people to whom one can make appeal for his identity, the easier it is to sustain life-meaning. Object-loss hits hardest when self-justification is limited to a few objects. But object-loss is not crucial—or even necessarily important per se—when there is the possibility of sustaining one's conduct as before. Action is the basic problem in object-loss, and people devise ingenious ways to sustain it. An excellent illustration is the phenomenon of vengefulness. Harold F. Searles (1956) showed beautifully that the revenge process can serve as a way of *keeping the object*. It cannot be overstressed that an object is never an object per se, in isolation. It is a means of coming in contact with the world, it permits action. By definition, to constitute an object is to create a behavior pattern. To lose an object *is to lose the possibility of undertaking a range of satisfying action*. This is foremost. In addition, for man, the object is a private performance audience. It is a locus to which is addressed the continuing identity dialogue of the self and experience. The continued presence of the object, in other words, serves as a purchase to the symbolic elaboration of the self. The object need not be present in the outer world; one needs only to have developed behavior patterns toward it, or modeled on it, and to keep its image in mind. Thus, the object, as we saw in Chapter I, exists on an internal-external continuum, it reflects a *process* of growth and activity in the actor. Just as the "external pole" serves as experiential contact with the outer world, so does the "internal pole" permit a continual fashioning of the identity. Hence we can see that object-loss means not only external performance loss, but inner identity loss as well. This bears repeating, because it enables us to understand the phenomenon of vengefulness. To hate and to seek revenge *is to create a continually present object*. Searles says that the vindictive person "has not really *given up* the other person toward whom his vengefulness is directed: that is, his preoccupation with vengeful fantasies about that person serves, in effect, as a way of psychologically *holding on to* him" (1956, p. 31). Vengefulness is a type of continuous performance, a way of maintaining an object that otherwise would not be there.

Initially, what we call the "superego" is the "internal pole" of our objects. We address our performance to them, by saying "See how well I am doing, as you would wish me to." Both action and identity are potentiated. The revenge-object is merely a variation on this. We keep it in order to be able to say: "See how great I have become, as you did not think I could become," etc. It has often been observed that the motif "I'll show the folks back in my home town" is a primary impetus to success. On the primitive level, revenge murders of the death of a loved one is simply a variation on this. One continues to perform *as if* the object were still there. The automatic nature of primitive revenge shows how important it is *to keep some kind of behavior pattern*, which serves in effect to keep the object. Vilification of the dead in mourning ceremonies is also a way of keeping behavior patterns toward the object. To remain silent is to be swamped by the action void.

Finally, "showing the folks back home" keeps the identity rooted in time, gives it the all-important duration and continuity. If one could not *keep* objects, the identity would have to be continuously recreated in the present. One would be in the position of Sartre's gambler: the entire past accretion of meanings would be severed. The identity owes its very existence to its rooting in the past.

We have a hard job—in our culture—in realizing how inseparable are object-range and performance-possibility. But consider the situation in traditional society. There the extended family is the rule, and not the small, tight, nuclear one that is familiar to us. The consequence of this is that the life-chances and life-meaning of the individual do not depend on a few parental objects. Meaning is generalized to a whole range of kin. The extended family provides a continuing source of esteem and affirmation for the individual actor, *even though significant figures drop out.*

In our culture we are familiar with the person who lives his life for the wishes of his parents and becomes depressed when they die and he has reached the age of forty or fifty. He has lost the only audience for whom the plot in which he was performing was valid. He is left in the hopeless despair of the actor who knows only one set of lines, and loses the one audience who wants to hear it. The extended family takes care of this problem: Even though it makes rigid prescriptions for the behavior of each individual, still each member can count on an audience for his continuing performance even after his own immediate parents die.

Thus, culture designs the action scene, and outlines the kind of crises to which the individual will have to adapt. One of the sharpest exposés of the grip in which culture holds the individual, and the breakdown which results from that grip, is Edmund Volkart's study of bereavement (1957). Volkart points out that restriction of the identity-appeal to only a few objects is a type of "psychological bondage." We train people to "love, honor, and obey" only a few others. And when death or some other train of events leaves the haplessly loyal person in the lurch, the psychiatrist is apt to hold a microscope to his body chemistry, or measure his saliva. Instead of providing for continuing life-designs, instead of training people in critical self-awareness, we actually facilitate the subversion of life-meaning. Volkart does not soft pedal this major personality issue, and I can do no better than to quote him directly:

Any culture which, in the name of mental health, encourages extreme and exclusive emotional investments by one person in a selected few others, but which does not provide suitable outlets and alternatives for the inevitable bereavement, is simply altering the conditions of, and perhaps postponing, severe mental ill health. It may, in the vernacular, be building persons up for a big letdown by exacerbating vulnerability (1957, p. 304).

In other words, in our culture we champion limited horizons— a limited range of objects—and call people "mentally ill" when they suffer its effects. We make no provision for sustaining meaning when the bottom drops out of someone's life. When a woman's children marry, when the mirror begins to reflect the gradual and irrevocable loss of her charm, her performance as a responsible person, culturally desirable, is over. She may find herself left with no part to play, as early as her late 30's— with nothing to justify and sustain her identity. Since this utter subversion of meaning usually coincides with menopause, psychiatry has labelled the depression that may occur "involutional depression." Medical psychiatry has only recently come to focus on social role;[14] clinically, it was easier to imagine that the depression is somehow due to bodily changes. Or, the psychoanalytic theory might see this as a pampered self-pity over the imagined loss of sexual capacity, over the inevitable diminution in instinctual vigor.

Thus, in sum, we bring people up to be uncritical children, and wrench them with electroshock when their lives fail. We draw a portrait of man as a creature of instincts, and examine him pityingly and cynically. All this we do, in the name of "scientific" medical psychiatry, because most of us find the unexamined life worth living.

Social Class and Meaning-Loss

Students of epidemiology first took to studying the social distribution of types of illness in the hope of turning up some answers. Since clinical research did not provide any real understanding of the etiology of depression and schizophrenia, it was hoped that perhaps social research might. These early hopes proved elusive. Fact does not precede theory, and no amount of counting can ever explain. But statistics on epidemiology did provide some kind of picture. It now seems generally agreed that depression occurs more frequently among persons with cohesive family groupings; among women, who are more cohesively identified with close ingroups; in higher socio-economic statuses; in highly traditionalized groups; and among professionals.

Schizophrenia, on the other hand, presents a radically different epidemiological picture. It occurs more among men than women; in the lower socio-economic brackets; among dislocated peoples—that is, generally where group membership and identifications are weakest.

Mental illness, as we have been surveying it here, is a form of cultural and individual stupidity, an urge to meaning by those poor in command over vocabularies. If this thesis holds up we should expect some confirmation from the epidemiological picture: action varies according to class, as does awareness; possibilities for self-justification as well as degree of cultural indoctrination vary by class. Indeed, the class picture does seem to give some kind of consistent reflection of the views we have detailed.

If depression is a form of meaning-stupidity in an overwhelmingly frustrating situation, we would *expect* it to be more prevalent in the upper classes, among women, and among people in close identification with others. These are all people who feel that *they should* find their situation acceptable—but who somehow do not. The upper classes, having achieved socially approved success, have no reason to be unhappy. Women are given their status in the social structure as a matter of course, and should not question otherwise. People in close and "loving" identification with others are taught that they should derive all their life satisfactions from the quality of these relations, and from the pattern of rights and obligations which they entail. All the more reason that guilt should present itself as a natural alternative for deep-seated dissatisfaction: one can well believe himself guilty for not being content where he *should* be content. On the other hand, among the lower classes, dissatisfaction need not necessarily terminate in depressive self-accusation. Any number of scapegoats can be found and other rationalizations used, to justify failure: the rich, the boss, the low status of women in the lower class *as compared with* the upper, "bad luck," "hard times" and so on (cf. Prange and Vitols, 1962). In terms of alternative vocabularies of meaning, the lower classes, paradoxically, are less "stupid" than the upper.[15]

But the situation is quite different with the lower-class schizophrenic. He lacks even that meaning which belongs to his own class—since he has failed to learn to interact effortlessly. He joins a personal "poverty" to a class poverty; and it has been observed repeatedly that the extreme schizophrenic is more obedient and conservative in accepting ideal formulas for proper behavior than are his peers. He tends to conform to idealized behavioral standards which deprive him of the possibility of easy scapegoats available to those who flaunt standards.

The upper-class schizophrenic, on the other hand, is in a more fortunate situation. In the first place, he can effect *some measure of correspondence between his fantasy world* and certain specialized symbolic achievements provided by society. He has more of a chance of having his fantasies fed, and his identity somewhat validated. Clifford Beers, for example, could assume the identity of a mental-hygiene reformer, and create some measure of conformity between his omnipotent fantasies and the real action world.[16] Possibilities of symbolic self-justification are more available to upper- than to lower-class schizophrenics. Also, it is worth noting that the upper-class schizophrenic can usually extend his identity back in time, to include family traditions, roots in the Old World, illustrious ancestors, and so on. This socially supported extension of the self in time gives some experiential depth to the personality, and helps buffer present ineptitudes (Strauss, 1959, Chapter 6). The lower-class schizophrenic, on the other hand, has no such time depth to his identity, and must rely solely on fantasy and on the unrewarding contemporary situation. Rogler and Hollingshead observe bluntly on the extremely stressful and unrewarding nature of lower-class life: "The afflicted individual moves from an unpleasant world into an unreal world of fictions. These fictions may be equally unpleasant. Class V individuals are trapped" (1961, p. 185).

The Syndromes as Stupidity: A Summing-Up

Meaning-poverty then, depends on the type of stupidity. For the schizophrenic, shallowness of meaning, as we saw in Chapter I, is a result of behavioral poverty; it reflects insufficient participation in interpersonal experiences. The depressed person, on the other hand, suffers instead from *a too uncritical participation in a limited range of monopolizing interpersonal experiences.* Here are two kinds of failure of the humanization process: the individual who has not been indoctrinated into his culture, and the one who has been *only too well* imbued with a narrow range of its sentiments. If both of these individuals end up in our mental hospitals, perhaps we cannot blame the psychiatrist for juggling chemicals and ignoring culture.[17] The problem seems to be individual rather than cultural. But this is only because one has a narrow medical view of human behavior. Individual and culture are inseparable. The individual finds answers to the four common problems in a cultural world. He finds himself enmeshed in the answers provided for by social institutions—by a whole ac-cumulated tradition of cultural learning. In view of this the psy-chiatrist may object that it would be much too big a job for the medical practitioner to bring under critical fire the institutions of his society. How can he undertake to determine how people "should be" brought up? Quite right, he cannot. This is the task of a broad, unified human science.

Happily, after 50 years of incredible deviousness, the data of the human sciences are starting to emerge, their relationships are becoming clear. If this revolution, like any other, is to be suc-cessful, no vested institution can escape critical review. Nature—in her constitution of *Homo sapiens*—seems to have framed the four common human problems. But man—by his cultural and social world—frames the answers. Nothing done by man for man can-not be undone and redone. It suffices to design the problem.

This seems a good place, then, to round out conceptually our whole discussion of schizophrenia and depression. We might say that the stupidity of the schizophrenic lies in the fact that he *may* have simple *awareness* of multiple vocabularies of motive, but no corresponding firm and broad range of interpersonal be-haviors. Hence, he has poor control over these vocabularies. The depressed person's stupidity, on the other hand, resides in the fact that he has firm patterns of interpersonal behavior, but a narrow repertory of explicit vocabularies of choice.

Now, one thing will be immediately obvious about this kind of sharp classification: it can rarely exist in reference to human nature as we have traced its complex development. Schizophrenic and depressive types merge into one another and overlap. They represent different kinds and degrees of adaptation to ranges of objects and events which are not mutually exclusive within one behavioral system. Thus we can see, at the end of this four-chap-ter presentation of the two major "syndromes," that they are not syndromes at all. Rather, they reflect the typical problems that man is prone to, the restrictions, coercions, the lack of control over behavior, and the confusions in symbolic reconstruction of himself and his experience. All this blends in varying proportions in the individual personality. If we can only rarely see clear "types" emerging from this, then there is all the more reason to reorient our approach to labelling the human personality. In Chapter VII we attempt to extend our cogitation to more fruitful areas for coping with human problems (even though we continue to use the shorthand syndrome labels for the sake of convenience; see the discussion of definitions and words in the Introduction).

Notes

1. This model is reconstructed here with some artistic license. Admittedly, it is subjectively satirical, but the theoretical literature is there for all to see. For a sampling: Greenacre (1953), Hoch and Zubin (1954), and Rado (1951). For what seems to me a singularly sterile, reductionist approach conveying psychiatric scientism at its most forceful, see R. R. Grinker, Sr., et al. (1961). For example, buried on page 96, we find that a person becomes depressed because of object-loss and low self-esteem, which hypothesis renders completely redundant the arid tables and charts which stuff the book.

2. Among others, Mabel Cohen and her co-workers have taken steps to broaden theory. See Myer Mendelson (1960). Also, Rado's recent views (1961) tend away from the libidinal formulation.

3. But the modern Adlerian view of depression still sees the depressed patient predominantly as a spoiled child, rather than as an adult whose world may have gone wrong (Kurt Adler, 1961).

4. The sociological explanation of funeral and mourning rites is that they serve as the social dramatization of solidarity at the loss of one of society's performance members. Ceremonies of mourning serve to reaffirm social cohesiveness even though single performers drop out of the cultural action plot.

5. I am of course omitting consideration of the nondiscursive arts, and of action reduced to subconscious habit.

6. Cf. D. O. Hebb's observation that for man, cognitive processes in themselves have immediate drive value (1955), (an observation

which indicates that psychology is belatedly emerging from its long scientistic moratorium; it is over eighty years since Alfred Fouillée elaborated the notion of *idées-forces*).

7. In this use, it is an inept attempt at coping—a feeble coping in Goldstein's sense—which, as previously noted, may avert a truly catastrophic breakdown.

8. Depression has also probably had a long historical connection with the self-effacement of mystics. John Custance (1951, pp. 61-62) compared his experiences during depression with the self-flagellation of Madame Guyon and St. Theresa.

9. Others make a similar observation: "Acknowledgment of personal sin or confession of guilt may sometimes be a defense against the possibility that there may be no meaning in the world. . . . Guilt in oneself is easier to face than lack of meaning in life" (Lynd, 1958, p. 58). But I would not say "defense," rather, simply, *the only language* one knows. M. Schmideberg observes also that "Guilt implies responsibility; and however painful guilt is, it may be preferable to helplessness" (1956, p. 476). For further remarks which are very much to the point of our discussion, see Charles Orbach and Irving Bieber (1957).

10. The nausea that sometimes accompanies depression may be due to the inability to place the world into meaningful interrelationships. This is the existential view—nausea as a reaction to meaninglessness. Alonzo Graves noted that he suffered attacks of nausea while engaged "in reflecting rather definitely over my situation and outlook" (1942, p. 678).

11. This is also very clear on the primitive cultural level, where hysteria is a common "syndrome." Cf. for example, Seymour Parker (1962).

12. Ingenuity in an infantile or "primitive" type of personality is often more clumsy. Cora Du Bois (1961, pp. 153-158) reports one case of "madness" from Alor that looks very much like the hysteric's "illness-language." This woman's attacks began a year after the death of her husband, when she was 35. She often repeated, in private, "This madness gives me much trouble." In view of her personal situation, and the abysmal cultural level of Alorese life, the phrase "This madness" seems very much like what Sullivan called the hysteric's "happy idea" (1956, p. 205), i.e., the ingenious language the hysteric hits upon to unplug a situation he does not understand. (See also Ch. VII below.)

13. In the light of our subsequent discussion on variations in range of objects provided by various cultures, see Seymour Parker's paper on the difference in symptomatology between the Eskimo and the Ojibwa (1962). Given the Ojibwa's narrow range of objects and upbringing, depression, as Parker notes, is a logical reaction to frustration. The broad range of objects and the communal life among the Eskimo, on the other hand, seem literally to make impossible a depressive reaction (as we understand it here).

14. Arnold Rose has correctly stressed the social role aspects of "involutional depression," namely, the loss of meaning (1962). His paper is part of a broad and growing attack on the narrow psychiatric jurisdiction over human failure. Its opening paragraph contains the keynote of this attack (p. 537). For some excellent case histories which reveal the restriction of interests to a few objects, the restriction of awareness, and the sudden undermining of occupational role, see: William Malamud, S. L. Sands, and Irene T. Malamud (1941).

15. In a random observation, it seems that even the suicide notes left by individuals in the various classes vary in verbosity. A mere cursory scanning of the literature—which may be erroneous—seems to reveal that upper-class notes are invariably curt, containing little vocabulary other than that one is "tired" of living. Lower-class notes seem verbose in accusations of specific individuals, and sometimes of definite circumstances. See H. P. David and J. C. Brengelmann (1960).

16. See C. W. Beers (1960). It is noteworthy that when Beers smuggled a letter to the governor of the state, the governor read it and replied to it. Szasz opines that a letter signed "Clifford Whittingham Beers" would be attended to; whereas that of a hypothetical lower-class schizophrenic patient, say, "Joe Kowalski," would not (personal communication, cited with permission). The class difference in possibilities of self-justification made itself felt immediately in Beers's case.

17. A *note on mania:* Mania, often found to alternate with depressive states, offers a picture of such puzzling lack of control that even Harry Stack Sullivan thought it due probably to a physiochemical disorder. (This is all the more strange for one who saw schizophrenia as an interpersonal problem.) The manic, in his states of hyperactivity, seems to go out of control and will often do things that normally he would never do. Perhaps most annoying to the others in our culture is the manic's tendency to indiscriminate sexual activity and heedless squandering of the hallowed bank account. There are various degrees of mania—in our culture it has been observed that salesmen are often recruited on the manic continuum. An individual can spend an entire lifetime as a "successful" manic,

earning high achievement and recognition, and even extreme states are not recognized by others as "abnormal" (Allers, 1961, pp. 62-64). Often the manic signals himself by becoming depressed due to some setback in his plans, and then he earns a diagnosis of "manic-depressive."

All this is well known; the problem is what to make of it in behaviorial terms rather than in physio-chemical ones. There are some interesting suggestions. In the first place there seems to be general agreement that the manic—like the depressed—has a very loose grip on his self-esteem. Despite the manic's appearance of boundless self-confidence, Federn (1952) noted that underneath was a weak ego. Kurt Adler says of the manic that he "intoxicates himself with false courage" (1961, p. 60). Generally, the manic seems as uncritical of his performance world as is the depressed. He is just as much caught up in it, and performs wholeheartedly on the basis of a narrow range of rules. The manic seems to intoxicate himself with an adroit, superficial performance of the rules, with the immediate stimulus of the moment (cf. Graves, 1942, pp. 672-673). He seems to carry himself along by his fluent command of the cultural fiction. This kind of immature and flighty omnipotence— not grounded in substantial ego-strength—is very much akin to the schizophrenic who is carried along to similar omnipotent feelings by mere word sounds: we seem to have here a difference between word-sound stimulus and "total organic sense" (see Ch. II). It is note-worthy that adolescents experience quick successions of omnipotence and extreme inferiority (Eissler, 1952, p. 104). This seems to indicate new behavior that does not have a firm basis in self-feeling: it seems as though the symbolic self, with a glib command over performance, is attaining to heights that the individual cannot really feel to be a part of himself. The adolescent stands torn on this very threshold: possibilities of unmeasured increase in social ex-perience of self-value, and in new ranges of behaviors, versus the accustomed experience of low self-value in the home, and the narrow range of objects and behavior it permits. The depressed phase is merely a surrender to the narrow object range. In this sense the manic is continually juvenile; to himself he is always unproven in the world.

As for the florid end-state of mania, this is analogous to the schizophrenic end-state. It is an extreme case of lack of control of a certain kind of being-in-the-world. Mania certainly should not be explained by splitting languages, and searching for a physio-chemical explanation. Past a given point, the whole organism can go out of control *behaviorally*, as the schizophrenic loses his world behaviorally. There seems to be no more need to split mind and body in the study of mania than in any other syndrome.

*We require a way of thinking that
takes account of the pull of expectancies as well as the push of tensions,
that recognizes that growth and creativity come as much or more from
instability as from stability, and that
emphasizes culturally created values as
well as the immediately observable external environment.*

CLYDE KLUCKHORN (1962, p. 264)

V

The Human
Personality

(1) A POST-SCIENTISTIC VIEW

IT HAS NOT ALWAYS been possible
to treat human institutions so cavalierly. First we had to discover that they were our own handiwork—and this has taken a
long time. The period of the Middle Ages to Darwin is a story
of Western man's enticement into self-exposure.[1] In the perspective of history, it seems inevitable that man should have
ended up by "seeing through himself," as it were. As soon as
human destiny and natural necessity drifted apart—as soon as the

theological world-view was undermined—man was doomed to examine his miserable condition. The Enlightenment gave man a new faith in himself, but he could not long sustain it. With Darwin's discoveries in the nineteenth century, followed by those of Freud and the wars of the twentieth, there was very little happy illusion left.

Modern Man's First Self-Exposure

Long before Darwin, Jeremy Bentham began peeling one corner of human illusion by examining man's use of verbal fictions. The nineteenth century discovered that man's whole verbal and psychological approach to the world was fabricated on the basis of human intent. Even mathematics was seen to be a creation of man's mind, independent of any necessary connection to reality. By the time the twentieth century was comfortably under way, Vaihinger had taken over from Bentham. He showed that concepts were merely tools for ordering and classifying experiences, they bore no necessary relation to reality. Man's whole psychological world was seen as a cognitive map that was largely fictional —a dream edifice which somehow (no one yet knows exactly how) served to make action possible. Man's symbolic world was almost reduced to the status of a figment of his imagination. Wittgenstein, Korzybski, the whole linguistic philosophy school offered support for the notion that the advent of language meant the limitation of perception in the interests of the ego. The pitch of disillusionment with man's private creations reached a high point. Kenneth Burke's semantic attack on the fictional nature of human meaning, and the verbal means of sustaining it, was remorseless: "If science would be truly atheistic or impious to the last degree, it should try systematically to eradicate every last linkage that remains with us merely as the result of piety or innate propriety, and not because of its rationally established justification" (1954, p. 119). Bentham had not taken up his cudgel in vain. Here was an attack with vengeance on the shackles in which cultural learning holds the symbolic animal. Burke wanted to subject language "to the same 'cracking' process that chemists now use in their refining of oil" (p. 119).

In the mid-twentieth century all of this is coming to flower. Man has rolled up his shirtsleeves, eager to tamper with his own creation. Freud, paradoxically, both helped and hindered this "new Enlightenment." He showed how culture was built into a fearful animal, how *Homo sapiens* is twisted into humanization. There could now be no doubt about the fact of man's self-creation—Freud had laid bare the process in embryo. But in doing so, he carried over too much nineteenth-century biology and physics, with the result that he accented the animal side, rather than the human side, of man's action. Now we see the full contradiction: If man is self-created via culture, the animal side has to count for less. Maintain that biological drives take precedence over cultural learning, and you take man "out of his hands," so to speak. The mystery of something prior to and greater than man's own efforts remains to mock his powers. Man may be able to see through himself, but he cannot see through nature. The long and bitter struggle against the full Freudian influence throughout the first 50 years of the twentieth century has been a struggle by man to take himself in hand with no "instinctual" strings attached. Freud's very monumentality rests partly on the self-contradictory nature of his formulations. He put subsequent thinkers in an enormous bind: as they chafed, his stature grew.

It was necessary, in sum, to abandon the idea that human action was motivated by some deep inner urges and instinctual essences. Only then could the cultural nature of motives be examined. To make this possible, people from many disciplines joined in the attack on the constrictive aspects of Freudian theory in particular, and of physicalist psychology in general. The story is only too well-known. There was an upsurge for a broader view of man. Adler, Binswanger, Sartre, Gordon Allport, Carl Rogers, Karen Horney, Hadley Cantril, Robert Lynd, Harry Stack Sullivan—the list is long. Everyone had something to contribute; either something to keep alive, to keep from being buried under physicalist and fragmenting research; or, something to call attention to, a larger whole, a more integral synthesis, something seen in a more wholesome light.

The focus of attention of the personality theorists was on the humanization process—the Oedipal transition. We saw in Chapter II how coercive it was. The child, in order to keep his objects and their love, in order to keep his self-esteem and the forward-momentum of his action, accepts to predicate his whole being on the vocabulary of motives learned from his parents. With the eagerness of Chinese communist youth who attend the "Revolutionary College" to learn "right action," the child similarly accepts his indoctrination without guile. Much of the bitter fighting within psychoanalysis, and dispute over the contributions of the men listed above, revolved around a search for the proper vocabulary with which to describe this humanization process. What were the basic and irreducible concepts, the dominant motives? Now that the dust is settling, we can see some of the results of the reaction against Freud. A major one is that the vocabulary has been stripped clean, and is being whittled down more and more. Not only are the instincts disappearing, but the words used to describe the total individual are simple and direct. Adler used the word "life-style" to describe the behavior that results from the child's indoctrination. Sartre uses "original choice for being." Both refer simply to the range of action that the child decides on in order to salvage his self-esteem and keep his conduct moving forward. So too with Sullivan's "self-system"—the series of "linguistic tricks" that the child learns for conciliating his environment. Rogers saw the humanization process as a gaining of "positive regard" from the parents, in exchange for fulfilling their "conditions of worth." The child is established as a locus of primary value by accepting the dictates of the culture. This is a variation on the theme that fear of object-loss is the basis for accepting indoctrination. Rogers points out (1959) that the greater this fear (based on unreasonable parental dictates and unusual difficulty in earning their "positive regard"), the more will the child's perception be rigidly twisted into an inflexible pattern. The tighter the controls and the more rigorous the training at the "Revolutionary College," the more straight-laced the recruits.

Any number of theorists could be cited, any number of variations sketched, in the description of the basic humanization process. We have already seen the broad outlines of this process in some detail. For our purposes all we need do is to note the remarkable agreement of the post-Freudian thinkers, how effectively they have gone beyond Freud to show that man can be understood only as a cultural animal; that *Homo sapiens* learns abstract, symbolic categories on the basis of which to act; and that the only biological basis for all this is a contingent one—the child barters animal behavior for human action partly because of a fear of object-loss, and a need for love. The constitution of the self, of the human actor, is based largely on social motives. Sartre, Adler, George Mead, Dewey—all were talking about the same thing. Thus, in sum, we have at last a picture of human motivation that owes almost nothing of its finished product to primary biological drives except the basic need for survival and action. We seem as near to an ineluctable law of early human development as we will probably ever get. And to arrive at this law we have not had to reduce man to "manageable" proportions: not to "x" number of drives or to "n" number of instincts, or to "q" number of needs. All we had to do was to affirm his extreme plasticity and his need to keep action moving forward. Man's motiviation is amply provided for by answers to the four common human problems. The possible answers, and hence the possible motives, are nearly as infinite as coherent word combinations themselves. A thousand humans pounding a thousand typewriters till eternity would probably not exhaust the possible predicates for deriving self-value. Symbolic animals, unlike other animals, actually live in castles in Spain.

The stream of convergence on the fiction and the social nature of motives has not been as smooth-flowing as this sketch makes out. If the reductionist and physicalist legacy of the nineteenth century is being abandoned, the idea of a precise science of man is not. This explains why the Lewinians—with all their brilliance —bogged down in artistic self-titillation with their "hodological" diagrams, and were ultimately obliged to think more broadly. Lewin made an early entry into phenomenology—into the actor's world as seen by him. But he left history out of his constructions of the "life-space" (McGill, 1949), which is equivalent to leaving the print out of a carefully designed book. Gestalt psychology reacted very early against the older physicalist and associationist psychology, which attempted to get at human action by measuring it from the outside. But although Gestalt pretended to be occupied with psychological phenomenology, it remained rooted to physiology. Kurt Koffka's *Principles of Gestalt Psychology* (1935) pretended to be a comprehensive text on the human personality, *and made cursory mention of language.* Physiology, no matter how molar or total the units considered, is still a study of a part-function of a whole symbolic animal. To leave history and language out of the study of human personality is like dissecting a corpse to study expression.

Modern psychology has been heroic in a quixotic way. Pick up any text on psychology and notice the painstaking care with which aspects of the personality are described and marked out, the history of psychology summarized, experiments detailed. The unaware student feels he is in for a feast of understanding, and up to a point he is. Up to the most important point, unfortunately. That is, the point at which the individual personality links with society and history: the point at which the symbolic animal becomes a locus of possibility, always in the making, never fully cast. Change a Venezuelan political party, the price of Camembert in France, or find a skin chemical that removes color, and you turn man's world on edge. Of course the best psychology texts have a good deal to say about "self-concept," and at least a word or two about social role. But even sophisticated works do little more than acknowledge with a pointed finger that "out there" lies the "social sphere"—very important for an understanding of the personality—"but, our job here is to limit ourselves to psychology." If man's world can be turned upside-down by a symbolic social event, then there can be no limits set by any discipline that pretends to understand his action. If a Stalin can study assiduously for the clergy only to shape himself into an ardent atheistic revolutionary, then psychology itself has to be turned upside-down. If we are going to study man then we need, as Maslow argues, a psychology of possibility. Those who really tried to understand human action never limited themselves to psychology. They studied it, digested it, and moved on—to philosophy, social criticism, history. James, Baldwin, George Mead, and Dewey are among those who took an understanding of man more seriously than the promotion of an academic discipline. Granted, they never pretended full allegiance to psychology as a science—because they understood what man is.

Psychology alone is not guilty—all the disciplines are. Anthropology, social psychology, sociology, history: each one cuts a vital organ or two out of the whole man, and lays it aside as beyond its special competence. The students think they see an integral body, but they don't know where to probe for the gaps (and their instructors will rarely tell them). Worst of all, the life is out of this body, and the disciplinarians pretend it is warm. Pick up any issue of a journal of sociology, anthropology, psychology, or social psychology, and glance over the articles. Here's a smell of the musty. A paleontologist's delight. The whole, warm, thinking, feeling, acting human is a stranger to these pages, for the most part. Why this lamentable situation? Mostly because the disciplines have decided to hug to themselves the little that each knows; to train "their kind" of specialist, concentrate on "their area" of knowledge. The hope in all this ostrich behavior is that one day each discipline would know enough so that they would all fall together in one big happy

Maypole ceremony, announcing the arrival of the Science of Man. It is all done, in sum, in the interests of "science."

But there is one big ominous "Frightful" lurking behind all these efforts; a "Frightful" that seems to be causing the moneyed foundations to gush more and more support for narrower and narrower research; a "Frightful" that for some decades now has led to a rededication to intensified fragmentation of academic interests. The "Frightful" is a variation on the secret of the Northwest Coast Indians, revealed to youth upon initiation into manhood. The lad is taken aside by his elders, and into his ear is whispered the coveted secret: The secret is that *there is no secret*. The "Frightful" is that there *can be no* "science" of man. That is, there can be no endless accumulation of data that will one day "add up" to sure knowledge; there can be no precise measurement; there can be no sure prediction. Least of all can there be a science of the individual personality. Man is composed of history and symbols; each actor contains a portion of the symbolic repertory of his society and of its past. Try spitting on the Alamo to see how a friendly twentieth-century Texan is made. Just as the elaborate panorama of history is continuing, unfolding, never finished, so too is the individual an amalgam of the continuously modifiable. The secret is that symbol-systems can be turned upside down and inside out. They can be tampered with beyond repair by a maliciously whispered word. They can be stretched to skyscraper height by a newly won literacy. They can be hopelessly crushed for life by a three-word confession, or carried by another to undreamed-of fulfillment. Where all this can happen there can be no question of science as we know it, or rather *have known it*, and have hoped for it. And if the exegesis in the following pages holds up, *that* kind of science can never be. The reason is that modern man is slowly realizing that symbol-systems *should be turned upside down and inside out*: that they were made precisely for that, that man's business is precisely to *become*. Let us consider this real revolution.

The Inside of the Personality

It was the phenomenological and existential "reaction," [2] in sum, which changed our ideas about the possibility of a measured, predictive science of man. Some thinkers could not stand the idea of building toward a science of man that would leave out the world of his experience, precisely what is peculiar to him as a human animal. Very simply, phenomenology showed that man looks at his world from the inside; and existentialism showed how important to man was the symbolic constitution of that world. Science, which was *par excellence* the technique of getting at things from the *outside*, measuring, weighing and counting them, found itself face to face with a most curious object. The human individual feels and believes; he *experiences* time, *lives* time, not merely measures and counts it; he exists in space, gobbles it with movements, shrinks it with yearning, stretches it with smugness. Science, which for a long time politely declined to deal with values, found an object whose very existence was to value: himself, his actions, the opinions of others. Here, in sum, was an object for study that lost its peculiarities when it was stripped of values. It then became an object like any other: corpse, in effect, equals earth equals organic matter. But the living man, the creature of values, had to be studied. In order to do this, his world had to been seen from the inside.

We saw at some length what man's world looks like as he constructs it in action. Seen from the inside the world has no greater mystery; it is largely a panorama of action-possibilities on the one hand, and on the other, a storehouse of symbols and images that subserve action or that take its place. Man's phenomenal world is a mixture of the possibilities of both action and dreams; a real world and an imagined world that cannot be unfused.

It is this very "fused" nature of the phenomenal world each

individual carries around inside, that has caused so much trouble to theorists and researchers. How is it to be studied, how is it to be described scientifically? The earlier phenomenological psychologists tried to improve on the older science by looking at man from the inside; but they didn't dare be "unscientific" about it. We noted that when Lewin tried to construct the life-space as seen from the inside he left history out of it in order to describe it in mathematical-geometrical language. Thus, even after shifting its focus, psychology strove to remain a "science" by fracturing its data. The problem in studying scientifically the phenomenal field is the problem of all science: when an area is "marked off" for close study there is a great danger of leaving some essential connecting link out. And the connection between data, as James saw, is as much a valid object for study as are the isolated data themselves. Arthur Bentley is critical of the phenomenological approach exactly for this reason (1954, p. 222). By talking about a "behavioral field" present in the subject's awareness, the researcher seems to be placing an unnecessary "something" between the subject and the object. Is the "life-space" separate from the external world of objects? (cf. F. H. Allport, 1955, pp. 156 ff.).

Problems of definition and precision are tedious. But if we slip by them to deal with larger, more inclusive units we are in danger of blurring important distinctions. The vast confusion that exists in this area at present is a result of nearly everyone having offered his version of a solution to this problem. What composes the phenomenal field; what are its limits; is it a system, and if so what are its boundaries? The Freudian schema of id-superego-ego has been superseded not only by the Sullivanian "self-system," but also by Gordon Allport's "proprium" (1955, p. 61) (a sub-unit of the personality as a whole); by the existentialists' *umwelt* (biological action world), *mitwelt* (interpersonal world), and *eigenwelt* (self-world) (May, 1958); by Snygg and Combs's division of the "phenomenal field" into "phenomenal self" and "self-concept" (1949), and by many more. The problem in this welter of conceptualizations is simply one of trying to order three aspects of individual action: (1) The person as a locus of control over his powers. (2) His perceptions (of himself and of objects) as formed by the cultural fiction (by answers to the four common human problems). (3) His transactions with objects. The problem is to define and limit each of these three, and to give them cohesiveness as belonging to one unit; at the same time, this unit has to be shown to be inseparable from the external world.

This is a post-Freudian dilemma. If thinkers had been content to see the humanization process and the resultant personality in Freudian terms, they could enjoy the equanimity of most psychoanalysts today. The id-superego-ego model is based on a tacit opposition of the individual to the world, and on a fragmentation within himself. It gives us a distorted view of human action—but it works.[3] The new problems in personality theory reflect precisely the willingness to take on new burdens, to see man in his greater complexity. For example, to psychoanalysts "projection," "transference," and "unconscious" are easy to understand. In their scheme, the ego maintains a guard over unconscious instinctual urges. Projection, and the other mechanisms of defense, are means whereby one distorts the external world to protect himself from being swamped by a recognition of these urges. In projection the ego says: "That is not my desire, it is his," and so on. The psychoanalytic scheme is not bad, because it accounts for perceptual distortion, for the cultural screen through which we have been trained to view objects. But, if we throw out the facile view of motivation by instincts, and deny the reality of the unconscious—as phenomenologists have done (van den Berg, 1955, pp. 25 ff.)—the picture thickens in complexity. Without a mysterious unconscious to spring instincts on us, our way of seeing the world must be a reaction to external events rather than internal urges. We can then understand that *everything* the individual sees, and his whole *manner* of seeing, is a unique result of a unique learning process.

The matter is enormously complicated by this, even though it seems a simplification at first. It results in the fact that clinically every person's view of the world has to be seen and understood in its own right, in its full uniqueness. The only thing we know is that it has been shaped according to the rough laws of the humanization process. Beyond that its forms are endless. If motivation is social, in sum, each actor is a unique symbolic creation.

The Human Sentiments

It is not surprising then, that to make some headway in the post-Freudian personality dilemma, theorists have had to overlook a large part of his theory, and have had to retrace personality theory from where Baldwin, Cooley and the social interactionists had left it. This accounts for the fact that social psychology, which had long since ceased to take Freudian instinct theory seriously, has kept alive a very vigorous view of human motivation. In effect, social psychology, by insisting that action is guided by sentiments and attitudes, allowed for a fully flexible approach to conduct. Gordon Allport, who insisted very early on the fundamental importance of attitudes (1935), has, consequently, consistently put forth a mature view of human personality. His fellow psychologists, for the most part following fads or trying heroically to shape themselves into a fantasied image of the "true scientist," have had difficulty keeping up with him. Here is a recent statement on personality that well sums up the present trend: ⁄

Starting fairly early in our lives we are propelled, I maintain, not by instincts, but by *interests*. In the earliest months of life a child develops systems of positive attachments. He loves his own mother, not someone else's. His initial undifferentiated adience is quickly polarized by objects. He soon develops attachments to groups of which he is a member: to his family, his church, his ethnic group, and later to his lodge, office, and his own offspring. The love and loyalty are concrete. They are fashioned into sentiments, and these sentiments are learned. To say that a person's positive attachments are nothing but an adventitious channeling of an instinct is simply not helpful. It is the sentiments that are the ongoing, postinstinctive motives of the developing personality. . . . The view of motivation that I am here proposing says that the important thing is the person's systematized design for living. This design—not his hypothetical instincts—is the dynamic force in his life. Whenever an adjustment confronts him he will make it with his *present* equipment—with his current prejudices, attitudes, sentiments (Allport, 1950, pp. 155-157).

Allport's position here is little different from Sartre's (1956).

Reaffirming the importance of attitudes or sentiments over instincts is causing something of a McDougall revival. McDougall, in effect, bears one close similarity to Freud. He put forth a brilliant and comprehensive theory of personality that likewise contained its own internal contradiction. Consequently, subsequent thinkers have had to pay him homage as well as to attack him violently. McDougall kept the idea of instinct, and at the same time insisted on the importance of sentiments (1923, 1960). In his usage, a sentiment is defined simply as a learned disposition toward objects (Adams, 1953). Lumping sentiments and instincts together in the same formulation was equivalent to maintaining at one and the same time that personality was bound by instincts and made infinitely flexible by learning. Thus, McDougall very early offered the key to a fully cultural view of motivation,[4] but he crippled his own contribution by carrying over the earlier notions of instincts.[5]

Little wonder then that McDougall's idea of sentiments was recently reaffirmed as the major theoretical underpinning of a massive community study (Leighton, *et al.*, 1959; Hughes, *et al.*, 1960). The post-Freudian epoch is in full swing. Leighton, in his use of sentiment, seems to be attempting a clean break with all earlier preconceptions about personality functioning. Recognizing that all the disputes in psychiatric theory center around the basic humanization process, that there is no agreement on what exactly is involved in this process in terms of fears, strivings, motivations and urges, Leighton attempts to simplify the whole matter. Fear of object loss, need for gratification of instincts, reduction of tensions—all these may or may not be true. But in order to avoid commitment to the particulars of any one theory, Leighton uses the term "essential psychical condition." This is conceived as a process, "perpetually being lost and recovered . . . maintained only through constant activity on the part of the personality system" (1959, pp. 138-139). With this view, Leighton joins a majority of post-Freudian theorists who assume that action and forward momentum of the organism are primary, and who argue further that this is best conceptualized with a minimum of theoretical baggage. Magda Arnold sums up this position similarly to Allport and Leighton: "Starting with the assumption of inherent activity rather than passivity (or strict reactivity), we do not have to look for special driving forces, be they instincts, drives, or needs, that spur the living being to action; nor do we have to assume that the environment pulls or lures it . . . the organism is already active . . . motives merely direct its activity" (1960, pp. 223 ff.).

How is the personality formed in this very neutral picture? Granted that the organism has no internal drives or instincts, how are the social motives built into it? Here is where Leighton has recourse to the idea of "sentiments." The sentiments enter into the theoretical picture as the bridge between the "essential psychical condition"—the perpetual striving—and the objects which help achieve and maintain this condition. Thus Leighton affirms the contemporary view that motivation is largely social, largely learned. The child is a thoroughly plastic creature formed in its individuality by the nature of its contact with objects. McDougall's sentiment finds it full usage in Leighton's scheme, without the self-contradictory assumption that it derives from instincts.

In some ways, however, Leighton has not improved on McDougall's scheme. By attempting to do away with instincts he has been forced to complicate the simple picture he aimed for. The "essential striving condition" cannot be entirely neutral. The organism is striving for something, for some kinds of satisfactions, for some kinds of avoidances. Each organism contains within itself certain conditions which must be met in order for it to develop. The human animal, as we know, contains peculiar conditions of its own. McDougall attempted to meet this problem by postulating certain instincts. Leighton attempts to meet it by postulating ten "essential striving sentiments" which achieve and maintain the "essential striving conditions" (p. 148): physical security, sexual satisfaction, expression of hostility, expression of love, securing of love, securing of recognition, expression of spontaneity, orientation in terms of one's place in society and the places of others, the securing and maintaining of membership in a definite human group.

At the summit of his system, McDougall had placed the "self-regarding sentiment." Leighton denies that any one sentiment can be accounted primarily responsible for optimum personality functioning. Instead, he suggests that the "ten essential striving sentiments," taken together, maintain the "essential striving condition" (pp. 404-405). But this conceptual substitution does not maintain the neutrality that Leighton seeks. Actually, it obscures the picture somewhat. This is best seen in the vagueness that results in the actual definition of what a sentiment is. On the one hand, Leighton has seized beautifully on sentiments as resulting from object-contact. The sentiment grows up in action with a specific object. But on the other hand, Leighton is obliged to talk about "ten essential striving sentiments," which would supposedly exist prior to experience with objects. Finally, his usage of sentiment shades over into the popular, common-sense usage. He makes sentiment synonymous —or nearly so—with "beliefs," "opinions," "attitudes," "perceptions," "themes," "patterns of culture," "values," and with Ortega y Gasset's words "conviction" and "beliefs" (1959, pp. 255, 256, 264). Thus, a consistent theoretical treatment of sentiments is undermined by (1) considering some sentiments to exist prior to contact with objects; and (2) by resorting to common-sense definitions.

Human Needs and Motivation: A Basic View

We have discussed the minor vagaries in Leighton's usage of sentiment in order to introduce a view of the sentiments that is clear and concise, and further removed from common sense. It seems preferable to have a scheme with somewhat less neutrality and, at the same time, a somewhat greater precision of definition of the sentiments. Thus we can support the post-Freudian convergence of personality theorists, noted at the beginning of this chaper, and, at the same time, keep some of the major accents of psychoanalytic findings. Let us take the question of neutrality first—how strict must it be? We know, for example, that in the higher primates a long period of postnatal dependency makes necessary extended nutrition and object contact. We seem, therefore, justified in postulating with the psychoanalysts that the child's basic anxiety is one of object-loss or separation. As we have noted repeatedly, children need secure object-contact.[6] We also know that in order to act as a symbolic animal the child needs answers to the four common human problems. These are supplied in the humanization process. Thus, the higher primates have to fulfill conditions found *in all of nature*—the basic conditions for *survival* and *action* on the part of any specified organism; but they are fulfilled in a special way. In the higher primates mere *survival* is assured by a long succoring-dependence relationship with the mother; *human action* is assured by learning answers to the four common problems. This twofold focus provides us with a very simple picture of human motivation, and at the same time a very elastic and still neutral one.

Now for the question of a more specific definition of the

sentiments. If we could talk about *one* basic need that *any* organism has, it would be the presence of other objects. The acting organism cannot exist in a void: it must have something literally to "bump up against"—this is the bare minimum. It can only act in a world which contains things to incorporate, to obliterate, to flow toward, to flee from. An organism can exist only in relation to other organisms. It can *act* only in relation to them: the existence of another organism makes possible our action. By definition, then, an organism in my field is an *action-potentiating object*. As we saw in Chapter II, when the maternal object cripples the child's ability to undertake action, she is subverting *her* main function as an organism-object in his field. Hence, David Levy's observation that interference with the child's action *alone* is illness-provoking; and our insistence that *the whole process of individuation consists in the creation of objects: the creation of loci of action-possibility.*

This is another way of saying that *the whole of life-meaning is invested in objects,* since they are the conditions of *our* coming into being. Man, due to his long period of dependence and his peculiar needs as a cultural animal, comes to invest his life-meaning in a similarly peculiar way. He doesn't only "bump into" objects, or recognize them vaguely. He recognizes them very acutely; he comes to understand the unique place that each object can fulfill in his strivings. On a simple organic level the organism attains satisfaction of its striving by union with an object, say, ingesting a food particle. Action becomes a continual rhythm of satisfaction and increased painful striving until a new satisfaction is achieved. The emotional life of these lower organisms would reflect this striving. Emotion is a sign of potential discord, a sign that the accustomed rhythm is not going to be maintained. For any animal, emotion is a way of recognizing objects and referring them to its own satisfactions. But for man, as Dewey observed (1934, p. 15), emotion—as interest in objects —becomes conscious. Not only do we "feel" potential accords and discords, but we realize *cognitively* the meaning an object has for us in terms of the satisfactions it grants. The whole of our life's investment in objects is contained in the explicitly conscious and implicitly emotional meanings we assign to them. The resultant sentiments that form around objects become our intricate rooting in the world. We merely carry to a higher pitch of consciousness and sensitivity a dialogue that takes place on all levels of organic life. For this reason sentiment is, as Leighton observed, "a good approximation to nature" (1959, pp. 245-246).

I think it is fair to limit sentiments to this specific definition of transactions with objects. On the human level, this would accord with Leighton's detailing of the three aspects of each sentiment. A sentiment would contain one or more of the following: (1) Thought-feelings regarding what has been, is, and can be—the reality aspect. (2) Thought-feelings regarding what ought to be—the value aspect. (3) Thought-feelings regarding what is wanted—the desire aspect (1959, pp. 247-248). Then, we could talk, simply, about the need for objects as basic both to survival *and* action. The sentiments would be seen as the *special indoctrination attendant upon the cultural initiation into action*—gained by answering the four common human problems in any variety of ways. This would retain Leighton's neutrality, as well as keep the definitions of sentiments more sharply focused on the humanization process itself. It would also keep an important place for McDougall's self-regarding sentiment. The human animal, in order to act, has to constitute himself a locus of primary value in a world of meaning. And this he does by gaining answers to the four common human problems. But before these answers are evolved in controlled action, the initial infusion of self-value is gained by the child in his early transactions with objects. Self-esteem, as the psychoanalysts aptly note, begins to grow with the intake of the maternal milk (Fenichel, 1945).

The problem of the place of self-esteem in human action is an important one, but not everyone gives it the same prominence.

Gordon Allport, for example, takes issue with the idea that self-value or self-love need be a dominant personality motive. "Pervasive as this aspect of selfhood is, it is not in all lives sovereign. And it is far from constituting the whole of the problem of self. . . . Self-love . . . need not dominate . . . only self-extension is the earmark of maturity" (1961, pp. 120, 285). It is difficult to argue with Allport's broad and sophisticated views, and easy to grant that self-love is not a dominant *motive* per se. But doesn't one have to feel warm about his acts wherever they extend? Doesn't he have to have a cognizance that they are a satisfying part of what he feels himself to be? As we will see in the next section, self-feeling and action are inseparably fused with objects. The three together compose the personality. We cannot act without self-value, not for long at any rate, and not without damaging effects on our personality. But when action is suspended we still try to feel good about ourselves—we try to construct a satisfying identity in fantasy. Even though self-value is inseparable from our acts, it exists while we contemplate them in our imagination. In man, self-value has become conscious. This is what may have led McDougall to consider self-feeling primary—the fact that it exists even in the suspension of action. Granted, there is a slight fallacy here. This is equivalent to postulating that mind as internal reverie has a *priority over* action in the external world of things because mind exists *apart from* action. Whereas, on the contrary, ideally mind exists to subserve action, just as self-value is built up in action and is dependent on it. When self-value comes to be fabricated *in lieu of action* the individual risks separating himself from the world— the same risk he runs when he develops internal symbolic meanings separate from action. This is the basic problem of schizophrenia as a mode of being in the world. Paranoia might be defined specifically as the fabrication of self-value in lieu of or apart from a specific range of action. In view of all this McDougall may have elaborated too much on what is basically an artificial separation. Some of his critics, on the other hand, seem to be defining self-love too narrowly (Allport is not one of these). With our modern appreciation of the centrality of self-esteem in human conduct, and our extensive knowledge of its genesis and dimensions, we close the circle on three hundred years of personality theory (cf. Lovejoy, 1961).

A Simplified View of the Personality: The "Action-Triad"

In its exact usage, sentiment should sum up the phenomenal world of the organism—the world as it looks from the inside of action. It serves perfectly to reflect this perceptual world as well as to establish a cultural view of motivation and striving. This usage of sentiment would be the same as that of Donald K. Adams: "It follows from our definition of a sentiment and the assumption about instrumentality that if you want to know the structure and the organization of a personality you can do it by ascertaining what objects his psychological environment contains and the relations that obtain among them" (1953, p. 58). Furthermore, the word sentiment should include or reflect the fusion of self and objects, the inseparability of self-feelings from the gratifying objects in one's psychological field. This would fit sentiment into Snygg and Combs's excellent conceptualization of the phenomenal field as permeated in parts by a definite and stable self-concept (1949, pp. 112 ff.). The self-concept is a reflection of transactions with objects, and the feelings this elicits. Thus, sentiments would have the same stability as the total phenomenal field, as well as the continuity of the acting individual which they compose.[7]

If we did not have the word sentiment, as it is used here, we should always have to specify three things which are meant by it. We should have to talk about the total phenomenal world as an inseparable unity of:

1. Perception and cognizance of objects. (Some are "full"

objects, others in various stages of "subsistence" and "existence.")

2. Each object as a locus of action-possibility. Each object, that is, calls up a certain behavior pattern. This behavior pattern is "internalized" or built into the actor as a series of rules or "actions-which-it-is-proper-to-undertake." These actions can be undertaken either *toward* the object, or they can be undertaken using the object as a *model*.

3. The cognizance of the object, and the rules for performance which constitute it, bring out a positive feeling in the actor, as he is set in motion by it. Thus, self-value is part of the objects and the rules which constitute them behaviorally.

These three aspects of every act are inseparable—this cannot be overstressed. The personality is part of the phenomenal field; it is the ensemble of sentiments. The personality, in other words, is the meeting ground of cultural fiction and social objects as action-potentiating. "Personality" is the manner in which the four common human problems are answered so that action goes forward; it is the composite of objects-as-action-possibility, rules, and self-feeling. If we did not have the word "sentiment" we should have to say that personality is composed of "action-triads."

The Post-Freudian View of Personality

This extended, technical detour into the usage of the concept of "sentiment" has traced the fully post-Freudian view of personality. Sentiment, phenomenal field, and a transactional view of organic life are part of a single comprehensive approach to human action. While this approach stresses the neutrality of human striving, it retains much that is good in the older views, namely, the psychoanalytic idea that the ego is composed of "internalized objects"—that it is "a precipitate of abandoned object-cathexes," to use Freud's succinct jargon. It includes automatically, in other words, the notion that the ego is formed by actions with objects. It also retains the view that the personality is a unique perceptual system, developed in action with a certain kind and quality of object world. So that, if we choose, we can continue to see personality as a special kind of "defensive system"—as a way of constructing oneself so that action can go forward. In simplified form, the new view of personality might be envisioned something like this:

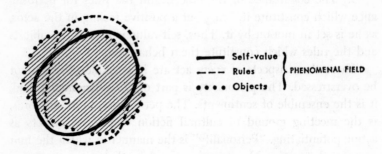

Where is the "unconscious" in this picture? And if no unconscious, how does one account for conflict, tensions—"mental illness?" We have already answered this question in the earlier chapters. It is not necessary to postulate *an* "unconscious." But it is indispensable to talk about a humanization process in which the child's perceptions (of himself and of others) are formed partly in a pre-verbal, extra-verbal, or otherwise unaware (to him) manner. This cannot be repeated too often: the child learns to invest his positive self-feeling in a style of behavior that is largely automatic, largely an unthinking mode of keeping himself satisfied and keeping his environment safe. Thus, while objects, rules, and self-feeling are mingled with and inseparably part of the action-field, there are important variations in each individual field:

1. Not all rules are explicit in the same degree. Vocabularies of motives are not all within easy reach of symbolization.

2. Not all objects permit the same range and degree of satisfying action. One does not possess the same fluent certainty

of rules (built-in behavior patterns) to all objects. Each individual has an object-world of a different degree of richness.

3. Consequently not all rules (built-in behavior patterns)
are invested with the same degree of positive self-feeling. Some
rules do not reflect dependable self-value.

*In each case we would need to determine the extent of the object
world; the level of self-value; the degree of sure behavioral and
explicit cognitive command over the rules.* So, we can see that
there is room for a clash between vocabularies of various degrees
of explicitness—two or more may apply to the same object. There
is room for object-poverty, depending on the strength and range
of built-in behavior patterns. There is room for low self-value,
depending on the early self-concept and on the degree of easy
mastery of rules.

Also, there is room in this personality scheme for "hate,"
without having to postulate an "aggressive drive": hate would
be defined as a (cognitive-emotional) technique whereby positive self-feeling is generated, when one is contemplating an object
toward which one can perform no satisfying action. Hate creates
self-reference and imagined behavior in an action void. Normally,
lack of rules equals lack of an object. But a hate-object is a
peculiar kind of part-object. It may be composed, as a part-
object, of symbolic rules only, and not behavioral ones; it may
be defined as, say, "Jew," without calling up any particular behavior, but unleashing a considerable amount of self-satisfying
fantasy. Or, a hate-object may once have existed as a satisfying
object, but is available no longer. (As when a person develops
new rules, during psychotherapy, toward parents who cling to
old rules. Or, when an object suddenly demands behavior one
is not capable of, say, a friend who becomes successful and enters
high society.) Thus, a hate-object is a definite part of our environmental field, but toward which one has no dependable and
satisfying behavior pattern. Much of so-called childhood "aggression," for example, seems to be an attempt by the child to
undertake *some kind* of action toward an object. It often arises

when the object could previously be related to with definite behavior patterns, but which patterns have suddenly been defined as taboo. The child—say on the birth of a sibling—finds himself with a maternal object to whom he can no longer relate in the same way as before. The object should be a locus of action-possibilities, but it is not. The child uses his poor ingenuity (aggression) to make this part of his world alive for action. Thus when we talk about fulfilling an "emotional need" in a newly rejected child, we are really talking largely about filling an "action" need. (See Burks and Harrison [1962]). Also, we see similar uses of "aggression" on the adult level. Married couples who relate to each other as part-objects may scrap and fight considerably: the gaps in behavior between sexual activity have to be filled somehow, and where a broad range of diversified behavior is lacking, mock or real aggression fills a void.

With this post-Freudian view of personality we pinpoint the great contemporary convergence on the creation of the cultural fiction. The study of personality is the study of the acting-locus of cultural motives, of a unique indoctrination. By viewing the personality as a locus of sentiments within a phenomenal field, a great advance has been made over pre-Freudian and Freudian psychology. Not only is the human animal constituted of uniquely cultural motives, but he is also drawn completely into the world. We can see that life as we know it, cultural life in a human world, does not act *on* the person: it acts *through* him (Cantril, *et al.*, 1949, Part 3, p. 517; Dewey and Bentley, 1949). We live and we become (in part) the objects that we help create. Constituted of the fiction, we in turn constitute it. Our life-style and our world create each other.

Notes

1. It is well to insist that I am talking specifically about Western man here. Eastern thinkers have traditionally played down the human enterprise and considered earthly happenings as illusive;

consequently, the early Buddhist logicians had no trouble arriving at a sophisticated rendering of the fictional nature of human meaning. But since they did not build a scientific tradition in the human sciences, or develop this-worldly values, these Eastern thinkers have never been in a position to make anything positive out of their discovery. We in the West seem to be in such a position now, as we will see better in Chapter VII.

2. Actually, existentialism did not "react" against positivism, but always developed along with it. The propensity to see man from either the outside or the inside is partly a personality characteristic, which seems to be epitomized at one pole or the other at certain epochs. For a good historical sketch of developments since the close of the Romanticist era, see Paul Tillich (1944).

3. It bears emphasizing that in all this reaction against the Freudian bind the human sciences are attempting to build a broad, coherent, and self-consistent theory of man as a cultural animal. Freud's place in the history of science is as secure as Newton's. And, now that we are breaking out of his conceptual system we stand to enter a period as flourishing as the Einsteinian reaction to Newton.

4. Continuing mention of Alexander Shand in the social-psychological literature is due to the same reason. Shand very early adumbrated the systemic character of the sentiments, the formation of the personality into a coherent striving unity based on learned reactivity to objects. See Shand (1920, pp. 21 ff.).

5. McDougall's *Social Psychology* (1960) has recently received its 33rd printing.

6. Harry F. Harlow's experiments with infant monkeys bear this out (1958). Cf. also Bowlby (1961).

7. Here we can understand the widespread dissatisfaction with the word sentiment, as with the word attitude to which it is closely related. Popular usage is too ingrained for sentiment to adequately reflect the specialized usage outlined here: the interpenetration of objects, rules, and self-feeling. Shibutani has also observed (1961, p. 365) that the common-sense treatment of the sentiments renders the word inadequate as a concept. McDougall had this very trouble with sentiment: it was too loose and nontechnical to reflect what he wanted it to stand for; he had something much more cumbersome in mind. Indeed, his definition supports this: "A sentiment is a system in which a cognitive disposition is linked with one or more emotional

or affective conative dispositions to form a structural unit that functions as one whole system (or, in more recent terminology, as one configuration or *gestalt*)" (1960, p. 437). After all this time perhaps someone will come up with a more precise, technical, but not cumbersome word. Sentiment has held out so long—despite its popular dilution—because it really says what we mean: cognitive attitude with total organic emotional disposition toward objects.

The distinction between sentiments and attitudes seems to be a useful one, if the specialized usage of sentiments is adhered to: the sentiments would refer strictly to thought-feelings growing up with objects in one's immediate behavioral world. Attitudes would refer more generally to thought-feelings transmitted symbolically rather than behaviorally with specific objects (cf. G. W. Allport, 1935). Thus, attitudes would refer more to broad allegiances, cultural beliefs, the ideational world. Granted, attitudes could not exist without reference to objects and events. Sentiments and attitudes could perhaps be conceived on a continuum: firm, behavioral rooting in objects on one end (sentiments)—and largely symbolic, abstract ideas more removed from specific behavioral objects on the other end (attitudes). In this usage, attitudes would be more available to conscious, symbolic manipulation; sentiments would be more uncritically fused with objects, more latent. (Cf. the difference between shame and guilt, in Chapter VI.)

In a railroad accident a menagerie-tiger, whose cage had broken open, is said to have emerged, but presently crept back again, as if too much bewildered by his new responsibilities, so that he was without difficulty secured.

Habit . . . thus . . . prevents the hardest and most repulsive walks of life from being deserted by those brought up to tread therein.

WILLIAM JAMES (1892, p.10)

VI

The Human Personality

(2) A CONTEMPORARY CRITIQUE

WE MIGHT HAVE EXPECTED that, seen from the inside, the human personality would hold more mysteries. A conglomeration of objects, rules and self-feeling seems a meager reservoir; it seems to rob man of some of the dignity of complexity. To paraphrase Whitehead: The scientist seeks simplicity but the public mistrusts it. Somehow, man wants his last remaining stronghold—the recesses of his own experienced being—to hold out against the prurient probings of the experts. We cherish what Susanne Langer called "the myth of the inner life." This is part of the identity problem: Man needs to be discovered by his fellows, and then chafes at the social limitation on what he "really feels" himself to be. The human being is a manifold of possibilities that strains at neat labels: "You say I am *only* this, but I assure you I am much more than that." Perhaps for this reason the fancy of earlier researchers was to the general taste: Jung probed deeply into man and found an "archetypal unconscious"; Freud fragmented the psyche into awesome Greek-named entities; the implication in all this was that however much man might know, the "unexplainable" transcended him from within.

Man offers enough bafflement when understood simply as an acting organism, directing his energies to movement in the external world. The sentiments vary infinitely in richness and complexity; action varies in range and competence. Man is a versatile performer in the cultural plot. There is enough here to justify puzzlement—Shakespeare proved that. We have only to pose two simple questions to see how far we still are from clarity of understanding: What does the average person want? Why does he have such a devil of a time getting it? Why, in sum, does life hang as such a heavy burden on the freest and furthest-ranging of all animals?

Every attempt to answer these questions must also be a guess as to where organic life is tending. What is an organic system, what are the conditions for its growth, maintenance, and decay? Ludwig von Bertalanffy offered his systems theory, which showed that an organism is an open biological system, transacting with the environment, maintaining some kind of steady internal state, reaching an optimum size according to genetic predispositions (1952). When the human personality came to be seen as a more-or-less coherent acting self, it too was understood as a system. Robert MacLeod suggested that we consider the self as a system with boundaries and self-regulatory maintenance (1949). Prescott Lecky offered "self-consistency" as a principle of organization of experience (1945). Does the human personality system have other tendencies? Kurt Goldstein spoke of "self-actualization" of the total human organism (1939); Andras Angyal cited man's need for developing a self-reliant "autonomy" (1941); Snygg and Combs (1949), developing the idea of the phenomenal field, considered that the individual tends toward "self-enhancement"—enlargement of the phenomenal self. Names and words could be multiplied. In general all agree that the individual acts in some kind of self-consistent manner, that he tends to organize his experience more or less coherently, and that he is striving for a growing mastery of experience. In all this the self, as a system, would have some kind of steadiness or "homeostasis" (Stagner, 1951).

Here the problem starts to loom. We saw in Chapter I that homeostasis was a poor word to describe the actions of an animal destined for the most part to be relentlessly striving (Toch and Hastorf, 1955; G. Allport, 1961, pp. 568 ff.), burdened by a past and a future that demand constant manipulation. At best, when used in psychology, homeostasis might serve as a principle of coherence rather than of balance. The difficulty with all system-principles like "self-actualization" or "self-realization" is simply this: The idea that an organism must "realize its inner nature" or fulfill its original design—or what have you—would presumably apply to all animals, from amoebas to dogs. It doesn't tell us anything about man, about our peculiar subject matter. Besides being metaphysical, it gives no real information. We watch a flower unfold and then call it "self-actualization." We see man striving to make his world safe and to increase his powers of action and control, and we call it the same thing. (For that matter, it is certain that the Hitler Youth Organization "actualized the potential" of its members.)

Furthermore, on the human level we should have to talk about a unique kind of system indeed to account for all that man does. The urge to order is always balanced and contradicted by the courting of confusion—at least in small doses. Man seems to crave a "touch of disorder" (Dewey, 1934, p. 167). Pleasure itself seems to be attained only in the face of conflict—the greater the conflict, the greater the attendant pleasure (Fite, 1903). Continuous pleasure, as Lecky saw, demands continuously new problems (1945, p. 67). The human being possesses an exploratory drive that constantly pulls him on (Claire Russell and W. M. S. Russell, 1961, p. 147). And on the level of human complexity, this urge to new stimulations can go so far as to put life in continual jeopardy. Witness auto racers and military strategists. Gardner Murphy sums it up very well by pointing out that no matter how much we talk about the rut of human habit, ". . . the pull *away from* the familiar, the demand for novelty and adventure, whether rooted in curiosity or challenge or the need to expand and grow, must never be minimized" (1947, p. 191). One explanation for the continued friction, deliberate outbursts of temper and nagging in close in-groups, is simply this: It is a way of creating novelty, a challenge to ego-mastery, within the safety of the same object-world. It is a fabrication of new experience in small doses—a sort of hothouse excursion into adventure. One prods oneself, and his better-half, out of the dull routine of the expected word, the usual reply, the flat familiarity.

Like all organisms man seeks self-involving action—this is one thing we can safely say. But every principle we try to set up, in order to get some kind of conceptual and orderly scientific grasp on human action, seems to fall short of adequately reflecting human complexity. System-principles like "homeostasis" seem too narrow to contain the push to the new. On the other hand, the idea of a constant push to the new, the "enhancement of the phenomenal self," is not secure either. The fact is that some people *do not* strive for autonomy, do not strike out after new experiences—except perhaps in the smallest of doses, like an agog contemplation of striped tooth paste. Fromm (1941) showed clearly that the individual can be trained to *fear* freedom and wide-ranging action.

A theory of personality must take this into account. A post-scientistic theory of personality thrives on it. We cannot look to nature to give us a clear-cut prescription for our efforts. The "self" is some kind of system—and then again it is not a kind of system that we know. People strive for self-consistency for the most part, but this kind of consistency can take in an infinite range of personality types. Human action remains marvelously complex, despite the lack of "inner" mysteries, largely because of the myriad ways in which the self is formed in relation to objects. We know man needs action and objects, and as we shall see later, choices and conviction. But whatever we find out about human needs, the fact remains that *the kind of people we make depends on the kind of people we want.* The social and moral dimensions of personality theory are inescapable. The kind of action-world one wants depends largely on the kind one is trained to want and to handle.

Modern Man's Second Self-Exposure

It is this "training" of the human animal that forms the focus for a truly remarkable agreement by personality theorists. Nearly everyone agrees that the humanization process, however it is specifically conceived, amounts to this:

1. *Each human actor is "twisted" in a certain way.*

2. *The early "twist" is usually fundamentally at odds with much of later experience.*

3. *Only the rare person is trained to be flexible, to appraise experiences anew with a minimum of early baggage.*

Basically, when the psychoanalysts say "You haven't gotten rid of your Oedipus" this is what they mean: that one has not *seen through* his early socialization, has not been able to evaluate its effect on his character. To talk about an '"Oedipus complex" may be a limited way of designating this early twist, but if broadly considered it is not an erroneous one.[1]

This remarkable agreement by personality theorists is destined to have an explosive effect in the long run, as resounding perhaps as was Darwin's theory—and likely even more. The twentieth century will go down in history as the age when man first consciously saw the desirability of throwing off the automatic bonds in which he holds himself via culture. Rousseau has been vindicated. *Most personality theorists agree that the constricting effects of early training should be undone.* We have come a further distance from Sparta than did Athens at her best. There was a time when Freud and a few analysts were lonely pioneers against the constrictions of society. Freud observed that he was bound to make himself the enemy of society since he sought precisely to undo its evil effects on the individual. But now he has been joined by a veritable throng of educators, social scientists, and clinicians. This upsurge has not yet caught Washington, Madison Avenue, or Hollywood, but in time (hopefully) it will.

Pick any personality theorist at random, and you find the same message:

Anthony Storr: "Part of the process of self-realization consists . . . in discarding introjected beliefs and attitudes which prove to be foreign to the developing personality. . ." (1961).

Claire Russell and W. M. S. Russell: ". . . we might almost sum up the fate of the human individual as the sabotage of intelligence, the mechanism of progress, by overspecialization to a too *familiar* environment—that of his early *family* surroundings" (1961, p. 128).

E. J. Cleveland and W. D. Longaker: "Ray Davis . . . seems quite unable to revise his chosen model of personality functioning and thus faces a neurotic dead end" (1957, p. 199).

Eric Berne: "While every human being faces the world initially as the captive of his script [i.e., his early training], the great hope and value of the human race is that the Adult can be dissatisfied with such strivings when they are unworthy" (1961, p. 126).

Donald Snygg and Arthur W. Combs: "A phenomenal self is adequate in the degree to which it is capable of accepting into its organization any and all aspects of reality. It must be evident that, on the basis of this definition, no phenomenal self is ever completely adequate . . ." (1949, p. 136 [emphasis on first sentence omitted]).

Aubrey Lewis: ". . . for a schizophrenic to live with his parents or wife is less conducive to his floating, or swimming, in the big stream with the rest of us than if he goes to live in lodgings with comparative strangers. . . . Those schizophrenics living with their parents who managed to keep their footing in the general community were, as a rule, separated from their mother all day . . ." (1961, pp. 223-224).

And a schizophrenic studied by Laing provides a personal insight: "My doctors just tried to make me a 'good girl' and patch things up between me and my parents. . . . No one seemed to realize that if I went back to my family I would be sucked back and lose myself" (1960, p. 190).

In the rational therapy of schizophrenics, one of the goals is to set him apart as an individual. Arieti says: ". . . he must not see himself any longer purely as the object of fate, chance, nature, persecutors, spouse, family, etc., but as somebody who thinks and acts as independently as the other members of society do" (1962).

The "authentic person," says Maslow: "becomes a little more a member of his species, and a little less a member of his local group" (1961, p. 55).

The existentialists, somewhat less clearly than all the above, mean the same thing when they talk about the "inauthenticity" of one's "original choice of being." Freedom, for the existentialist, is precisely a striking out for one's own life, for new choices, for a break with the accidents of one's birth, place, and training. They consider that the individual is born into a random en-

vironment. Faced with the need for action, he learns an "unau-
thentic" form of behavior. This is his "original choice of being."
He lives in the world of "the many," does what "one" does,
sinks into the crowd and babbles his "empty talk" (Allers, 1961,
pp. 44-45). Culture determines the individual; it is up to him
to be free.

But everyone imagines that he strives to be free, authentic,
himself—we all nurse greedily our uniqueness. Then why the bitter
struggle against a change in life-style, even when the individual
senses (in psychotherapy) that he is not free? It is partly this
bitter struggle against changing one's accustomed action-style
that led the psychoanalysts to affirm the correctness of their
instinct theory. It is barely imaginable that one should struggle
so hard, except against the relinquishment of real basic inner
drives, of irrevocable natural urges. The force of the "resistance"
was thought to be here. But this is to fail to understand human
action: the patient is not struggling against himself, against forces
deep within his animal nature. He is struggling rather against
the loss of his world, of the whole range of action and objects
that he so laboriously and painfully fashioned during his early
training. He is fighting, in sum, against the subversion of himself
in the only world that he knows. Each object is as much a part
of him as is the built-in behavior pattern for transacting with
the object.[2] Each action is as much within his nature as the
self-feeling he derives from initiating or contemplating that action. Each rule for behavior is as much a part of him as is his
metabolism, the forward momentum of his life processes. The
fund of his early experiences is as strong as any instinct could be.

The individual grows up learning to cope in a certain kind
of world, and is at a loss to act if faced with another. The
iron force of habit needs no instinctual underpinning: where
rules, objects, and self-feelings are fused, sunder one and you
literally "split" the individual. The "conflict theory" of neurosis
is a facile way of saying this. Perceptions are fused to feelings
and actions. Schachtel reports a patient who was pervasively angry

because he was not sufficiently loved. He imagined that the analyst always wore a frown. When he finally did look at the analyst's face, and discovered that there was no frown, he was at a loss for what to do and how to feel. He wanted to see a frown, and could cope with nothing else (1959, pp. 197-198). Schachtel observes that distorted perception does not easily give way to clear perception because it means that the individual *will have to let go of the attitude* which causes the distortion. The differences between our early formed perceptions and the adult realities we face are often as great as those between the schizophrenic's fantasy world and the real one.

Part of the reason for this is that our early transactions with objects take place on a direct, concrete level. Much of this learning, as we noted, is not available to ready symbolization. In this sense it is truly "built in." Jean Piaget's studies (1932) showed that every child goes through two general phases in learning moral rules: an early phase, which is characterized by what Piaget calls "moral realism"; and a later phase called "moral relativism." In the early phase, all rules are inflexible, learned by rote, not capable of exception; the child has no judgment to exercise over the rules, their derivation, their rightness or wrongness, a possible exceptional case or extenuating circumstances, and so on. This phase is gradually superseded by a "moral relativism" in which the child gains increasing command over the rules. He becomes interested in them "for their own sake"; they lose their shrouding authoritarian aura; they become manipulatable, controllable, flexible, objectified. Piaget is talking here about explicit rules for games, morality, and so on. We can extend his observations to rules as used in our sense—as the behavior patterns learned in early transactions with objects.

Strictly speaking, this kind of behavior can never be wholly objectified, *because each set of transactions is peculiar to a particular existential (parental) object.* Since rules (behavior patterns) are inseparable from the objects which make action possible, there will be a heavy dose of the uniquely personal in each pattern.[3] We might say that each early object *contains its own personalized, reified morality*. In a sense this is only natural; as animals we are taken in by the stark object quality of the existential thing. It is infinitely more overpowering than shadowy word-rules. The heavily personalized childhood training in our culture literally strikes at the heart of the symbolization function. Each transaction with early objects leaves a mystical, authoritarian residue. Each child experiences something similar to the one who grew up in a polyglot family, and imagined that each separate individual on earth had his own peculiar tongue. Similarly, close ties in the nuclear family cripple some of the individual's later ability to abstract.[4] Every authoritarian figure in later life may possess the father's face—he has only to utter the father's stern commands. Schachtel's patient was unusual only in degree of distortion, but everyone's perception is colored by the early concretization of rules. To say that we "introject a superego," and that its dictates are "concrete" means just this: we cannot separate rules and self-feeling from the very objects which bind them. The politician relies on a liberal use of "home" and "mother" because they are strings to the very heart of the puppet creature: it is only by symbolization and objectification that man attains a full human dignity.

The unavailability of early experience to symbolization is what we mean by "unconscious bonds" (Miller, 1961), the early "layering effect" (McClelland, 1956), "pre-perception," "sub-ception," and "regressive behavior" in the sense used by Rogers (1951, p. 491); and this is also covered by the distinction between "manifest-overt" and "latent-covert" values (Cleveland and Longaker, 1957, pp. 182 ff.). The individual is "divided against himself" not in the sense that Freud used it—as a battle of instincts vs. conscious ego control—but rather in the sense that *one learns to transact with objects before his full powers of symbolization are developed*. He shapes himself into an actor without even knowing what is going on. The result is that he is divided against himself in terms of varying explicitness of vocabularies of motive. We saw in Chapter I that there can be confusion among vocabularies of motive even on an adult level; it is easy to imagine the confusion when some of these vocabularies are built into the system on a pre-verbal level. It is this confusion that causes "neurotic conflict," and not any underworld struggle of dark, instinctual forces vs. "respectable citizen." One way of phrasing the new view is to talk of a clash between the self-concept and various "sub-identities" (Miller, 1961). The individual's problem of maintaining a consistent identity is undermined by the various levels of inexplicit messages or rules. For example, one can try to be a perfect husband according to an explicit definition of this identity. But all the while the wife as a female object may embody some concrete reminders of other possible definitions learned earlier from mother: "You must not replace father," or "I will never allow my baby to act like a dirty boy," and so on. Thus the bridegroom may be impotent on his honeymoon, or enjoy full potency only with prostitutes. The various sub-vocabularies mine at a straightforward definition of one's identity.

Some objects and situations cause these rumblings, some do not. Sometimes we feel the total identity congruity more than others. Ideally we should like to transact only with objects that call up a congruent identity—one that is a composite of action, rules, and self-feeling not threatened by vaguely (or sharply) felt alternatives. The "perfect object" is one that calls up everything we want to be and everything we feel we can be—straightforwardly and with no inner rumblings. But obviously, there can be no "perfect object." Every object makes some demands on us that are not congruent with secure self-feeling, with tested strengths (see Ch. VIII). The humanization process leaves its scars: felt incapacities, concretizations, fusions of symbol-meanings and body-meanings, inexplicit urges and fears. Every object calls up several different voices, so to speak. In one respect, the object plays on something congruent, in another, not. This is what we mean by ambivalence: definitions of action and urges that are not consistent, that change from one moment to the next. The same object points in different directions at different times; we cannot forge a consistent identity in our relations to it. A mother is ambivalent if she explicitly supports one's full masculinity at one time, and at another quietly invites one to yield to his infant dependence. Objects that arouse many vocabularies, at various levels of explicitness, threaten our self-consistency.

We can see then, that it is a fairly easy matter for the individual to "lose his world"—he doesn't have a very secure possession of it in the first place. Objects, situations, vocabularies, strike at him in manifold ways. If the individual has such a difficult time constructing and keeping his world, it is easy to understand that he will be even more reluctant to move out of it.

The Post-Freudian View of Anxiety

The fundamental problem of the clash between early training and the possibility of new experience is best summed up in the idea of anxiety. Man moves forward with extreme reluctance because to do so causes him anxiety. Anxiety, in effect, reflects the basic dilemma of human action and meaning. Now that the air has been cleared of Freudian instinct theory we are able to see that anxiety holds no mysteries. Despite the many books that have been written about it, the aura of awe that surrounds it, anxiety is a remarkably simple phenomenon.

In Freud's early formulations, anxiety is shrouded with the mystery of the subterranean instincts. Anxiety was seen as a signal to the individual that he was about to be overwhelmed by "instinctive urges." Normally the child would have given free vent to these "drives," but he had been taught by society—by his parents—that to give expression to them was to incur the displeasure of the loved objects. The choice was clear. To give way to instinctive gratification was to run the danger of losing one's world. If the dependent primate infant loses his parents he loses his life. Anxiety was felt as a signal that such doom was impending; the child learned to sit tight on the lid of his instincts whenever the signal arose; he learned to control his "inner forces" by taking himself in hand and shaping his action according to the dictates of the parents. Thus, Freud saw anxiety as the fundamental phenomenon in the humanization process.[5]

And fundamental it is, even if the hypothetical instincts are left out of the picture. The early anxiety of object-loss gives way to other sources for anxiety, sources which are as comprehensive and clear as the whole problem of humanization. As the infant gradually ceases to be a biological actor and becomes a cultural one, anxiety comes to depend on symbolic rather than physical necessities. Human anxiety comes to be derived from one or more of three things:

1. The constricting effects of the early indoctrination process in which the child learns one world view out of many, and so closes off the possibility of an infinitely broader range of experience. Hence, anxiety in the face of new experience. This category would include, of course, the anxiety learned in association with prohibited body functioning, so that sub-verbal and pre-verbal somatic confusions are part of the constriction on one's world-view.

2. The basic identity problem which consists in *symbolically* constructing a durational identity. But if the identity is a symbol-system, it is as precarious, airy, and flexible as are symbols themselves. At any moment we can define ourselves anew, come up with a new label, a new allegiance, a revocation of the past that destroys all painstakingly accumulated coherence. Hence, anxiety in the face of discontinuity of identity.

3. If one can change the rules learned from the parents, if one can uproot them from their grounding in the existential parental objects, then they too are airy and flexible. This means that the individual comes to see *himself* as shaper and maker, symbolic juggler of his own meaning. Neither he nor his symbols

have any root in a timeless reality. Hence, anxiety in the face of fragility of human meaning.

The broad view of anxiety as a condition of human symbolic existence explains why Kierkegaard is still contemporary. Kierkegaard seems to have divined the human condition as one of infinite symbolic possibilities succeeding the constrictions of early training. Thus he defines anxiety as "the dizziness of freedom," as a "desire for what one dreads." The symbolic animal looks out from his closed world, and dizzies himself with the realization that he can become something different than he was made. He can overcome the accidental determining circumstances of his early indoctrination. Anxiety is a "prospective" emotion, it is a leaning to the future, to eventuality (MacKinnon, 1954). Rollo May points out this basic connection of anxiety with the problem of freedom: "If the individual did not have some freedom, no matter how minute; to fulfill some new potentiality, he would not experience anxiety" (1958, p. 52). Schachtel talks about the child's "embeddedness" in the objects of his early experience, and his continuing emergence into a more open, freer, less determined world (1959, p. 77).

Little wonder that Paul Tillich calls Kierkegaard's work on anxiety his psychological masterpiece. The ontological categories of existential philosophy fit perfectly the vicissitudes of ontic development.[6] Tillich says: "The *angst* of finitude drives man to action and at the same time to an alienation from his essential being and to the profounder *angst* of guilt and despair" (1944, p. 63).

Translated simply, this delineates perfectly the humanization process: The "anxiety of finitude" is the child's early helpless inferiority, an inferiority that he can overcome by *basing action on the psychological, symbolic categories given to him by his early objects*. This creates a cognitive world that makes for *an alienation from possibilities of broader perception and action*. The "profounder *angst* of guilt and despair," refers, finally, to the specific constrictions necessitated by the arbitrary boundaries of one's cultural behavioral world. The child becomes a prisoner in his own symbolic mansion (Becker, 1962). The free action of an infinitely plastic, instinct-free animal, becomes bounded into a narrow range. Anxiety connotes specifically "pressure," "narrowness" (Riezler, 1960). As the individual peers over the edge of his arbitrary horizons, the glimpse of freedom becomes the dizziness determined by this very narrowness.[7] "Not being able to come to terms with the world" sums up aptly the clash between new experiences and the early built-in rules. As Kurt Goldstein says, the "capacity for bearing anxiety is the manifestation of genuine courage . . ." (1951, p. 113). Courage enables one to realize his "own nature"—the inner expansiveness made prisoner by arbitrary learning. To be courageous is to choose new ranges of objects and experience in spite of the old rules, in face of them. As one pushes beyond the early rules and objects to new experiences, he must submit to the anxiety of stepping into the unknown. Thus, the drama of the humanization process was perfectly summed up in rough outline by Kierkegaard. It remained for modern research to pinpoint this process, to show exactly how the individual constructs his action-world.

The existentialists have, too, summed up better than anyone else the anxiety attendant upon the problem of identity. Sartre uses the example of the person who, overlooking a precipice, cannot decide either to jump or to draw back: "The possibility of my remaining safe on the height and the possibility of my throwing myself over are both equally my possibilities. Anguish as well as dizziness comes as I realize that nothing prevents my deciding one way rather than the other and as I perceive the possibility that my self might make a decision contrary to all that earlier I would have expected" (1953, p. 17). Thus, Sartre aptly illustrates points two and three listed above. Anxiety arises *from the possibility of abrogating an entire meaning framework.* A new choice, phrased in mere symbols, may undermine an entire coherent cause-and-effect sequential pattern established in the past. This sums up an acute and peculiar human problem: *the possibility of discontinuity of existence on a uniquely symbolic level.* This possible discontinuity is aggravated by the fact that in our identity struggles, in our fashioning of ourselves, we cannot rely upon someone else's knowledge (cf. Riezler, 1960, p. 148). The individual finds himself increasingly alone in his world, increasingly thrown back on his own resources. The "nausea" of the existentialist is a glimpse of the utter randomness of the world. This randomness can attain meaningfulness only under the magic touch of the symbolic arranger, but the magic touch itself has the firmness of air. There is nothing necessary about our fictional arrangements.

Thus, the post-Freudian view of anxiety sees it as a basic phenomenon of several aspects of human action. Anxiety loses its obscurity, its mystery: it is an accompaniment of the peculiarly human venturesomeness in this world. It is not a reaction to some "deep inner threat" as it is simply a "fear of the unknown" (Magda Arnold, 1960, p. 272).[8] Walter Coutu has seized on the nature of anxiety for a symbolic animal: basically anxiety is the same as *curiosity* (1949, pp. 165 ff.). It is a leaning-forward into the unknown, a groping from the blindness of one's meagre symbol-repertory. The human animal scans his psychological world for clues to action. When dependable and coherent indicators are not forthcoming, the anxiety of the unknown arises (cf. Kelly, 1955, Vol. 1, pp. 495 ff.). For the symbolic animal, anxiety derives largely from *lack of words—lack of conventional reasons for action.*[9] Aim and purpose, for man, can only be had by a clear-cut mental attitude (Nina Bull, 1951, p. 10). The symbol gives point, focus and reality to vague feelings of suspense, restlessness, excitement, and tension. We are not too far here from the Freudian view; if we leave out the unconscious drives, the psychoanalytic thesis on anxiety stands. The situation in which the organism feels overwhelmed, unable to put up sufficient resources, is one in which action-possibilities do not occur. By "learned anxiety" we denote those situations in which the possibility of choice is obscured by heavy threats learned earlier, by the possibility of failure. The fewer situations the individual can verbalize, the more the anxiety. The schizophrenic who has the fewest objects-as-action-possibility has the most anxiety. The depressed person, on the other hand, has objects, but the rules are so inextricably entwined with the concrete object that there is no backing away from them, no grip on them for critical review, no symbolic dexterity possible. The depressed patient is as buried in his object as the Sphinx in the desert sand, and is as hopelessly dumb.

Now we can see why the early learning period, the early indoctrination, can be a most important and pervasive influence in one's life. To a symbolic animal whose main strength lies in symbolic manipulation, it is the one area *unavailable to explicit symbolization*. It is his one big blind spot. The individual would have an easy time changing his early "inauthentic" style if he could somehow disengage his own commitment to it. But rules, objects, and self-feeling are fused—taken together they constitute one's "world." How is one to relinquish his world unless he first gains a new one? This is the basic problem of personality change. Actually, what occurs in psychotherapy is that the individual gains a new object, *which becomes a wedge for inching himself out* of his old world. The new object-as-action-possibility brings in its train a transfer of self-feelings. One gains his feeling of worth from his relationship to the new object (therapist). Finally, new rules are elaborated and solidified—one has changed his world.

Some individuals are fortunate in their early training. They have had to fulfill fewer "conditions of worth" as Rogers has it. They gained positive regard from their parents with a minimum of ambiguity or fastidious discipline. The result is that they have their own feeling of value pretty much in hand, so to speak. If they experience anxiety in certain areas, they inch into the unknown a bit more boldly; they feel that they have less at stake, that the sword of Damocles is suspended by a stronger cord. As a consequence, they tend to verbalize the rules better, assay their choices more clearly. Situations tend to be appraised more on their own terms than in terms of past perception. This is what Rogers calls the strength of "continuous valuations." It seems that a principal strength of these individuals is that they feel secure in their possession of objects. Which is another way of saying that they have developed a broad range of behavior *for the creation of* objects. Hence, they can "back off" from any *particular* object and examine it critically; they are not bound to narrow action needs. To be able to withdraw from any action-commitment long enough to appraise it critically needs the secure possession of one's own positive self-feeling. Ordinarily, when the object-as-action-possibility slips from one's grasp, he feels himself falter helplessly—his world is edging away. But security in a broad range of behavior *makes the particular object of less vital importance.* The self-image does not depend hopelessly on any one object, or on any unquestionable rule. Maslow quite aptly observes that the functionally autonomous person is most capable of withstanding a loss of love and popularity (1954, p. 106). And one of the major findings of Leighton's Stirling County study was that the ability to substitute objects was a primary resource of the strong personality (1959, pp. 160-161).

Obviously, this strength will be absent where: (1) self-esteem is insecure, (2) the range of objects is narrow and undependable, and (3) the rules are uncritically and inextricably fused with a *particular concrete* object. Any of these conditions makes for "neurotic constriction." And there is only one feasible definition of neurosis for a symbolic animal: *namely, constriction of choice-possibilities* due to failure to symbolize (Becker, 1962, pp. 185-186). Slavery to single objects, uncritical acceptance of rules, blind investment of self-feeling in a narrow, inflexible action range—all these signal failure of man's primary strength and only uniqueness: his symbolic dexterity. *Homo sapiens* cannot choose to focus narrowly with his splendid distance receptors—memory and sight. He cannot wilfully remain dumb with his unique tool—language. He cannot shun broad ranges of experiences with his 1450 c.c. brain capacity. We saw that for any animal, restriction to a narrow reservoir of powers to act is equivalent to stupidity. Now we can close the circle. Neurosis is the typical stupidity that results from early learning: by definition neurosis is the dumb hugging of a meager range of actions and objects, in order to feel worthwhile. Anxiety is the spur; it reflects both stupidity and peculiarly human tragedy: It signals a word-poverty based on the accidents of early learning; and it reflects as well the hard knowledge that no matter how rich is *Homo sapiens* in words, words themselves are fragile building blocks for identity.

The Changing View of Emotion

To the view that anxiety is due to lack of words rather than to inner impulses must be joined a criticism of the "inner reservoir" theory of emotion. The view of emotion that is now being developed makes a further attack on the old Freudian scheme (Arnold, 1960; Asch, 1952; Benda, 1961, pp. 188 ff.; Bull, 1951; Coutu, 1949; Hillman, 1960, pp. 254 ff.; Lecky, 1945, pp. 94 ff.; McGill and Welch, 1945-1946; Rogers, 1951, p. 493; Sartre, 1948). It used to be thought, for example, that one major function of psychoanalysis was the "cathartic" release of "pent-up" emotions. This is part of the reservoir-in-the-tank schema that we saw in Chapter IV. But the emotional-purge theory has been criticized from within psychoanalysis itself. Gregory Zilboorg complained that the term "emotional insight" was obfuscating the clinical picture and had no realistic meaning (1953, pp. 203-204). The idea of an "emotional insight" was useful only when we thought of the individual as a repository of antisocial drives—hates, fears, lusts. Now we are seeing that motives are social, and that insight depends on words. Man directs his feelings, he does not purge them.

Actually, there are two primary conditions for the inability to experience emotion. If one has no mental attitude toward an object, one cannot feel any emotion. (The schizophrenic inability to experience emotion, as we noted in Chapter II, is probably due to a total lack of mental attitude or intention toward an object.) On the other hand, where intentions are automatically executed, explicitly and without delays, one will feel no emotion. Emotion arises where intended action is delayed (Bull, 1951). Now, when the therapist complained that his patient was not experiencing sufficient emotion, what he was actually up against was one or the other of these two situations: no intention, therefore no emotion; or, automatic execution of explicit cultural meanings, therefore no delay and no emotion. The therapist complained that he could not work with such a patient because all his efforts remained on the surface. But the reason he could not work with him was not that the patient refused to "look within himself" and acknowledge "buried emotion." Rather, it was because the patient would not assume any self-reference in relation to a problematic line of behavior. Only when the patient could see alternatives for himself was the necessary delay—and consequently emotion—possible.

Franz Alexander and Thomas M. French, for example, in championing the old view, considered "emotional insight" to be basic to the corrective effects of therapy (1946). They cite the case of Jean Valjean as an example of what can be accomplished by a corrective emotional experience. But Valjean proves something quite different: it is not that he "brought up emotion," but rather that he proceeded to examine himself intellectually from a new point of view. He got outside and beyond his accustomed world and himself, by seeing his acts in a different light. (His normal attitudes were frustrated when he was not punished for taking the silver candlesticks.) The "release" is not the release of an "inner reservoir." It is, rather, the re-initiation of positive forward movement that accompanies the learning situation. First, something about one's conduct must become problematic. Then, as the individual finds words with which to understand his present and past situation, present conduct finds available to it a new surge of directiveness. It only *seems* as though emotion is being "released." Actually, however, what is taking place is the adumbration of new possibilities of forward-momentum of conduct.[10]

Shame and Guilt

As we unfold this reading of the revolution in psychiatry, one thing stands out: Man is learning where to pin the blame for human failure. In one major focus of our time, twentieth-century thinkers have laid bare the flimsy symbolic basis of human meaning. In the second, clinicians—beginning with Freud—have for a half-century been heaping up evidence on the noxious effects of early learning. There is very little about the peculiar "human condition" that is not somehow in man's potential control. Symbols are learned and juxtapositional: No one arrangement is timeless—even if carved on tablets of stone—unless *man* chooses to make it so. Sentiments are not brought into life, they grow in transacting with things. Anxiety too, grows as we learn to inhibit our powers. Not surprisingly, then, we have found that guilt and shame—the typically human—have been made by man. Rather, it would be more correct to say that they are part of the human condition, but that they have been elaborated by man in facilitating the living of his designs. The more uncritically the design is lived, the heavier the burden of shame and guilt.

So much has been written about shame and guilt that they have assumed an aura of needless complexity. (In this they resemble anxiety.) It used to be thought that shame was a common social sanction, used by most societies to keep the individual in line. Guilt, on the other hand, was considered rare. Western culture was thought to be the primary guilt culture, the carrier of a harsh Protestant superego. The child, growing up under strict parental dictates, internalized a rigid moral code. He had only to transgress it, or think or imagine it transgressed, in order to feel guilt. Thus, guilt was thought to have marked a break with more primitive, easy-going, earlier cultures. Theoreticians spoke of "guilt cultures" and "shame cultures." Guilt was considered to be an "internal sanction"—the rigid introjected superego. Shame was considered an "external sanction"—the ever-present possibility of social disapproval. Furthermore, since the superego was learned in early interactions with the parents, guilt was thought to be an accumulation of past threats; shame, on the other hand, was a threat always in the present, referable to some present audience rather than to a past one. The guilty person carried around his own "internal audience" in the form of parental images; shame was more realistic, referable to real people in the external world. It remained for Milton Singer, in a much-cited work (Piers and Singer, 1953), to mark an end to this era of speculation, and to show all these differentiations to be undependable. Shame and guilt could not be reliably distinguished from one another along these lines, even though they contained a good deal of truth.

In the same work, a psychoanalyst tried to put some order into the problem from a theoretical point of view. Since the psychoanalysts themselves were guilty of much of the confusion, this attempt was fitting. But despite Milton Singer's generous citations of Gerhard Piers' formulations, Piers did nothing to clarify the issue. The psychoanalytic developmental framework served to order his ideas, and once again reduced everything to a rigid formula of infant development. Piers saw shame as the typical reaction to the anxiety of object-loss; shame was a fear of losing the parents by a failure to live up to their ideals. Guilt, on the other hand, was reaction to the anxiety of mutilation—specifically castration; the child feared his body would be harmed by the parents, for failure to obey their dictates. Shame = reaction to the threat of object-loss; guilt = reaction to castration-threat—a neat scheme. It fit perfectly into the psychoanalytic theory, too, because it allowed one to distinguish between "unconscious" shame and "unconscious" guilt (whatever they may be). In other words, it bolstered theoretically what could not otherwise be substantiated. A time-worn skill of psychoanalytic theorists.

Guilt and Early Objects

We get closer to the core of the problem of differentiating shame from guilt by trying adequately to define them. What is guilt? What does it mean "to feel guilty toward someone?" It means, simply, to be somehow stymied in satisfactory action with reference to them; it indicates a bogging down of self-satisfying action in relation to specific objects (the object being either a *locus toward which* action can take place; or, a *model on which* action can be patterned).[11] We get a clear picture by taking the extreme case: The schizophrenic feels guilty "just for existing." Action is so constricted that he cannot say: "Forgive my act," but is forced to feel: "Forgive me for existing." This is guilt carried to its extreme: "identity guilt." It is a function of a total inability to initiate self-satisfying action in relation to objects. The more thoroughly the individual feels a baffling constriction of his would-be powers, the more burdensome the guilt. In this view of guilt, the accent is on the *bind* on *action*, rather than on the *fearsomeness* of the *object*. This allows considerable clarification. Especially, it explains directly how one can feel extreme guilt toward loving, understanding, and very mild fathers (cf. Alexander, 1953). If guilt is severe where the object is kind, it means that guilt is related to the disposal of *one's own* powers, rather than to the prohibitions of the object. It is noteworthy that the Old English root of the word guilt carries the meaning of both guilt and debt (Lynd, 1958, p. 23). Parents may avoid harshness only to make the child even more sensitive about his acts (Schmideberg, 1956). In effect, guilt exists in massive doses precisely where the prescription for behavior is not clear-cut. Schizophrenic identity guilt is synonymous with "no behavior," because there are *no* dependable formulas.

Heidegger defines guilt as "the call of Being for itself in silence." The existentialists get to the heart of the matter, and again obscure it with ontological categories. Being calls for itself in silence because it is being hampered, constricted. What hampers it?—the early indoctrination, of course. The life powers (being) are narrowed down by the particular prohibitions learned from specific adults in each culture. Guilt is the action-bind that reaches out of the past to limit new experiences, to block the possibility of broader choices. Guilt is the "persistent operation of past experience in the present" (Frank, 1938-1939, p. 306).

Our previous discussion in this Chapter is now pertinent. How does past experience operate in the present? We saw that it does this on several levels, or rather as an amalgam of concrete, sub-verbal, and symbolic, verbal experiences. The individual carries over from his early training an inextricable fusion of often very incompatible information on who he is, and how to act in the world. Guilt and shame can, I think, be conceived as *different points on a continuum of accessible rules for being and behaving.* Guilt is felt with reference to rules that are less available to symbolic manipulation. Shame is felt in reference to rules that are more explicit, more amenable to clear and rational scrutiny. In one sense, Piers is not wholly wrong, guilt is more concretistic. Therefore one might say that it has to do with somatic phenomena. But, guilt is concretistic in the same sense that we talked about any rules being concrete: *they tend to be fused uncritically with the existential object from which they emanate.* Guilt and shame do not refer so much to *different* phenomena; rather they are different words for the same thing: They describe the fact that early learning is available to symbolic manipulation in different degrees. With guilt, the rules and the object-as-action-possibility are more fused; with shame, the rules and the object are more detached, the rules are more "mobile," more capable of being examined independently of interference by the concrete object representation.

Another way of looking at the difference is this: shame and guilt both refer to action that is blocked. In shame, the action block is clear-cut: there are no possible actions that could be undertaken, or (as we say below) no "valid private motive." In guilt, action *may be* possible, but one does not know, one is not sure. The matter is confused. It seems that there *should* be possible action. In shame there is no question about it: action is simply *not* possible. Again we see the difference in explicitness of behavioral rules.

Thus the old formula adumbrated a truth: it held that shame is a reaction to the judgment of *others*, whereas guilt is a feeling of depreciation emanating from within *oneself*. This is another way of stating what we are here stating more precisely, namely, that "judgment of others" is more explicit than a "feeling of wrongness" from within. One thing we noted about all rules learned in early transaction with objects is that they must possess *some* concretization. It is impossible to totally disengage the rule from the early object; the existential *thing* always has a power and immediacy that no word-sound or behavioral formula can achieve. Guilt, then, must have an inextricable component of object in it: In learning our rules we never disentangle ourselves completely from the object. Consequently guilt must exist wherever man learns rules in close contact with others of his kind. Indeed, David Ausubel has affirmed just this, that there are no cultures without guilt (1955). Empirical studies thus join to support Hegel's philosophical observation, that innocence can only exist where there is complete suspension of action (1910, Vol. 2, p. 465).

If guilt reflects the fact that the existential object is present inextricably in the formulation of the rules, it explains another thing: the so-called "intrinsic guilt" (Maslow, 1962, p. 182). Many theorists on guilt hold that some guilt is a desirable thing, that man must feel responsible to something. Maslow

188 THE HUMAN PERSONALITY

contends that "superego guilt" is derived from others, from the culture, and therefore it is relative and artificial. Intrinsic guilt, on the other hand, is guilt felt because of deviation from something very real within oneself; it results from being untrue to one's own self or inner nature; hence it is desirable. But there are no "rules" for "intrinsic guilt." There is only a feeling that one is not doing right *by himself*. This is the guilt that the schizophrenic feels *for feeling* guilty all the time, his "authentic" guilt (Laing, 1960, p. 144).[12] Here truly is Heidegger's "voice of Being calling for itself in silence." Since there are no rules for this intrinsic guilt it is plainly guilt to oneself as an *object*.

Guilt to the object itself, then, in the complete absence of even implicit rules, comes naturally to man. The living organism carries within its very existence a quietly insistent command to move forward. All the more reason to suppose that the impressionable child can feel guilty to his parental objects as flesh and blood things, unique in nature. He would need no rules at all. This extreme kind of object-guilt is wholly arbitrary, because it calls for conduct as *singular* as the object is in nature. Small wonder that youth sometimes has recourse only to antisocial aggressive behavior (cf. Alexander, 1953, pp. 47-48). The object is so overbearing, or its rules so ambiguous, that it takes the place of the rules. Its morality, therefore, becomes as singular as itself: it *is* its morality. This is so inhibiting that to obey it would only be possible by complete dependent surrender. When one lacks a valid private motive his only recourse is to capitulate to the object. There is no justification for any behavior that he might undertake.

Object-guilt also explains why the self-sacrificing parent is the most guilt-inducing of all. She (or he) holds up to the child all she is undergoing for his sake—all she is undergoing as a unique, existential object. There can be no question of detaching rules from an object such as this, or possessing any valid private motive in the face of it. *The parent's historical destiny itself* is a set of rules which are superordinate to any motives of her offspring.

Shame and the Self

Helen Merrell Lynd, in her searching study of shame, decided to concentrate on shame rather than on guilt, because shame "goes deeper" in the personality (1958, p. 22, note f). By this I think she means that shame derives from the blanket human condition; whereas guilt is more a part of the person's relationship to particular objects. Guilt is the result of one's "facticity," the mere circumstances of birth and place; shame is a key to one's openness. Shame, in effect, shows the social nature of the self. After all, what is the "self" if not a composite of social motives, of learned self-justifications? As a presocial organism, the child is literally "empty": empty of interpersonal motives. As he fills himself with social motives he acquires a self. Hence, a paradox occurs. What is at the same time the most thoroughly social is taken into the individual to become the quintessentially personal. The internal object, the behavior pattern, is one "pole" of the external object. But it is this pole that becomes inseparable from our self-feeling. Thus, we invest the "inner side" of the social motive with our own feeling, and it becomes the uniquely private. This is what Josef Nuttin means when he says that the sense of shame is connected "with one of the most characteristic features of psychological life in man, namely, the combination of the privacy and penetrability of human consciousness. . . . The private interiority of psychological life, combined with this inherent possibility of its exposure, constitute what we may call the *functional conditions* for the origin of shame" (1950, pp. 344-345). In other words, the individual has a private life, but since this life is only the "inner pole" of the social motives, it is private only *by location*. It is not private in the sense that it is *known only to oneself*.

Shame arises *in the moment of acknowledgment* that the private is merely the "inner pole" of the social. It is the confession that one *really has nothing private per se to oppose to someone's scrutiny*. Scheler has conveyed this in the example of the mother who saves her child from a burning house (Williams, 1941-1942). She may run out quite naked in saving the child, and she will feel no shame. But the moment the child is saved and she feels the gaze of the crowd, she will experience shame. What has happened? While the child was being saved, the private and the public self were inextricably fused in a publicly approved act; afterward, when the act was over, the woman found herself publicly exposed with no valid private motive. So too with the model who poses in the nude, and the woman who submits to a physical examination by a doctor. No shame is felt, simply because the social definition of the situation completely blots out the need for a private one. But let the artist give a hint that he is regarding his model as a desirable sexual object, let the doctor do the same, and shame floods the woman (Williams, 1941-1942). Again, the social definition of the situation was lifted for a brief moment, and the women found themselves in a position in which they could initiate no valid personal action.

The same thing is conveyed strikingly by the pubescent girl who enters a room full of men and for the first time feels herself being scrutinized as a sexual object (van den Berg, 1955, p. 57). She has nothing private to oppose to the social motives. She may cover her eyes *in extremis*—anything to close the open window to the self, to shut out the penetrating gaze of others into one's personal emptiness.[13] Instantly a blush floods into her head. Exposed and taken completely unawares, with no valid private motive to oppose to the social situation, the total organism seems to reply: "I do have an inside." The blush protests the "right of habitation" of the body by the self. It is a total organic resurgence, a unique phenomenon in the only animal who has a social self—hence the only one who needs such a protest. It is an affirmation of personal existence by an organism that is a socially standardized object. We see the same thing in the blush of a rival at the announcement of another's successful achievement. This is not a blush of mere "envy," it is a positive manifestation that declares: "I (too) am here."

Embarrassment is related to shame in the same manner as a struggle to a surrender (cf. Lynd, 1958, p. 38). It seems to be a delay in which one scans himself for a valid private motive, something to oppose to the imminent exposé. Embarrassment is the period of groping before one gives in to shame; it is a temporary helplessness. Often embarrassment is punctuated with a cough—seemingly another form of total organic affirmation (cf. Arnheim, 1949, p. 168). While the search for a valid private motive is in progress, one puts forth a willfully controlled expression, announces his presence. This is akin to the repeated glancing at one's watch while one is waiting, exposed and seemingly without motive, in a public place. It announces that valid inner workings are going on—somewhat like a sign over an open manhole.

We find those who blush quickly, "cute" precisely because society likes to see its members thoroughly socialized. Women blush more than men in our culture probably because the culture gives them less justification to possess private motives. Not to blush is to declare that the social has not taken hold. We like people to admit that, when the group desires it, they have nothing private to oppose. Hence, we sometimes let ourselves blush deliberately—when it could be suppressed—to show how "nice" (social) we are. But just as the organism blushes to affirm itself, people can die when they realize they have nothing valid to affirm—primitives, as we noted earlier, have been said to die of shame. Having committed, say, a terrible community outrage, the individual finds the social claim on the self so total, so irrevocable, that his personal life has nothing left to do but expire. To commit suicide over a shameful offense known to oneself alone is merely to admit that the phenomenal self has been obliterated, and that as an individual one is already dead. Adolescents who undergo psychotherapy often refuse to divulge everything to the therapist. They want to keep some of their secrets, or their whole fragile self will disappear.

The symbolic stuff of social motives is so fluid that the child has to be trained to cultivate "pride." In other words, he has to be trained to cultivate *the appearance of private motives.* Children learn that society desires this, and that they can make themselves desirable by running and shouting "I have a secret." The point is this: the motives that compose the self are so completely social that we run a great risk, namely, the risk that the individuals who compose our society will not seem really unique, and therefore the whole social circus will seem somewhat trumped up. To cultivate pride is to give the whole thing some inward reality (Becker, 1962, Ch. 8). In a sense, the symbolic animal is caught in his own bind. He wants the social motives to hold sway so that everyone will fall into line. On the other hand, if no one makes an appearance of having valid private motives, we will not be able to feel that our reality is both individual *and* social. Thus, we teach people self-love, so that pride will give the appearance of private motives. But at the same time, self-love reduces the possibility of shame, and the autonomous individual separates himself from the group.

Shame and Guilt in Historical Perspective

We saw that the difference between shame and guilt is a reflection of the early time in which social motives are learned. Guilt refers to less explicit command over the rules. If this thesis is borne out, then some further interesting points suggest themselves. Why is guilt so much a part of Western history, more prominent than in most other societies? The distinction between "shame cultures" and "guilt cultures," we noted, is on the whole untenable; all cultures humanize their young in contact with person-objects. Therefore, there must be some guilt—some concretization of rules—in each humanization. Nevertheless, some cultures do seem to operate more along the shame-axis, others along the guilt-axis. Certainly Western culture operates along the guilt-axis.

Historically and sociologically this difference seems explainable. In the first place, Western society is characterized by an extensive and rapid development of commerce, trade, and individual mobility. Western society is synonymous with the break-up of traditional society, the original development out of tribalism beginning with the Greeks. In a world of confusion, change, and mobility, shame sanctions would operate with difficulty, if at all. One is truly shamed before his cultural peers, rarely fully before foreigners. This is logical: if the self is social, only one's own society contains the key to the "inner pole." Added to this mobility, is the fact that the nuclear family developed as the extended family of traditional society broke up. With easy travel, industrial manufacture, and economic mobility, smaller mating groups were formed for rearing young, independently of the larger family of uncles, aunts, grandparents. This is the picture we are seeing in the breakup of traditional society in some countries in Asia and Africa today; and from this several interesting conclusions follow. Shame sanctions, being less effective in a society in which one is a stranger, could not be widely used. The cattle barons who ruthlessly killed and machinated to carve out enormous land domains during the United States western expansion, had no need to care about anyone's "opinion." Their loyalty was to the values they had learned from the parents, and not to the impersonal, lawless, and fluid world in which they were immersed. The only sanction they could feel was toward the parental object itself, with its own unique rule formulas. Thus, one condition for guilt being operative occurs

194 THE HUMAN PERSONALITY

when the rules one has learned differ from those of the society in which one is immersed. Shame would be more likely to be operative when the two are congruent. Shame sanctions reflect the fact that the parents' values are similar to those of the society at large. In this sense, one might say that "the parents" are always "there" to appraise one's performance, since everyone in the society has the same standard. The performance standards are "exteriorized" in terms of the sheer numbers who share them. When the performance standards are not possessed by others in the immediate object world, they are perforce "interiorized" (cf. Leighton and Kluckhohn, 1947, pp. 105-106; and Gerth and Mills, 1953, pp. 98 ff., on "the social relativity of the generalized other"). Thus, when we talk about the prevalence of shame sanctions among primitives, we are referring to the fact that the values one has learned are congruent with everyone else's.

This uniformity is aided by the further fact that among many tribes, child socialization is permissive. Often rules are learned very late, and from others besides the parents. These rules would be less inextricably fused with particular concrete objects. A. M. Hocart once observed (1952, pp. 205-207) that in many tribes he questioned the natives about why they did a certain thing one way rather than another. The answer was surprisingly uniform: "Because it is the custom," or "Because that is the way we have been taught," or "That is the way our people do it." Hocart noticed that they did *not* say "Because it is the right way." Late rule-learning, in other words, seems to contribute its share to separating the rules from the objects.

Shame and guilt, in sum, seem to have little to do with the sternness of the father-figure, the religion, God-image, or "type" of conscience one has learned. They have even less to do with the dogma of psychoanalytic theory. They seem to have very much to do with the number of people present in the child-indoctrination teams (cf. Spiro, 1961, p. 120); with the age at which firm indoctrination begins; with the fluidity or mobility of the society in which one is immersed; in a word—with the full range of social conditions which shape the exercise of our powers.

If shame connotes greater possibilities of explicitness of the rules that form the social self, we can understand why Helen Merrell Lynd found shame desirable (1958). Shame wrenches the individual away from the insidious grip of his early objects, from the quiet pollution by early obscurities in learning. Guilt signals the hopeless fusion of self and others; shame allows the full social searchlight to penetrate one's inner recesses. Little matter that shame shows that one has no valid private motive to oppose to social scrutiny: at least shame allows motives to be brought into the open. Here they might become objectively scrutinizable, as motives fused more solidly with objects can never be. The anxiety of guilt is the crippling of future possibility with the obscure looming of past objects. Shame operates in the present, changes as the present changes. It is a matter of fashion. With shame, the symbolic animal has half a chance. Thus Lynd thought that shame should be faced, and only thus possibly forced. Guilt lames the human animal, shame stops him dead.[14] Totally blocked action has nothing ambiguous about it, and so leaves room for invention. Which seems to be the same idea that Emily Dickinson had in mind (Lynd, 1958, p. 210):

> Shame need not crouch
> In such an earth as ours;
> Shame, stand erect,
> The universe is yours!

Modern man, in his quest for autonomy, is forcing his own culture's hand. Disentangling the rules from the objects, it is but a step to examining critically one's whole society.

Notes

1. See Becker (1962, Ch. 6) where the Oedipal learning period is treated as a broad, developmental phase, rather than narrowly as a "complex." See de Beauvoir (1953) for an existentialist reaction against Freud, treating the early human personality in all its complexity and plasticity.

2. A woman who becomes a man's mistress in the hope of eventually inducing him to marry is not using bad intuition. The range of behaviors that he cultivates toward her become an integral part of his personality. To sever relationships with her is actually to cut out a part of himself. The feel of the object is as much in his fingers, the smell as much in his nose, as is the object in the external world.

3. Thus, Thomas Szasz (1961, p. 161) quite correctly argues that the sharp theoretical distinction between "primary gain" and "secondary gain" should be effaced. The satisfactions we gain from the actions and those we gain from the objects are difficult to separate—especially for the immature person.

4. Thus we can understand further how the depressed patient has been "too well indoctrinated," as we observed in Chapter IV. He is hopelessly dependent on familiar objects in order to define his situation: he cannot call up the rules for abstract, critical review. His self-concept is "object-anchored" in effect, rather than "role-anchored." To be able to step back and frame a definition of the situation in abstract, analytical terms, is not a strength that he possesses. (We will review and continue this discussion in the section on shame and guilt, below.)

5. John Bowlby has opted for a most simple view of the child's basic anxiety as the "Primary Anxiety" of object-loss or separation. This anxiety is not reducible to terms other than the rupture of attachment to the mother (1961, p. 253). It would have nothing to do with later, learned gratifications. In his later formulation Freud also swung over to this position (Bowlby, 1961), but he never abandoned his earlier views completely.

6. The humanization process (Oedipal transition) reflects nicely the philosophical speculations of the existentialist philosophers, as we note below. Unfortunately only a few—like Sartre—have been

able to pinpoint the union between the vicissitudes of early child training and the peculiar tragedy and beauty of human existence. Tillich's comment sums up the whole problem of translation of concepts: "It remains, of course, an open question how the psychological meaning of these concepts can be distinguished from their ontological meaning. Most of the criticism directed against Heidegger deals with this problem; and it appears that Heidegger implicitly admitted that he was unable to explain the difference clearly, and that he himself has increasingly emphasized human nature as the starting-point of the Existential ontology" (1944, p. 58). In this chapter and in Chapters III and VIII we offer a translation of some of the most important points. Once existential categories can be seen in the light of the rough laws of human development, they become crystal clear. Furthermore, they become scientifically meaningful. This is another great modern convergence between philosophy and psychiatry.

7. Kierkegaard observed that the more original a person is, the deeper his anxiety (Goldstein, 1951, p. 113). This can be interpreted in several ways. For one thing, the original person will strain more at the early rules, find himself more dissatisfied with the narrowness of his world. Or, in another sense, the original person may well be recruited on the schizophrenic continuum as we saw it in Chapters I to III: He may be unable to construct a secure world, unable to rely on dependable rules. His originality is thus one which flees anxiety by the fabrication of a world of his own, or a new version of old rules. Historically, the anxious person, or, the misfit, is the one who attempts to resystematize the cultural symbolism.

8. "Fear of the unknown," of course, has somatic dimensions which make it seem akin to "inner threat." Especially would this be true of the residues of early, presymbolic conditioning, which can hang on tenaciously: The heart will beat violently in certain situations long after the need for excitement has passed, in the life-history of the individual; and long after one has ceased to remember why the situation causes the excitement. W. Horsley Gantt (1960) calls this "schizokinesis," to describe the difficult-to-extinguish early learning, and the discrepancy between old conditionings and new experience.

9. This is an insight evidently inspired also by acquaintance with linguistic philosophy; it was put forth by Professor Alfred Louche at a guest philosophy lecture to the Department of Psychiatry, Upstate Medical Center, Syracuse, New York, January 18, 1962.

10. For an important paper on this subject see Robbins (1955).

11. I am omitting discussion of the conventional usage of guilt, in the sense of "I am guilty of a crime," or "I am expiating my guilt." This usage is not included in the way guilt is defined here because its meaning and the behavior it reflects are explicit. I am concerned with matching the concept to a specific range of behavior where its meaning has been far from clear.

12. There is also an "intrinsic shame"—shame for feeling ashamed. The difference is that one knows more why he is ashamed, than why he is guilty. Cf. Kafka (1948) for a literary rendering of the dumbness of guilt.

13. The experienced woman is self-assured under the prurient gaze of a roomful of men precisely because of her accumulation of private experiences. She is thus "full" of private motives, and can respond to the social scrutiny by feeling and thinking something like this: "You imagine that your definition of my sexual identity prevails, but I assure you that I have a sexual identity (or, a total identity) of an experienced richness that you cannot exactly grasp." (Cf., in this context, the definition of masochism [in Chapter VIII] as a bankruptcy of private motives. For another way of looking at the self-body relationship when one is stopped under the gaze of another, see van den Berg's excellent discussion (1962). I use the term "valid private motives" when the individual can muster reasons for continuing action; when he cannot call up such reasons the body becomes a burden and a potential focus for shame. He can no longer take it for granted. Thus, the schizophrenic who lacks motives for interpersonal action may find that his body is almost always a point of interference at the disposal of others, as we note in Chapter II above [cf. notes 2 and 12].)

It is in this sense that we can perhaps partly understand the extreme importance of polite "face ritual" in a traditional society such as old China. The interlocutor with whom one interacts, in a closed society, might know all about one's family, one's past history, one's wife, and even one's hopes and plans for the future. Thus, extreme care has to be taken to handle the self delicately, to pretend that indeed *there is* a private self. Face ritual is relatively unimportant in an open, mobile society, where the self is private and unknown. Tactlessness and crudeness would not injure one, because one could always marshall some private facets of his personality to oppose to the interlocutor's probing.

14. The shamed animal, stopped dead, has the recourse of becoming shameless. Like the criminal about to be publicly hanged, he can answer pitiless scrutiny with a defiant "God damn your eyes" (Erikson, 1956, p. 200).

It almost always happened that among all the people in the world only our own parents, and perhaps a few people they selected, were right about everything. We could refuse to accept their rightness only at the price of a load of guilt and fear, and peril to our immortal souls. This training has been practically universal in the human race. Variations in content have had almost no importance. The fruit is poisonous no matter how it is prepared or disguised.

      G. B. CHISHOLM (1946, pp. 7ff.)

VII

The Scope

of the Revolution

IT IS TO BE EXPECTED that once man began unveiling himself his self-scrutiny would be pitiless. With equanimity the scientist opens the top of a dog's skull and jerks him about with electric charges in the brain; we may not open the human skull for the same trials, but the investigation into human motives is just as cool and matter-of-fact. Besides, man wants the better life; when he detects the poisons in himself that sap it he is apt to kick himself. Certainly, Chisholm's eloquent statement has a tenor of wistfulness about it. In fact, future historians could well call our age "The Wistful Age"—never before had so many seen man's shortcomings so clearly, and been able to do so little about it. Chisholm says that the training of children is making "a thousand neurotics for every one" that psychiatrists might hope to help (p. 9). We know where to lay the blame: at the point of indoctrination with the cultural fiction. The existentialists have added their massive protest to the clinical unmasking of the child's early "twist." Sartre points out that any number of writers "have made their rejection of childhood training a point of departure for working out a more acceptable ethical system" (Barnes, 1959, p. 329). Human "authenticity" lies precisely in rejecting the excessive constraints of early environment, in liberating oneself from its fetters.

Freud versus Dewey

But Freud saw this as the beginning of the century. Why is it taking such a long time to spread the message more broadly? It would require a thoroughgoing sociology of contemporary knowledge to answer this question, but one fact is indisputable. With all its revolutionary zeal and vision, Freud's system remained inherently conservative. Freud himself is not entirely to blame: His greatest fear for psychoanalysis was that it would fall into the sectarian hands of the medical profession who would prevent its broad, social dissemination. In this he proved himself again a prophet. But psychoanalysis carried within itself the Freudian seed that made possible this monopoly: namely, the idea that human achievements were reducible to physio-chemistry, that man contained ineluctable deep-seated instincts, that the drama of human life was consequently one of man *versus* society. Thus, we noted earlier the implicit contradiction in Freudian doctrine: on the one hand the contention that symbolic man was shaped by society during the early humanization process; and on the other the notion that man's instincts prevented him from ever being fully shaped by society. The consequence of this was to hold thinkers in a chafing bind for a half-century. Was man a social animal or wasn't he? A further consequence of this bind was even more subtle. That is, the settled-in notion that no matter what society does to or for man, nature (via man's instincts) has arranged to abort the best human efforts. The paradox was complete; Freud's revolutionary doctrine bogged down into an inherent conservatism. It remained for neo-Freudians like Horney and Fromm to appear revolutionary by their social criticisms. In two contradictory ways Freud's revolutionary thunder was stolen by his disciples—by the medical profession and by the critics of culture.

Dewey—Freud's great contemporary—put forth a different and more self-consistent view of human experience. It will remain for future historians to tally up merits and demerits. At this time it is clear that of the two, Dewey's view of human "dualism" was nearer the mark: in a symbolic animal the bind on action is due to a suppression of symbolic choice, and not to a repression of instinctual need. The human animal is not torn apart by an instinctual "unconscious," but rather by the stifling grip of early constrictions in learning rules for action. Admittedly, Freud got at the *actual* difficulty of human action—the fact that it bogs down, becomes inappropriate to some new challenge. Dewey is saying nothing more than this, but he is saying it less ambiguously: human need is merely the need for the possibilities of choice. The possibility of choice permits the forward-momentum of the organism in a blocked situation. Choice inheres in the nature of organic life, in the accumulation of experiences for future action; the organism stores memories which facilitate these future choices. Man differs from all other animals in that only in him does choice become conscious. Man differs further with a peculiarly unique tragedy: He is given the gift of conscious choice, and is saddled with an unusually long, deep-going early training that hobbles its free use.

The fundamental fact is that success of action is measured by only one criterion: simply by matching appropriate means with consciously chosen ends. The whole power of any organism resides in bringing about the realization of chosen goals. All organisms attempt to do this—to match their repertory of means to the challenge of the situation. With man, of course, the matching of means to ends contains a unique element: *he alone decides* upon what the ends are to be. Control of natural processes thereby reaches its acme: free purpose enters into nature as man determines goals and rationally weighs and scrutinizes fitting means for their realization. With man, experience, purpose, and choice become fused with prescription or "morality."

Yet with all this potential, man has done precious little for man. In the twentieth century mankind at large is as far from the proverbial "Good life" as ever. Like the nascent rationalists at the time of Louis XIV we still see ruin and reason in grotesque coexistence. Furthermore, we have unwittingly brought to pass a situation in which we are as unsure of surviving tomorrow as was Nanook the Eskimo hunter. The explanation is not far to seek—we have covered it at some length in these pages. Man builds a symbolic world on a foundation of anxiety-proneness, on a fear of object-loss. In order to act he must learn answers to the four common human problems; and it is these answers which in most cases bind him forever to a narrow range of vision. In order to exist in any society one learns to "do as the Joneses" and everyone joins in dedicated protection of the stupid, the useless, and the stale. The Plains Indians died fighting and so proved their means inadequate to the end in view. Guardian Spirits plus bow and arrow are not equal to the task of survival when the enemy has Winchester and Gatling Gun. Rigid answers to the four common human problems are as binding and as merciless as the impulse that drives lemmings to the sea. Man answers the problems of his action and finds thereby his equanimity. A whole society does the same—everyone supporting everyone else in a plodding self-contentment. The liberal sprinking with tears that drench every life is due mostly to the failure to see that "Mother Necessity" may be only a reflex of the ignorance of proper means and ends. Thus the bellies of Hindu children swell with starvation while sacred monkeys pillage scarce crops and sacred cows fill the streets with sacred dung. The equation cow = steak = full stomach never comes to mind. Nausea would ensue if it did—not nausea over ingestion of prohibited meat so much as nausea over a shattering of the delicate equilibrium of life-meaning. Kingsley Davis sums up nicely the bizarre picture offered by restriction of means and the creation of artificial ones, that man undertakes to further his symbolic designs: "To an observer outside the society . . . it seems almost that the actors are blindfolded or walking in a daze, because they do not see the possibilities that lie at hand for the realization of their desires; or else it seems that they are doing things which seem elaborately unnecessary for such realization" (1948, pp. 132 ff.).

Because of early constrictions in learning, the range of means available is always less than it might be. There are at least four ways in which people everywhere shut off a potentially rich source of means (Davis, 1948, pp. 132 ff.): In the first place, answers to the four common problems set up goals which man can never realize—like claiming rewards in a future life for good deeds in the present. Since there is no way to show such goals to be true or false, people accept the means passed down from their elders. Secondly, early indoctrination, we saw, leaves the child with a style of behavior that is usually automatic. He has no idea why he wants what he wants, or why he insists on getting it in certain very definite ways. He only knows that acting in this manner is satisfying, and that acting in any other way is anxiety-provoking. Thirdly, since each individual gets a different early training experience, some are less fortunate than others in the range of means that they can contemplate without anxiety. The schizophrenic, never having developed his powers, has few or no dependable means in his repertory. Finally, social prohibitions and laws themselves limit the means that are available for reaching specified ends. To "borrow" an automobile in order to rush oneself to an important appointment is punishable as theft.

Man's chief strength, intelligent appraisal of a broad range of means, is thus hobbled in a number of ways (cf. A. S. Luchins and E. H. Luchins, 1959). The problem of rationality, of what man *will allow himself* to know and do, is the major problem of human existence. Little wonder that Dewey made the idea of balancing means and ends central to his whole philosophy (1934, 1958). For Dewey the major issue of contemporary life was how far man would allow rationality to govern his actions. Was twentieth-century America to continue to live as uncritically as the Kwakiutl? (And with nearly the same central values.) Or was man's reason finally going to come to grips with the full range of problems of living in society? This is not the place to review Dewey's work. But we can show how Dewey neatly summed up the constrictions of irrationality and culture, in terms of two kinds of means-end relationships.

External-coerced means-end relationships. Dewey's paradigm example here—like Marx's—is the contemporary scheme of working for wages (1958, pp. 361 ff.). The means-end relationship is simple: I want these goods, *therefore* I have to get a job. In other words, in order to enjoy what I have been taught to enjoy, I have to spend the greater part of my time in mostly tedious labor for wages. There is no free choice involved. Only when I receive the wages can I then get the goods. In this wage-work scheme there is one prominent feature. On the surface it looks like a fair bargain; do this for that; means employed to a given end—nothing, in sum, that any organism in nature does not undergo to satisfy its desires. The key word here is precisely *undergo*. This is not creative fashioning of experience in order to attain a given end. Instead, there is a long duration *of dead time and dead effort*— merely a barter toward the end desired. The individual "puts in time" in order to get a wage (cf. Murray, 1952, p. 446). Seen from the point of view of the acting organism, the period of wage-work is a suspension of its own initiatory powers. This is not to be compared to what looks like a similar process in nature, say, the cat who waits patiently for the mouse to come out of the hole. The locus of willfulness, the locus of decision, lies *in* the cat. *He* is matching the means and ends. Barter of one's powers, the divorce of ends and means exists only on the human level. In experiments even the ape shows himself reluctant to make the sacrifice that man makes daily: he will refuse to undergo a frustrating series of trials, even though the reward rate is 50 per cent.

Internal, free creation of matched means-end sequences. Here the individual has full control over the means, and appraises them with reference to the goal. The situation is fully explicit, fully verbalized, the connections of means and ends are judged *intrinsically.* For example, one is about to do therapy with a patient. One wants him to be free of his phobia, therefore one will employ a certain range of means. They seem balanced, appropriate. As the process of therapy is initiated, the organism (the therapist) is alive under his own chosen effort to reach the goal with means decided on by himself. Contrast this to the wage-earner: He has little idea of the factors that make his wage-work situation necessary. He sees only the *accidental* connection between means and ends, and *conforms himself to it.* The work has nothing *intrinsically* to do with the end: There are a thousand different ways to earn the same wage. An effect is not an end, says Dewey; it is only an end when the conditions for realizing it have been freely chosen. Otherwise it is an accident, a coercion. To be unconscious of the crucial factors in the situation to which one is adjusting, is to repeat as an adult the early slavery of the child. It is to consent to have one's choices constricted by the accidents of being thrown into a certain kind of world, a world beyond one's powers, beyond one's right to question, beyond one's capacity to change.

Dewey's view of coerced means-end sequences goes to the heart of mechanical action. "In all ranges of experience, externality of means defines the mechanical" (1934, p. 198). By definition, then, the coerced means-end sequence stands for everything that is *not* human, *not* freeing, *not* fulfilling. With the coerced means-end sequence man abdicates the exercise of his own powers. This is the perfect definition of "alienation," of the mechanical hollowness of contemporary life (cf. Levi, 1959, pp. 16 ff.). It can be said most emphatically: *Human failure is performance under coerced means-ends sequences.*

The Psychiatric Syndromes as Coerced Means-Ends Performance

Human failure shows itself most clearly in the psychiatric syndromes, in the constriction of action that we call "mental illness." The syndromes are, par excellence, examples of the failure of man to practice and promote a fully rational approach to interpersonal living. This notion has been in the air for quite some time. Freud talked about the "quiet voice of the intellect" persisting until it is heard. Horney cited the neurotic's conflict between early family training in means-ends and later cultural exigencies. Kingsley Davis, who gave the problem of means-ends a prominent place in his sociological theory, offered a view of mental illness as a means-ends conflict: the individual lacks consistent order of preference in the ends he seeks, or he lacks the means to achieve the ends he desires (1948, pp. 263 ff.). Personality theorists cite the constriction of the phenomenal field on the choices one has to make (Hall and Lindzey, 1957, pp. 481 ff.). The individual has to act in the world according to how he perceives it—and we have seen at some length that perception varies enormously between individuals. Carl Rogers insists that the individual can only move forward when choices are *"clearly perceived and adequately symbolized"* (Hall and Lindzey, 1957, p. 481). Inadequate perception leads to inadequate behavior (Snygg and Combs, 1949, p. 119). Abraham Maslow offers a view similar to Davis's, giving a prominent place to the conflict of means, conflict of goals, and the total disorganization that ensues from lack of choice in the face of threat. The neurotic, says Maslow emphatically, is not only emotionally sick, he is "cognitively *wrong!*" (1954, p. 204). Thomists also join in saying that "Ignorance rather than 'unconscious' forces accounts for the seemingly 'irrational' behavior of the mentally ill. . . . Reeducation is essential to true recovery from mental illness" (Barta, 1952, p. 27). In mid-twentieth century even the physicists have their say on the human personality. Percy Bridgman, for example, does not doubt "that the majority of people find the concept implied in the statement 'only I am conscious' entirely unintelligible, so completely has any possible freshness of perception been atrophied under the bludgeoning of society. As part of the same picture, when the individual realizes that he cannot get away from himself, he will see that his most important personal problem is to find his springs of conduct within himself, a vision of which very few people are capable" (1959, p. 316). There is a growing rallying of people from all fields on the problem of human rationality.

It is not difficult to make out a clear case for neurosis as stupidity. We substantiated this in some detail in Chapter VI. But in order for the revolution in psychiatry to get under way, this was hardly enough. The fact is that the main attack in this revolution is the upsurge to take *all* the "syndromes" away from the jurisdiction of medical psychiatry. Psychiatrists and society are quite willing to admit that neurosis represents human "confusion," and can best be ironed out by throwing some rational light on the matter—"talk therapy" suffices for this. But the malfunctions we have discussed in detail in Chapters II to IV were surrounded with the awe of medical mystery: Here, surely, was *real* "disease" and not *merely* "stupidity." The psychiatric medical practitioner might exclaim: "How dare anyone treat profound human suffering with such a flippant label?" How dare they indeed. How dare the medical professsion pretend to understand what *human* suffering is when all their basic training confines their knowledge to the animal body? We have shown how frightfully people can suffer when they risk losing their *human* world, and we have seen how this suffering comes about in terms of a total, cognitive, behavioral block or constriction in action. Only a symbolic animal could suffer so—an insight that led Goethe to be grateful at times for the short span of human life. The full grotesqueness of human suffering *has* to be explained on its own terms—least of all can it be reduced to physio-chemistry. One word can sap a human life.

We noted in the Introduction that Szasz took the most recent step in the revolution by showing that hysteria—the syndrome on which the myth of mental illness was predicated—was not an illness at all in a medical sense. Rather, it was a failure in human communication by someone with restricted perceptions, poor command of means, in an overbearing situation. The hysteric sums up in one vast amalgam of dumb ineptitude the constrictions on the exercise of human reason. Accidents of birth, time, education, place, and sex, combine to render the individual grotesque. The hysteric, with his body-language, reflects perfectly what Dewey meant by coerced means-end sequences. There is no possibility of effectively matching means and ends when the individual is not free in several ways to cognize the total behavioral picture. Sullivan aptly called the hysteric's language of stupidity the "happy idea" for unplugging action. But it is a pathetic happy idea; a perfect illustration of a rash invention of means in a situation in which ignorance prevents one from getting a desired end.

It remained to show that the long-mystifying "disease" of schizophrenia was also stupidity—stupidity in a very basic area of experience, in primary enculturation data. The schizophrenic, lacking behavior patterns, has no chance for manipulating means and ends. When his world begins to slip away, his only recourse is to constrict his means-ends control to such a narrow range that he turns into a ludicrous caricature of cultural man. Depression, nearly as mystifying a "disease" as schizophrenia, is more akin to hysteria. The depressed patient is similarly a paradigm of external coercion of means-ends. He has no idea of the main coordinates in the situation to which he seeks to adapt, he is entirely uncritical of the important factors. Within this divorce of causative, known means from prospective end, he employs his peculiar guilt-language. He keep his inadequate means within the confines of his closed performance world—and here they work. They would not work for ends beyond this closed world. In a sense, this situation is similar to the crucial humanization process that we have repeatedly sketched: the child makes heroic adaptations to pressures that he cannot rationally assess. It is a blind adaptation in which one has adumbrated needs, but no real choice over the ends wherewith to reach them. The result is that the child succumbs to the best available formula (a life-style) for keeping action moving forward; the depressed person does the same with his guilt-language.

The New Meaning of "Normal"

And so we close the full and final circle. If mental illness is stupidity, and stupidity is behavior under coerced, external means-ends sequences, then we must proceed to redefine "normal." *Normal no longer can mean "not ill"—it must mean "not stupid." And "not stupid" means "not coerced."The normal individual, then would be the creative one, the one who exercised control over his choice of means and ends.* Indeed it is just such a definition of normal which was put forth by Dewey, and which is again coming to the fore in modern psychology. The normal man is one who "is habitually *oriented in a creative sense.*"[1] In other words, if man's unique characteristic is his free exercise of rational control over means and ends, then his primary strength would be full expression of his unique characteristic. The logic is ineluctable. The conclusion that is forced is even more striking and apodictic: For man, *the normal cannot be anything else but the ideal* (McGill, 1956-1957, pp. 101 ff.).

Public Policy: The New Science

And now we can see better the fallacy of a "science" of personality, or a "science" of psychology. We noted this fallacy in Chapter V where we sketched a view of the personality as a symbol-system capable of complete changes in functioning. The orderliness of closed systems, the prediction that science seeks, none of this is possible when we deal with emotionally charged symbol-systems. The history of psychology, in effect, is a history of its own disillusionment as a science. Psychology's early revolt against its linkage with philosophy in the latter part of the nineteenth century has now run full course. Psychology has evolved back into philosophy. Only this time it must be social philosophy rather than transcendental metaphysics. Units of cogitation have gradually become broader, the attempts to localize "soul," "consciousness," "meaning," have spread from cells and reflex-arcs to the whole society. Actually, Dewey, who dealt a telling blow to the early associationists and psychophysicists, sums up this development. From his early critical paper on the reflex-arc (1896) he developed a thoroughgoing social criticism. In less than 50 years psychology thus found itself back in the lap of speculation, promotion, values, ethics. Psychology, having rid itself of vitalism and transcendentalism, at last has to rid itself of the pretentions of being an integral science.

Only in the mid-twentieth century can we see clearly why this must be. Personality, as a symbol-system, *cannot fully be studied apart from the social fund of symbols which constitute it.* If human failure on an individual level is a failure to rationally match means and ends, we must understand that this is only one aspect of *a total social failure to pair means and ends.* It happens to be best focused in mental illness, where control over action possibilities is at a minimum, where means-ends matching is largely external, coerced. It should be abundantly clear by now that the stupidity of mental illness is nothing else than a precipitate of social stupidity. Personality ineptitude in commanding appropriate means, or in choosing ends, is always shaped by the society into which one is born. If we want to "stamp out mental illness," it will mean putting the control of means-ends sequences back into the hands of the people who need to make choices, or who want to make them. It will mean making rational means-end matching explicit for as many as possible.

Why have the "scientific" psychologists refused or been unable to recognize this? There are any number of reasons, and this is not the place to review them. But one reason comes to mind, and is pertinent to our discussion. We saw previously that personality could be likened to an open system, and system-principles could be ascribed to it: that it tended toward "self-actualization" (Goldstein), "self-consistency" (Lecky) "self-realization," and so on. Some psychologists, haranguing their colleagues, insisted that the science of personality must be a science of possibility (Maslow, 1954, p. 77), a science of developing open systems. Quite correctly. But in doing this, they spoke lavishly of psychopathology as a "twisting of man's essential nature" (Maslow, 1954, p. 340). Thus, we see the danger of positing system-principles, and trying to speculate about what nature is up to in her fabrication of *Homo sapiens*. By trying to find a scientific underpinning for the promotion of human possibility, these maverick psychologists left themselves open to the charge of a new vitalism. The fact is that we have no idea of man's "essence," of what he can become, or should become. Traditional psychologists quite rightly objected to this kind of promotion, which tried to sneak by under the guise of a scientific establishment of system-principles and organic tendencies. The impetus to a broadening-out of psychology was thus hampered.

Human possibility, like normality, is inevitably something to work toward. The only hint in nature is that organic life seems to thrive best when the organism has command over appropriate means for given ends. But we cannot build a science on this, for the simple reason that man chooses and fabricates ends of his own free will. And, to repeat, individual means and ends are always distilled down from social means and ends. It was Lester Ward and Dewey, in our time, who showed most clearly the way. If we insist on having a science of man, then it must be a science of social man, a science of man in society. This is the only solution, and it will be fought the hardest. It has already been evaded for 50 years by a fumbling capitalist economy, which steadily balks at placing reason over the unthinking game of private profit. A science ignored by a democracy dedicated precisely to the rational balance of means and ends. A science evaded also by academic compartmentalization—a fiasco of fungus luxuriance, nourished generously by the moneyed, private foundations. Students in the future will surely snicker at the first generation of twentieth-century man, at the efforts of serene specialists in sociology, anthropology, psychology, and related "disciplines" to fashion themselves into the scientific father-image of physicists. One cannot escape the impression that we are financing mightily the privilege of burying our separate disciplinary noses in the sand. We are financing, in sum, a culturally concerted effort to look everywhere but at the true problems of social and human values.

But if all this were entirely the case, this would not be a book about a revolution. A distinctive science of social man seems to be in the making, but so quietly, and so unexpectedly. The first rumblings started with Rousseau, only to fizzle out with Marx, in historical dogma. Possibilities took a new surge forward with Freud when he observed that he made an enemy of society every time he effected a psychoanalytic cure. Today the matter is unmistakable: For the source of most human misery, social arrangements must be examined, with a view to serious changes. We have seen people from all disciplines converging on the source of human ineptitude. The United States today, in fact, is so concerned with "mental illness," that we are devoting an increasingly huge effort to its eradication. And so we have a rather paradoxical picture: a society that does not want to change its values, but which fears ill health perhaps more than anything; consequently, it is forced to scrutinize itself as a *source* of that very ill health. No amount of generous grants to physio-chemical research can long delay the full vigor of this social self-scrutiny. Dewey's social philosophy, a criticism of the dilemmas of irrational man, is now being quietly echoed by social psychiatry. Social psychiatry is not a medical science in the narrow sense of the term. It is, as Lasswell insisted, a policy science, "along with law, education and the social disciplines at large" (1962, p. 120). The function of policy sciences is precisely to proceed to the kind of piecemeal social engineering that Dewey championed, the only basis on which a science of man can ever be built. As Lasswell observes, cultural catharsis is not enough. The mass rituals and irrational patchwork which society uses to keep its values intact cannot be protected by a true policy science. We cannot have our streets lined with cheap Negro bars on one side, and self-righteous "rescue missions" on the other. "We do not want to protect democracy by manipulating the community into a variety of activities deliberately encouraged or designed for the purpose of preserving as much of the status quo as possible. Any status quo observes rational, selective, progressive change. . . . This appears to be the program of social psychiatry, in particular . . ." (Lasswell, 1962, pp. 131, 146).

Alexander Leighton's massive Stirling County study gave a glimpse of just how far social psychiatry can go in tracing down the noxious effects of cultural values. In our discussion of depression, in Chapter IV, we detailed some of these effects in terms of the range of objects a culture makes available, the degree of awareness of its members, and so on. Leighton's work gives full psychiatric substantiation to a focus on purely social problems. Issues of personal freedom, of economic freedom, of rationality, of social arrangements, type of family, goals for achieving statuses, means for achieving them, and so on, come up for critical review. Although Leighton seems reluctant to carry through conceptually on the full implications of his findings, the new social psychiatry gives promise of being (potentially, at least) culturally ruthless:

"In what way are certain *situations* in a given society particularly threatening to the psychological functioning of the individual? . . . For instance, among people who have a striving background and strong upward mobility tendencies, is it particularly stressful to be in an area where the chances of fulfilling such ambitions are slight or where success, if it occurs, produces hostile attitudes and social disarticulation?" (Cleveland and Longaker, 1957, p. 180). The ramifications of answers to such questions will hardly allow for the maintenance of status quo. *The society which invests in mental health* (as here defined) *had best be aware of what it is bargaining for.* Now that we have been able to phrase all the syndromes in behavioral language, psychiatry can be nothing less than full social criticism. The early insights of psychoanalysis have now been extended to their appropriate range. Lasswell echoes Paul Schilder's call for a "new culture pattern" (1962, p. 241).

The naively hopeful study of "comparative psychiatry" will be a study of comparative stupidity. (Or, it will be a pseudoscientific farce, as it now is [Becker, 1962, Ch. 9]). The much-vaunted TAT (Thematic Apperception Test) is after all a stupidity test—it assays the cultural distortion in perception. The study of "adaptive mechanisms" across cultures is not a study of something that can be compared in a laboratory, according to any scientific tables (cf. Du Bois, 1961, Vol. 1, pp. xxv-xxvi). The "adaptive mechanisms" are life-styles; the mechanisms by which one perceives *are* the individual himself. They are a summation of the range and capacity of his powers in controlling means and ends. The "adaptive mechanisms," in sum, are an IQ test. Not any pseudoscientific IQ test as we now know it, but rather a test against values *to be decided on,* a test against *chosen* human possibility. The new science of total social man will seek to broaden the range of human capacities. It will not attempt, ostrich-like, to tally up the *present* score of human stupidity, and use *that* as a basis for working out "laws." The new science will work for an increase in human freedom, by attempting to increase the total social rationality of means-ends matching. Thus, it will not be a science as we have known it in the narrow domain of physics. It will not try to delimit fixed and certain laws. On the contrary: It will try to multiply the possibilities of greater numbers of uncertain *choices*. Here truly is a challenge and a dedication worthy of man: the maximization of possibilities for his own action. It is worth pausing to consider this. There are many signs that our whole conception of science will have to change, and is changing. The model of the physical sciences as a paradigm for all possible sciences once seemed indisputable. Now it seems downright silly. Part of the reason for the early development of the physical sciences, and their continuing ascendancy, is simple: *We are reluctant to build a social science*, that is, we are reluctant to tamper with deep-grained traditional habits. We simply do not want to bring cultural values up for critical review.

But science is par excellence a frame of mind and a method of inquiry that seeks understanding and control. The historical question is, *what* do we want to control? Very early we decided that we wanted to control the physical world. Now we are faced with the opportunity to control the social world—indeed with the necessity of controlling it if we want to solve real human problems. Here is where the matter becomes complicated. Most of those who hold up physics as the model for all possible sciences imagine that one day we will be able to control the human world, if only we can work patiently to reduce symbolic and social phenomena to their physical constituents. They claim that once we locate, in cells and in body chemistry, the roots and mainsprings of action, we will be able to proclaim a science of man in society. *The fallacy here is evident* even if we grant that reduction is possible (and there are—as we have seen—many powerful reasons for not granting this). The fallacy is simply this: if once we are in a position to determine man, are we going to use this control? How? Who is going to use it—scientists?—philosopher-kings? Toward what end? Obviously the question is insurmountable; we cannot even entertain it if we value freedom. The point is that control of human life by a physical science is antidemocratic and antihuman. Therefore we cannot envisage it as a goal of science. Further, the conclusion is ineluctable: *if we had a science of the precise determinism of human behavior we should have to repudiate it!* It would be incompatible with a belief in human possibility. Samuel Butler and William James, among others, appreciated this long ago. E. A. Burtt has recently forcefully summed up the whole problem (1962).

What is the alternative? We have seen it in these pages (and will see further below). We have seen that the psychiatric syndromes epitomize human failure, because they represent lack of human control in situations where choice is called for. *This is not a matter of ignorance of laws in a chaotic world, but of ignorance of possibilities in an ordered world.* The science of man in society —the science of control over human action—must then be a science of the maximization of individual choice. This means that the locus of control will reside in the individual actor himself, rather than in "science" as an esoteric, controlling institution. Human science in a democratic society must be a science which places the shaping of human possibility in the hands of the individuals themselves.

Thus it seems fair to say that the revolution in psychiatry will give the strongest possible support to the new views of science. Science and human values are inseparable; science exists only to further human values; science can further human values by accelerating atoms—but accelerated atoms cannot undertake to further human values: only humans can do this. Man must take a moral stand with regard to the facts of social science (cf. Kapp, 1961; Kattsoff, 1953, p. 381).

Identity and Personal Choice

To talk about the need for a science that would increase the numbers and the possibility of rational choices is not a starry-eyed idealism. Not at this stage in history at any rate. There is every reason to believe that maximization of choice is the only way to meet the challenge of living in twentieth-century society. What is the challenge exactly? We have been led to feel that it is very complex. But this is only because so many pundits have stepped forward to give their own impressionistic version. Nearly everyone in some kind of authority has his say. We have seen the fallacy of the Freudian version of individual vs. society. Trigant Burrow, who early broke with Freud, had his own system (1949). He saw man's ills in terms of an overdevelopment of the cerebral cortex. Man was thought to be split against himself phylogenetically, as his old brain and new brain worked at odds. Burrow proposed that man's natural "harmony" with the world was being defeated by his learned symbol systems. Others give a more sociological interpretation to modern man's plight. It would stem from the plural numbers of roles that each individual has to fill: the number of roles is so great, and sometimes so incompatible, that the individual comes to be torn against himself: "loving husband," "ruthless business tycoon," "devoted son," and so on, stand in some contradiction to each other. Others would focus on the problems of society at large—its fragmentation into interest groups, the loss of old community bonds, of fellow feeling, of common purpose in the pursuit of agreed social goals. They lament modern man's turning in upon himself, his preoccupation with his own welfare and personal acquisitions, his use of society as a personal grab bag whose fruits are to be snatched and greedily consumed in private. This would be the anomic or "inauthentic" man (Tiryakian, 1962, p. 164).

There is a grain of truth in all these views, as well as in those that accuse "mass man" and "mass society." Trigant Burrow, for example, is really and quite rightly lamenting the indoctrination of the individual into a segmented, cultural world view—however much he speculates about an "improper" phylogenetic development. The only phylogenetic or biological basis for the human condition seems to be the long period of helplessness of higher-primate infants, their large brain, and freedom from instincts. We traced out its effects: Due to his need for a succoring object, the infant's principal anxiety is one of separation from the object, fear of object-loss. Thus the social self is built on an unsteady foundation. The child's feeling of self-value is dictated by parental recognition of what *they* consider to be a desirable self. The child's cortical controls and cognition—his ego—comes to exercise its powers in a limited range. The result is that free choice of means and ends is crippled from the start. The child invests his feeling of value uncritically in a limited range of cognitions and actions. Later, this is complicated by the addition of vocabularies of motive, which overlay the pre-perceived or sub-ceived earlier rules. The human tragedy is thus basically simple, and we have phrased it again and again: It consists in a potential abundance of available vocubularies of motivation over which the individual lacks internal, free means-end guidance. The reason for this lack of guidance is his failure to learn to act confidently in the interpersonal world; or, a relatively rigid and unaware commitment of his feeling of worth to the earlier rules he had learned. In either case he is denied a sure command over a broad range of behaviors.

The real "problem" of modern society emerges very clearly. Largely it is a problem of individual integration. Role diversity is less important than the plural number of vocabularies of various degrees of explicitness that can underline a single role (see Ch. II). To talk about promoting "social cohesion" and "social solidarity" is to cover only one small segment of the whole problem. The well-integrated individual, in a socially cohesive society, is one who has a narrow range of vocabularies of motives (G. W. Allport, 1937, p. 143; Lynd, 1939, p. 45). Social cohesion and individual integration, in other words, join to limit the possibilities of personal tension by cultivating stupidity (a narrow range of vocabularies of choice). There seems to be only one way out of this dilemma: namely, to increase explicit vocabularies of motivation *and at the same time to give the individual a consciousness that he has choices among them,* as well as make it possible for him to implement these choices. Thereby we do not aim to "turn back history" to the comforts of social cohesion in traditional society—with all the constraints over personal freedom that it entails. Nor do we reduce the individual to a manageable stupidity in a complex society that he does not understand. Instead, we accept the increase of social diversity and personal complexity and attempt to arm the individual so that he can cope with what history is doing to him. Then it becomes a fair game —we educate him to face up to the world, to be able to verbalize the choices he is presented with, and to translate them into behavior. This is the basic problem. No amount of institutional "homogeneity" or social solidarity can legislate it out of existence.[2] I would venture to guess that some of the tensions in the Soviet system result in part from these facts. That is, the plurality of vocabularies of motivation continues even in the face of social homogeneity and the rational ordering of most institutions. The individual still has to be armed with self-knowledge about his *own* diversity. The tension comes when cultural criticism is not made an explicit part of his education. The human animal is by definition inauthentic when he does not know why he is doing things.

In a recent critique of contemporary utopian theorists, Winston White (1961) forcefully presents the sociological nub of the problem. In traditional society the individual had his life cut out for him. He did not have to choose for himself either life career or marriage partner, or many of the less important roles. It was laid out for him by his elders. Modern man can count on no such ascribed choices, and many do not seem to want them. In sum, says White, modern man has a new freedom, making new demands on his personality. The situation is increasingly confused, socially and morally, as a concomitant of this new freedom. But so far we have not faced up to the remedy, which is to educate modern man properly in his ability to "explore and choose for himself" (1961, p. 115).

Individual integration, however, is not the whole problem.

White, in his eagerness to show that the utopian critics of contemporary society have oversimplified or distorted the picture, seems to imply that society is not at fault in all this, that it would suffice to "increase personal integration." But we have no "science" of individual integration. I think we have demonstrated quite adequately that the symbolic nature of human striving makes man's integration a most peculiar task; the symbolic animal has to juggle a volatile world.

Dewey, George Mead, and the existentialists have made abundantly clear one thing about this juggling; we noted it in discussing the problem of identity: Man lives in the present; only the present is real. The past happened largely as we think it happened. That is, we choose to remember events out of the past according to our present purposes. We reconstruct a past to bring it to bear on present problems. Every new present, said Mead, brings a new past; in each age a different Caesar crosses a different Rubicon. Dewey might go so far as to say that present purposes so determine our reconstruction of the past, that it is conceivable that in some age it will be possible to say that Caesar never crossed the Rubicon at all.[5] Historians such as Collingwood and Carl Becker maintained that this kind of personal reconstruction of the past is exactly what historians did. The version of history that we get depends irrevocably on the personal world view of the historian (cf. Toynbee's "Christian" history). So too with the individual and his past: we are each our own historian. The existentialists saw the implication of this for psychotherapy (van den Berg, 1955, p. 81). The neurotic patient recounted a miserable past, because he saw it in terms of his hopeless present. Take, as a direct illustration of this kind of reconstruction, our changing relationships with single individuals. If we fall out with a friend we might reconstruct our whole past with him in terms of the nasty things he once did, and so on. But if we become friends again, we could throw a warm glow over an entirely new past, recalling happy events shared in common. The whole problem of identity, as we noted in Chapters I and II, depends on one's ability to rework the past, according to his chances in the present. (The future, finally, never exists anyway; we always live in the present. What we call "the future" is merely a bundle of word-expectations that we put together, depending on our present frame of mind.)

All this is very relevant to the problems of modern man. If the present determines past and future, we can understand why Erikson saw the problem of identity as the cardinal one of our time (1950, p. 242). The reflection one gets of his identity *is a measure of his control over his present world.* Never before have the vocabularies of motivation in the present been so many; never before have so many possibilities of self-justification had to be handled by *such little cognitive control and awareness of possibilities of choice,* of means and ends. Why is man's identity so poor, so shallow, so fragmented, in such a rich world? We have answered it: Because he has none of the requisite cognitive control over the richness, quality, choice, and flexibility of the action-alternatives available to him. We educate people in the twentieth century to live in a New Stone Age. In the technical jargon with which we are now familiar, the identity problem boils down to this: The individual learns from his parents to anchor his self-concept in a narrow range of culturally approved choices: consequently, he may not be free to choose from the range and quality of present new experiences. In a superbly indeterminate world, the identity of the rigid individual is helplessly bound to a determinate past. Flexibility in bringing to bear a past of one's choosing depends on flexibility in using behavioral styles and objects of one's present choosing. The problem of fashioning a satisfactory and coherent identity is precisely one of having control over a fluid past—and this kind of control *depends on control over a complex present.* For this reason, existential therapy concentrates on man's problems in his present world. What is the available range of present satisfactions? What is the extent of the person's object world? What is the range of conduct available to him? How explicit is his command over his vocabularies, his awareness of choices? This is what modern psychiatry must determine first and foremost (Szasz, 1961, p. 288). The therapist's digging around for the patient's past experience is a necessary accompanying archaeological excavation, but only because the present is in ruins.

Identity and Cultural Choice

And so we sum up in detailed perspective the ultimate argument against the possibility of a "science of personality." The personality is a symbolically equilibrated past-present-future which depends on the whole panorama of the present. To assess the individual personality it is necessary to assess the state of his world. But—(as we have stressed and as White seems to overlook)— the state of the individual's world never depends on himself alone, or on any direct cause-and-effect influence of his past. To plead for individual integration is to plead for a criticism of culture. The quality of all one's lived experience derives from the dominant cultural values and the kind of world they permit. A good deal of what the individual is depends on how his culture has chosen to answer the problem of survival. The Hindus saw survival as less important than the problem of reincarnation. Therefore, they set up elaborate routine to assure that this problem will be met. The individual's life is routinized to this end, and the area for the exercise of his spontaneity is limited by this. Each culture determines the challenge from the environment in its own way. This becomes the "problem frame of conduct," the area in which routine is instituted (Burns, 1958). The fundamental question of values in any culture can be phrased in simple terms: What kind of control over what kind of environment? What kind of basic routine to which individual spontaneity will be subserved? In other words, what kind of prearranged means-ends schema is the individual born into? Whatever it is, his spontaneous control over means and ends will be inhibited by it. This is what we mean by the great burden of tradition, the unquestioned value option that precedes the birth of the individual. The unquestioned answers to unscrutinized problems form the binding mold.

For most societies, the problem frame of conduct to which individual spontaneity is sacrificed has traditionally been a religious one. The environmental challenge was met by instituting religious control over a supernatural world (as in the example of the Hindus, above). In America today the problem frame of conduct is largely one of formal control over an exchange world. No society has ever defined its environmental challenge wholly in terms of human control over a physical world. This definition, however, is the one to which a small minority of scientists are devoted.

Erich Fromm, Dewey, the existentialists, all joined in criticizing, in effect, the problem frame that we have decided on in contemporary America. The individual is born into a world in which it has been predecided that the promotion of free enterprise and the sale of goods is the dominant problem in meeting the challenge of life. As ludicrous as this is, it is so. The necessary routine, therefore, to which the individual will have to submit, is a routine designed to ensure meeting this problem. *The curb on human spontaneity in twentieth-century America comes about largely in the interests of furthering a merchant value system.* This answer to the four common human problems does not appear, of course, in such stark terms. The indoctrination is more subtly pervasive. Each individual grows up learning to derive his feeling of value from the routine designed to preserve and promote this central value option. That is, each individual derives his self-esteem from subjugating his critical spontaneity to the sale and consumption of goods (cf. Veblen, 1932). Therefore, to threaten the merchant values is to threaten the individual with the loss of his world. Thus, everyone joins in supporting a routine *devoted to a mythological environmental challenge.* The individual routinizes himself willingly to protect a certain kind of arbitrary distributional system, because this system has set up an artificial prestige code that enslaves his self-esteem. Here we see external, coerced means-end matching in its most ruthless sense, as Marx and Dewey saw it in the wage-work system. The individual feels his self-value to be dependent upon obtaining a larger share of the merchant goods as well as upon distributing a larger share of these goods. As he goes about fulfilling the routine to this end, he imagines that he is putting means and ends together himself. Actually, as Al Capp would have it, "any fool can plainly see" that the real environmental challenge of man has been met: namely, the problem of subsistence. American industry and agriculture have heaped such stores of goods that the world is justly envious. But historians of the future will surely not be kind about the thorough and cavalier manner in which we waste and destroy these goods. Butter, eggs, and grain rot in million-dollar-a-day storage; manufactured goods become outdated because we are taught that they are. All the while we derive our smug feeling of self-value from the pace of distribution and consumption—a mythology of such magnitude, a bankruptcy of critical acumen of such ludicrousness, that the commercial babble of an idiot disc-jockey seems to make sense.

This kind of voluntary surrender of rational means-ends matching is bound to take its toll. As we saw earlier, it is precisely this cultural fiction that social psychiatry is beginning to come to grips with. People who try to draw their identity from this miasma of unreason are bound to end up in psychiatric clinics. It is no longer possible to pretend that all is right with our world, and calmly go about looking for chemical imbalance in the brain. The great myth, the life-sapping one, is that *Homo sapiens* is an "owning" animal (Knight, 1960, pp. 123 ff.); whereas we have seen that human satisfaction seems to be approached by doing, by matching means and ends, by choosing, by creating. These strictures are not "mere impressions" of a "proper human destiny" by "idle philosophers" or "dreamers." We are not pretending to know what man "should" be, but saying only that there are enough indications that he is not merely an "owning" animal. Now that the myth of mental illness (as a narrowly medical province) is dead, empirical confirmation of our cultural constraints is starting to trickle in: the high incidence of schizophrenia in areas afflicted by poverty, illiteracy, blind industrial mobility; the frequent incidence of depression among the upper classes, that is, among those who derive their feeling of value best by wholehearted devotion to the cultural mythology, and full success in it. *In itself this is the beginning of a factual critique of the "owning" culture*: the individual forfeits his critical reason and his spontaneity in order to make himself a locus of possession, and in order to demonstrate automatic loyalty to inherited values. He occasionally pays the price by being reduced to a babbling caricature of an adult, whose relentless self-accusation strives to hold his mythological world uncritically intact. The surrender of critical reason in the service of blind indoctrination could have no more appropriate issue for *Homo sapiens*—the "wise" animal.

The New Hedonism

We can see why many psychotherapists and psychoanalysts become social critics and reformers, or turn to Oriental philosophy, Judeo-Christian religion, or some kind of ethic. The problem of identity that plays itself through on their couches is not confined to the office alone. The patient can be educated to see and to seize choices, but once out the door the cultural world swallows him up again. The culture decides the problem frame of action, what conduct will be routinized and to what end. The culture, in sum, contains the key to the coffer of choices, and decides what it will offer even to those of us who are most gifted with spontaneity. Consequently, we seem to be calling for nothing less than a total reenlistment of society in the furtherance of human design. We seem to need to create richer worlds of the self, to make it easier for people to derive a feeling of value from their acts. Rebecca West said it bluntly: "I take it as a prime cause of the present confusion of society that it is too sickly and too doubtful to use pleasure frankly as a test of value" (quoted by Menninger, 1945, p. 92).

And Karl Menninger seconded her: "I believe we psychiatrists should come out squarely and courageously for hedonism and lend the support of our convictions and experience to the bewildered, fearful and hate-inspired peoples of the world" (p. 92).

The idea of using pleasure as a test of value, the promotion of hedonism, is well known. It has a habit of coming to the fore when the conditions for creating the good life seem to be present everywhere, but mankind seems nevertheless to be miserable. Thus, Jeremy Bentham's frank hedonism has retained its perennial appeal. Perhaps in the twentieth century more than ever, human effort seems to be suffocated by human misery. The panorama for viewing possibility against actual achievement has become world-wide. Where the social disruptions are not downright bloody, or the obvious contrasts not too glaring, then, as in America, the identity problem is severe and mental illness rampant. Can't man so design his life as to give himself pleasure? —the sensitive person asks. The matter is not quite so simple. What *pleasure is* remains always to be determined. It is not merely possession of certain goods or the performance of certain acts. An "objective" assaying of pleasure is never possible because, in effect, pleasure is a matter of involvement of the total identity (cf. also Snygg and Combs, 1949, p. 360). A hundred years after Bentham and Mill the problem is still very much with us. Hedonism is not yet defunct by any means, and the debate over it has never been allowed to rest (cf. also G. W. Allport, 1954, pp. 10 ff.). Philosophers as well as psychologists continue to argue the matter (Sheldon, 1950; Williams, 1950). "Must the sadist be denied his pleasure?" (Williams, 1950)—and so on. Some have attempted to be "scientific" about it, and have suggested a "higher-need' hedonism—a hedonism that would be based on fulfilling "truly human" needs, rather than merely animal needs (Maslow, 1954, p. 151). The only trouble is, as we saw, that it is difficult to be precise about basic, "truly human" needs because man is so plastic (cf. Lee, 1948). Man needs objects, self-esteem, answers to the four common human problems, rich experience—the whole thing bathed in a healthy aura of conviction and abiding meaning. But we must remember that the "scientific" problem is inescapably moral, because satisfaction of identical needs can find radically different cultural and individual expression. Oil tycoons, revolutionaries and atom-bomber pilots all seem to be operating at high levels of *Homo sapiens'* functioning.

There is no need for eternal discussion of hedonism; the matter is clear. Man is a rule-following animal. He comes to derive pleasure by getting back a satisfying self-image from actions he learns in society. He builds up a dependable cause-and-effect action pattern that becomes inseparable from his identity. This action map is his "mind" in a narrow sense. Anything that is consistent with this pattern is meaningful and potentially pleasureful. The pattern is followed out to its conclusion even if it means death. Once self-esteem becomes inseparable from a pattern of action-meaning, then even kamikaze is preferable to the pain of breaking the rules. Man is trapped by his own rule-schemes. When self-esteem and social motives become inseparable, individual destiny becomes a part of the social pleasure, the whims of the society at large.

This means that if we are going to talk about a new hedonism, about a social furthering of human pleasure, again we cannot talk about it in any "scientific" sense. The identity is comprised of social motives, and these motives become the limits of human pleasure. If we would maximize pleasure we must program for it. There are no sure guides to the specific forms of the pleasures which *Homo sapiens* craves as a species. However, we know several things that provide an excellent basis for a program of hedonism; the question remains whether, at this late date in human history, we value man enough to use them:

Man everywhere wants a feeling of value based on his acts.

Feeling of value and action are inseparable.

Man must construct a cause-and-effect, durational identity that draws its justification from a satisfying present. Firm identity and satisfying action are inseparable.

Man overcomes present problems by having conscious command over the widest possible gamut of choices.

Educating for choice, and making choices available, are a problem for broad, social policy.

Human pleasure, in sum, the warm feeling of self-value that derives from one's acts, is a total social problem. In the final analysis, of course, the individual will still decide his own pleasure. As Rousseau saw, society can make itself responsible only for promoting individual freedom: which means that our realistic attempts will have to be directed toward decreasing pain by increasing the range of man's command over action. And this can only be done by increasing the field of choices. Thus we can program for the *possibility* of greater pleasure, gained through the exercise of fuller human freedom. With these vistas, and with man's new explicitness about the reach of his problems, the twentieth century is witnessing a revolution in self-awareness that has not been seen since the Renaissance and the time of the Greeks. For the first time in history man has the opportunity to be truly authentic in the only sense in which this word can have meaning for him: fully aware of the basis for his acts.

Notes

1. V. J. McGill (1956-1957, p. 100) quoting Fr. Duyckaerts in a review of his *La notion de normal en psychologie clinique. Introduction à une critique des fondements théoriques de la psychothérapie.* (Paris: Librairie Philosophique, J. Vrin [1954]).

2. Besides, the idea that the homogeneous society is the happy society because everyone shares the same world-view is a facile fallacy. Every individual perceives the world differently from every other; constraint via custom and rules holds groups together. For a critique of the fallacy of the idea of cognitive-sharing as a basis for social harmony see J. M. Brewster (1936); Lewis A. Coser (1956).

3. This is what Bertrand Russell thinks Dewey would do (Russell, 1960, p. 826), and he feels that this is carrying things too far, that it would nullify completely historical reality. Of course Russell's protest is well taken—events *do* happen. But we must not lose sight of the force of Mead's and Dewey's argument, which was intended to underscore the massive dose of human purpose in any symbolic appraisal of experience. This "symbolic instrumentalism" is a proper antidote to positivist, mechanistic, reductionist science. Russell, finally, does not have Dewey's fully transactional view of reality. For Dewey, as for Kant, fact is "notoriously two-faced. It is cosmos as noted by a speck of cosmos" (Dewey and Bentley, 1949, p. 74).

VIII

Epilogue

POST-PSYCHIATRIC MAN

NATURE MYSTIFIES US. We don't know what she is up to in the conduct of life. But we do see that organisms have a better chance for satisfaction when they control a broad range of means for the attainment of goals. And we do know that organisms seek satisfaction, safety, control. Moments of satisfaction are fleeting, equilibrium quickly bypassed, unity always severed—the rhythm of organic life is a ceaseless interchange by a restless life process in a chaotic world. Little wonder that the organism strives for dependability, for a firmer grasp on the flux of experience. Dewey thought that amid such a troubled world, the organism longed for perfect being. And he added that it was a fallacious longing: if the world were perfect, and striving stilled, there would be no organic existence as we

230

know it. Disharmony and longing alone serve to make satisfaction possible (1958, pp. 62 ff.).

This is a simple way of saying what Sartre (after Hegel) elaborated into a needlessly complicated and verbose ontology: that "being-for-itself" (organic life) seeks to be "being-in-itself" (perfect, untroubled being); but at the same time, it does not wish to lose its quality as a "being-for-itself" (conscious experience). Since this is not possible, life, says Sartre, is a hopeless passion, a shuttling back and forth between a desire for boundness, and a desire for freedom, a desire to be stilled and a desire to remain in a state of striving. But Dewey's view does not have the hopelessness of Sartre's. The organism, as a residue of funded experience, is always bringing something new to bear in its strivings. It undergoes, accumulates, reorganizes experiences, and creates thereby a new quality of interchange with the world (1934, p. 103). When the organism achieves its fleeting union, that union itself is a growth in richness. In Dewey's words, "In the behavior of higher organisms, the close of the circuit is not identical with the state out of which disequilibration and tension emerged" (1938, p. 31). The organism, in other words, is continually moving into new states of integrated relationships. Momentary integrations are not mere passivity, not a return to former equilibriums, but the creation of something new, to which the organism brings its accumulated experience. In this kind of transaction the organism and the world are in continued states of transformation. The organism comes into contact with the world, loses it, then comes into contact with it again in a different way.

The Nature of the Esthetic

An amoeba has an easy time of it, in its temporary integrations. It extends a pseudopod, ingests a food particle, and the moment is complete. No simpler matching of means and ends is possible. We saw in Chapter I that the problem of integration depends on the equipment of the organism, that an animal with distance receptors like sight and memory has much greater spans to bridge in order to bring itself into satisfied contact with the world. On the human level the task of attaining satisfaction is prodigious. The ordinary separation of subject and object is pushed to a point of extreme complexity. Man is presented with a whole new range of integrative problems: time, space, identity, anticipation, hope, belief. Each human word is almost a problem in itself; taken together they make literally worlds and eons to span and circumscribe. For a symbolic animal, in brief, integration is immensely complicated. The use of symbols in coping with the world magnifies the problems of a straining organism. Dualisms are felt in several areas (Baldwin, 1915, p. 232):

—The symbolic self or ego. We saw in Chapter II that the early humanization process itself creates a split: The ego and the body tend to differentiate themselves; the symbolic self and the physical body often seem like two unrelated ways of being in the world. This problem is exacerbated in the individual we call schizophrenic—he may feel that his body is a strange object.

—The symbolic and the material tend to be different kinds of stuff—we sense a difference between a thought and a real, material thing. This extends to a felt difference between word-sound stimulus and total organic sense. A variation on this occurs in the problem of fashioning an identity. We saw that the purely symbolic constitution of the identity is a source of disquiet: at any moment a new life situation can cause it to be undermined or radically changed. A further variation on the same problem is the difference between "total identity" and "social identity." There may be a strain between an identity that one "really feels" and one that is earned through symbolic, social performance.

—We also know, as we use abstraction, that the singular real object and the universal class we put it in are not completely congruent. The abstraction treats only a fragment of it—the object is always greater than its class properties.

—When we meet a problem in action, we are aware that the

means to be used and the end in view may not be matched at all. —There is also a difference between the private motive and the social motive: the "inner pole" of the self and the "outer pole" are not congruent. We may feel either hopelessly separated from the social—as in loneliness; or, we may feel helplessly monopolized by it—as in shame.

—Finally, there is the often deep antagonism between old rules and new experience.

None of these are absolute dualisms. But they are felt dualisms. The self-conscious symbolic animal, furthermore, feels them very keenly. This complex of strains, tensions, drifts, antagonisms, plagues man like no other animal in nature is plagued. No integration is possible here with the extension of a pseudopod. Far from it. If one is going to pull things together out of this sort of confusion, a superb effort is necessary. And even then it is understandable that success will be rare.

When we realize the complexity of the problem of fusion, and the rarity of the possibility of success, then we can understand one thing further: The fundamental importance of the esthetic in the life of the symbolic animal. In recognition of this, many thinkers worthy of note made the esthetic an important part of their preoccupations—most recently James Mark Baldwin, Dewey, Sartre, to name the few that interest us here. For man, the esthetic object is the consummatory object; contemplation of the esthetic object draws the multiple fragmentations of felt experience into one fused whole. The symbolic animal attains thereby a coherence between his striving and the world. The esthetic object shows man the possibility of the unity and integrity of his peculiar experience.

What gives the esthetic object this quality, this unprecedented power? Dewey answered it very simply: The esthetic object shows that the perfect union of ends and means is possible, and it does this by containing within itself the perfect matching of ends and means. Thereby, it embodies, in one moment for all to see, the vision that fulfillment is possible. For the self-conscious animal, drawn in a dozen different directions, the esthetic object affirms this one thing above all: That human powers, properly rallied, are not brought to bear on the world in vain.

Let us look more closely at this affirmation. If the esthetic object mirrors integration on the human level, it is reasonable to think that it provides us with some idea of what man is up to.[1] How does man convince himself that his powers are not brought to bear in vain? How does he achieve fulfillment? In the preceding chapters we left two threads dangling on this question. In Chapter I we noted that human integration was difficult to the point of rarity—and this rarity we now define as the creation of the esthetic object. In Chapter VI we indicated that an animal who must predicate his world on mere word-symbols is bound to feel anxiety over its precariousness. Now we can explore the interesting question of just how a symbolic animal goes about securing his world by means of esthetic integrations. We will see how a symbolic fiction is infused with reality and, in a final section, some major reasons why love is a central human preoccupation.

The Embodiment of the Fiction

The problems of human integration are best summed up in the schizophrenic: Here we see at its sharpest the basic dualism of the physical and mental, the material object-world and the cultural symbol-world. The dualism, as we note above, extends through the self and the body, the word and the thing, the single object and the sum total of similar objects. The effect of this dualism is to make the world a kind of eerie place, never fully under human control. The schizophrenic experiences this eeriness at its fullest: the external world of objects is so free, so indeterminate, so obtrusive, that he gives up the human struggle altogether. Instead of attempting to come into possession of the external physical world, he takes refuge in the internal symbol-world. In the dualism of the material and the mental, the word and the thing, the schizophrenic relinquishes man's hoped-for hold on things, and withdraws into a substitute comfort with the word. The dualism, instead of being overcome, is accented to its fullest. This often results in losing the external world altogether. Thus, the stakes in the game are high. If nature has blessed one animal with the powers of unprecedented control, she has also provided the rub: failure to cope adequately with the tensions between the symbolic and the material can result in a total loss of the world.

At the other extreme from the schizophrenic is the well-enculturated actor. In his hands the symbol serves its function well. The external world is harnessed for use: objects are treated by their use-aspects, put in their place, subdued, subserved to the intentions of the human agent. Things are named and tagged, cultural man looks out upon a world that belongs to him, that answers to his names, his labels, his purposes. Everything is ordered, as tidy as symbols can make it. The once-chaotic world is seen through rose-colored cultural glasses. By means of sure answers to the four common human problems, behavior is decisive, objects are created and enslaved.

But it is not only objects that are enslaved. The fully performing cultural actor is enthralled by his own world view. His very fluid mastery becomes a rigidity—the rigidity of habit, of accustomed perceptions, of the smug, the not-to-be-questioned. As he wears his well-beaten cultural path through the world of things man keeps his nose to the ground and passes that world by, for the most part. Full possession of the external world is like full possession of a woman's virtue or a friend's loyalty,—one need no longer bother. Don't ask a Parisian what Notre Dame looks like from the rear, seen at twilight from the Ile St. Louis. Chances are he has been too busy making his way through the world to have noticed. No one has put it better than Bergson:

Between nature and ourselves, nay, between ourselves and our own consciousness a veil is interposed: a veil that is dense and opaque for the common herd,—thin, almost transparent, for the artist and the poet. What fairy wove that veil? Was it done in malice or in friendliness? We had to live, and life demands that we grasp things in their relations to our own needs. Life is action. Life implies the acceptance only of the *utilitarian* side of things in order to respond to them by appropriate reactions: all other impressions must be dimmed or else reach us vague and blurred. . . . The *individuality* of things or of beings escapes us, unless it is materially to our advantage to perceive it . . . (1910a, pp. 151-152).

The schizophrenic, in sum, never gains the world; fully cultural man gains it only to lose it—to lose its freshness, the uniqueness of its objects.

Why doesn't cultural man look up from his path? We saw the answer in Chapter VI. The familiar is safe and sure. We train our perceptions to see the expected, and if we see the unexpected we are at a loss to act, to know what to do: the analytic patient may want to see a frown on the therapist's face because he doesn't know how to cope with a smile. We cling to our abstractions because, even though they show us only a tiny facet of each object, to see more would be a threat (cf. Schachtel, 1959, p. 195).

The average person is only too happy to succeed where the schizophrenic fails. He wants to build himself into the world as solidly as possible. If this can be done, the problem of human action is solved. The average person, therefore, doesn't take to symbols for their own sake. They are meaningful only if they are intimately connected with things. Once we find that our symbols work, that they help us chart a dependable path through the threatening jungle, we tend not to consider them as mere symbols any more. We try to build them into our world as solidly as the objects, make them stand for the object, *be* the object, become inseparable from it. In other words, we want to see our cultural fiction incarnate—give it permanence by weaving it into a real world of things (Becker, 1962, pp. 184, 189, 190). This seems to bring about something very vital to man, namely, the conviction that his culturally constituted plan for action has a deeper than merely man-made significance.

Martin Buber has this in mind when he says that man needs to "imagine the real. . . . Applied to intercourse between men, 'imagining' the real means that I imagine to myself what another man is at this very moment wishing, feeling, perceiving, thinking, and not as a detached content but in his very reality, that is, as a living process in this man. . . . The human person needs confirmation, because man as man needs it . . ." (1957, pp. 103-104). For man to see that other organic existences are acting, living, breathing, throbbing—literally permeated—with the symbolic cultural design, seems a necessary support for his equanimity. This is the function of ritual, to interweave inextricably the symbolic and the organic, by gesture, sound, body balance, measured movement. Our voices resonate in our heads, our studied steps take command of space, our banners and flames fill the world with color. Thereby the world takes shape as a truly human world, a world in man's possession. Things without thoughts are meaningless, thoughts without things are hazardous. Sartre says this in another way (1956, pp. 386-392) by pointing out that we desire a (woman's) body only because it has consciousness in it. We like another human organism because thought processes are going on in it. We want things only because they engulf the symbolic in the world, and this engulfs us most convincingly. Sartre also gives an excellent example of the esthetics of skiing as the weaving in of personal intent, personal movement, into the concrete world. This becomes a kind of private ritual exercise of power. With the tracks of the skiier on the snow, he possesses the slope, claims it for man, makes a humanly meaningful unity out of it (1953, pp. 109 ff.).

Now a paradox emerges. For the sake of his equanimity and power man is trying to entwine cultural rules with objects. But by thus incarnating the fiction it becomes real and enslaves him. This is precisely the problem of the depressed patient, or the guilt-ridden child. The rules are so concretized in the objects that he has no symbolic command over them, no purchase by which to proceed to a critical appraisal. The paradox is that for conviction man needs to merge rules and objects; whereas for manipulatory control over the rules, for the power to change his designs, man needs to *disentangle* the rules from the objects. That which convinces, in sum, gives us power by rigidifying. At the same time, it removes our powers to back away from the object, to proceed to fabricate other designs, other rules, other life-schemes. For equanimity's sake we become slaves to the objects. We no longer see the rules critically, nor do we see any more of the object than the limited facet that the rules reveal to us, for our behavior. Little wonder that guilt is rampant in human life. Man is hoist with his own petard, with his need for conviction. The child or the adult who concretizes the rules does so under the impetus of a primary esthetic desire to merge the mental and the material. He is hardly to be blamed when, for the sake of certainty, he finds the concrete hardened around his own feet.

For the most part, these esthetic mergers are too convincing. They serve only too well the purpose of blending material and mental: Mother and her rules become inseparable; the boss and his, likewise; the simple greetings and niceties of everyday social ceremonial are given their dose of conviction; man "imagines the real." The plodding everyday drama that we act out for each other's conviction seems right for all time. We can think of no other word for "tomato"—and when we hear a foreign one we snicker. A glimpse of other possibilities, of other life designs, of other words for the same objects, threatens us, and we giggle off the tension. The fact is that most people are poor artists. Their works have conviction, but conviction alone is esthetics at a low grade. Conviction integrates our world by sealing us in the mold of the familiar. At best, the everyday citizen who "imagines his real" is a fabricator of girlie calendars, of portraits of presidents, of "Home Sweet Home" or "In God We Trust" signs.

That is why the true artist is so rare. He creates an esthetic product that fuses the private and the public, the subject and the object, the symbolic and the material—but it does not imprison. On the contrary, it liberates us somewhat. It makes us secure in our present meanings, and also reveals a sliver of new meanings, of new possibilities. It shows the object all wrapped up in its appropriate rules, but it shows an object that is a little different than we expected to see. It defeats the usual routine of abstractions, and shows us more of the world. The artist breaks through the cultural mold at the same time that he reenforces us in our strivings.[2] Here is his gift. He gives us conviction without blindness or without sameness, which is why it is often said that the true artist holds up a picture of the ideal that for us should be the real. The truly esthetic object affirms human victory over the chaotic, and with it affirms human possibility. It fuses man with the world,[3] and at the same time opens that world out somewhat.

There is a total unity in the esthetic object. The unity is so perfect, the parts so harmonious, so appropriate to each other, that we cannot doubt that the symbolic is the real. We feel that man transcends nature with the means that he has, and that these means are proper. Any doubts we may have about the adequacy of our symbol-systems is momentarily stilled. The esthetic object, as Dewey saw, is the consummatory object par excellence. With it, man transcends the arbitrariness of his symbolic fiction by blending it in perfect proportions into the hard world of things. The esthetic object demonstrates that life is not in vain, by holding up tangible proof of human creativity. Thus we see the difference between the true artist and the everyday esthetician: The everyday esthetician secures conviction by nestling the human spirit in its familiar cultural bounds. The true artist, on the other hand, overcomes the arbitrary cultural fiction *by allowing man to believe in his basic creativity.*[4]

If the esthetic solidifies human meaning and carries man forward we can understand that Baldwin and Dewey did not want to define it too narrowly. It could be a part of any human activity as long as that activity was characterized by a perfect matching of means and ends, by a full and free exercise of human powers. Science could be esthetically consummatory as well as art. The scientist, by a free exercise of means, builds man into the world and opens new vistas at the same time—as surely as does the artist. It is not for nothing that both Baldwin and Dewey made esthetics the keystone of their mature thought; that Dewey culminated his philosophy with a work on art; and that Baldwin was led to affirm, over a century after Schiller: "The time may come, and the stage of human culture, when the realization of aesthetic values will supply the last and final ground of judgment, both individual and social, if not of the truth and utility of this or that objective product of thought, still of its comprehensiveness for the insight and enjoyment of mankind" (1915, p. 241). The esthetic object, in other words, is the human hedonic object par excellence. It represents the triumph of the forward-moving organism over the conventional systems which hold it in bondage. It extends man's self-feeling to a new range. It signals the triumph of the organic life process over the stilted symbolisms of a particular culture.

Thus, an esthetic view of human strivings has implications as broad as a critique of a medical approach to mental illness. Further, this view is a part of this critique. If human malfunction cannot be discussed without talking about the constraints of culture, then similarly we cannot ponder the problem of human action without considering how man goes beyond culture. With esthetics he does this intrinsically, with his own creative energy. Baldwin and Dewey, with their championing of an esthetic approach to life, meant to insist on the importance of a continuing critique of culture. Furthermore, by focusing on the esthetic, Baldwin and Dewey meant to hold one thing uppermost in mind—the one thing perhaps that we have most miserably failed to see: *that man is the measure of all value.* Consequently, a science of man must subserve human values. Nothing could be plainer. Nor could anything be further from this than the mechanistic, reductionist approach to human striving with which we have for so long been saddled. Not only have we failed to make man the measure, but under the influence of Freudian theory we have largely reduced Leonardo and Michelangelo to studies affirming the correctness of a psychosexual theory of infant maturation.

Love and Esthetics

Love is closely related to esthetics, in fact, it is a kind of esthetics. Love pulls man's straining world together; love carries man beyond the constrictions of culture. The love-object can be as consummatory as the esthetic object, and in much the same ways.[5]

In the first place, love attacks a major dualism—the strain of self and body. Sartre has understood this with extreme clarity (1956, pp. 368 ff.; cf. also van den Berg, 1955, pp. 54 ff.). I look at the veins on the back of my hand, says Sartre. Why do they run just this certain way, why are they different from other hands, why is this one fat, this one thin, and so on. I am annoyed by this fortuitousness. There is no reason for my hand being any special way, it is an accident, an unlikely thing. But let the woman who loves me and whom I love caress my hand. Instantly the situation changes. The caress banishes everything that was accidental about my hand. It turns it into exactly the hand that I should have. I am reseated in my body. This is *my* hand.

The self, in other words, is always somewhat of a stranger to its body. The symbolic amalgam of social motives that we call the self sees nothing necessary about the body it is lodged in. The self is fictional but free. The body is existential, determined. Love fuses the self with its body. It does not create a mere *modus vivendi*, but goes further: it converts the accidental into the necessary. We *want* this body that the other affirms. If we appear to the loved-one as *this* body, then the self has no reason to shy away from it. Our timidity is banished. Thus love banishes shame, transcends the fictitious learning, the sham morality (cf. Lynd, 1958). The loved-one by her affirmation breaks down convention. Areas of the body that may be charged with anxiety, taboo areas established by early learning—from which one's own attention and thoughts shrink—are now opened for mutual exploration and acknowledgment. The self discovers its earthly situation and finds it good. To be loved is to be placed beyond all established values; one becomes a measure in oneself. Sartre explains the frequent requests for proofs of love in this way, as a desired confirmation of one's primary value (1956, pp. 369 ff.). "Do you love me enough to kill for me? Steal for me? Leave your whole family for me?" The insistent entreaty is: "Am I [as a unique object] the ground of *all* value?"

We can see how miserable the schizophrenic is. He is never established as the ground of all value—neither by his mother, nor, usually, by a real love relationship in later life. He must always be an accident to himself, a misfit in his own body; he must always be measured against all things, and have nothing measured against him. When one comes to be cherished in and for himself an important transformation occurs in one's world. *It* becomes necessary and *one* becomes necessary, no matter what has occurred in the past. If one is loved for what he is, as a unique, existential object, *then the crucial awareness dawns:* He would *not* be loved if he were anything else. Everything that happened in one's past comes to be regarded as necessary to what one is in the present. One is unique only because his past is unique, if it had been different, then *one* would have been different— and would *not* be loved for what he *is now.* The individual accepts his whole past, his accidental parents, accidental neighborhood, accidental peer tormentors—everything. A primary endeavor of psychotherapy is thus accomplished by love: the individual accepts his past and his uniqueness as irrevocable, as necessarily and desirably so. A major identity task is fulfilled.

In all this, love is addressing itself to overcoming another primary split in human conduct: the strain between old rules and the lure of new experiences. The lover and the loved-one build a world where the old rules are never perfectly applicable. The world of the "We" creates new obligations, provokes new challenges, permits one to be different (cf. Riezler, 1942-1943, p. 461). The loved object spurs one on. If one is to act in relation to this object, some modification of the old rules is in order. The major problem in modifying the old rules is overcome with the aid of the loved object. That is, the problem of the self-esteem which is committed to the old rules. If one is loved thoroughly for what one is, this is no problem at all. *The loved object functions as the psychotherapist. It is permissive of one's individuality.* The self-esteem is given a new freedom, a liberation that it could not otherwise enjoy, as soon as one is constituted by love as the primary ground of all value. As the self-esteem is thus unconditionally reenforced, the commitment to the old rules becomes more mobile. Ideally, love is a process of self-education in new action possibilities. Sustained by the love object, living with full self-esteem in the new world of the "We," one finds the liberation from old rules greatly facilitated.

We can see why love is so central to human conduct. It is potentially and naturally therapeutic. But it is a frightfully inadequate word. It can refer to two totally different kinds of self-affirming action. The potential for changing the old rules is only a potential, and the fulfilling of this potential depends on the love object chosen and one's own preparedness to change. Otherwise a love object can be extremely threatening. One can go two ways. Either one can be led out of the old rules by seeking to conform to behavior demanded by the new relationship, or, one can continue within the old rules, if one chooses a loved object who affirms and soldifies them. In this sense, kinds of love are like kinds of esthetics. Everyday love, like everyday esthetics, builds the individual firmly into the world, gives him conviction by settling him more solidly into his accustomed habit. Liberating love, like true esthetics, gives conviction while it leads one on to a newer range of experiences, to new rule performance.

Erich Fromm had this distinction in view when he talked about "neurotic love"—the love in which one or both of the lovers have remained attached to the figure of a parent (1956, pp. 28, 94). The result is that they transfer the feelings, hopes, and fears learned in the past to the new love object. The wife is seen as the mother was. The husband continues to see his world in terms of the old rules, in other words. Again, he is like the analytic patient who sees the world as he expects to see it, but cannot and dare not look at it afresh. Thereby, a major function of the love object is defeated, namely, to carry one, by means of new perceptions, somewhat beyond himself, his old rules, his old world. Fromm observes very aptly that respect comes from the root *respicere*, to look at (p. 28). In order to be carried beyond one's accustomed perceptions one has to *look at* the uniqueness of the loved object. But this requires some flexibility because fuller vision of the object is possible only when the old rules do not monopolize perception.

Perception is fundamental to love, which is the reason why the notion of beauty is inseparable from it. The old rules, after all, stamp the world with sameness; they outline the expected perception. In this sense, the objects they refer to are akin to fantasy objects. As we saw in Chapter II the fantasy object is always shallow, always poor, always a mere shadow of what is given in reality. The full force of the existential object is a shock that at least partly uproots us from the accustomed, the usual, the expected. "Lo-o-o-k at th-a-a-t!" The awe-filled and hushed tones of this drawn-out enjoinder, the whistles of admiration, are not an aberration of modern street-corner society. Neither is the youth's appreciation of the striking face and figure a throw back to lower-primate hypersexuality. It is much more than that, much closer to the core of a central problem of life: namely, the problem of overcoming the split between self and world, between subject and object. Perception of the existentially unique draws us directly into the world. The object is a bridge. We don't desire the unique object in itself, so much as we aim to use it to take hold of the world, to draw ourselves into it. Sartre notes that for this reason Stendhal describes love as a mode of being in the world (1953, p. 56). That is why we make such a vocal fuss about the unique object. In endless popular songs we record the striking details: dark eyes, red hair—"love," "love," "love," "love," "love"—the higher primates monotonously scream out their problem. With man, possession of the world, integration with it, has become conscious. The perception is the point of contact, the locus of momentary unity. We acclaim it vocally, consciously. The lower animals, on the other hand, lay hold of the world constantly through their perceptions. But this laying-hold has not become conscious with them—and neither has the separation risen to awareness. The lower animals are not self-conscious, are not cut off from the world by their self-absorbed thoughts. The cat makes a thousand striking visual contacts daily—the same quickening, alert, pulsating fusion that we make only rarely. In this real sense *it is always in love*, as much in love as it need be. Human love is a sentiment for life of a peculiarly alienated animal, an animal who has to urge himself into the world.

My discussion, of course, omits mention of the purely hormonal, physiological urges to sexual union with objects, which, in the higher primates, are continual and not seasonal. But this is intentional. Beauty and sexual desire are separable; the sexual is bound to the flesh; the beautiful is supreme because it can seal the contract with life even beyond the span of one's own. Which is what the poet of the *Flûte de Jade* conveyed so well: "*Vous me demandez quel est le suprême bonheur, ici-bas? C'est d'écouter la chanson d'une petite fille qui s'éloigne après vous avoir demandé son chemin.*" (You ask me what is the greatest joy here on earth? It is to listen to a little girl's song as she goes off after having asked you the way.) Harkening back to our earlier discussion we can see that this example contains the basic prescription for the esthetic. Here, culture takes the form of the song, and the directions for the way, which are interwoven with organism—the little girl; the organism is the new generation, the directions it seeks are the same as those of the dying generation (of the poet). The whole, then, seems beautiful in the timelessness with which man's symbols are interwoven, across generations, in the real world of organisms and geography.

Perception of the unique, existential object, then, brings our world to life because it brings us into it. Every theorist on love has understood this. It led Scheler to remark that the lover is not blind—the rest of the world is (McGill, 1941-1942, p. 282). The lover thrives on the unique qualities of his object, particularities found nowhere else in the world (cf. van den Berg, 1955, p. 56). This is the *individuum ineffabile*, the unspeakably unique, that cannot be described or expressed in conceptual terms. It can only be revealed in nature (cf. Heider, 1958, p. 160). Schachtel sees the uniqueness of the concrete object as containing the *mysterium tremendum* of life (1959, p. 182). It is full, boundless, overpowering. For this reason we do not tire of contemplating the love object; the contemplation itself is a source of joy. Here is a constant quickening of perception that is truly life-enhancing. This is probably what led La Rochefoucauld to his reflection that constancy in love is a kind of inconstancy, since our thoughts never remain fixed on any one particular charm of the loved object, but roam from one charm to another (Shand, 1920, p. 549).

Perception and contemplation of the unique, existential, loved object, in sum, helps us overcome another primary strain: it commits us to the organic life process. At the same time, it substantiates our being in the world. Like the true esthetic work, it affirms that the symbolic is the real, that the fictional is an irrevocable part of nature. Human design and life process are felt to be inseparably one. If the splendid existential object is so real, and so much a part of the world that includes me, then I too am an irrevocable part of a meaningful world. The possibly fictive nature of symbolic meaning is overcome, as the perceiving organism is quickened and committed. The ultimate message is direct and clear: If the world can be so rich in existential objects, and if each beautiful thing is just as it should be, *then life itself must be of value.*

I suppose the reason that love is one of the principal sources of anguish in the higher primates is because it stands at the threshold of a this-worldly liberation. It pinpoints the great contradiction we noted above: The new perceptions lead one beyond the old rules, to a broader life, a different object, a new commitment. But in order to perceive the uniqueness of the loved object, in order to see it and accept it more in terms of what it is, one must already possess some flexibility, some disposition to be weaned away from the stale old rules and perceptions. Otherwise the object is painted in the pale grey of one's own familiar world. Anguish at the threshold of new experience is heightened by the grip of the past, as well as by the lure of the new. Just listen to the endless conversations at every corner and in every coffee shop: "And then he said, and then I said . . ." "Don't you think I'm right—wasn't that a nasty thing for her to do?" And so on. There is a bundle of rules for each actor, and no final arbiter but one's best friend. With very few knowing what they really want, or how to go about getting it, it is understandable that most of life should be a saga of man's incomprehensibility to man. Man needs objects as much as life—objects *are* life, they permit action. But every object dangles its own rules, and we get caught up with each other as innocently and as pathetically as a kitten in a ball of yarn.

Every single object we meet is a potential wedge into a new world, or a potential link into the old chain. The love object, especially, promises much, but depending on it and on ourselves it may give little or nothing. The "great loves" in history are exemplary precisely because of their rarity. And even in many of them we see people who know how to compromise, who are somewhat suited to each other's weaknesses as well as strengths and hopes. John Stuart Mill, for example, seems to have found in Harriet Taylor (Hayek, 1951) the perfect affirmation of his identity strivings. Here was a woman who accepted him for all he was trained to be—a thorough intellectual. Here was a woman who gave him a worldly identity at the very time when he felt most the need to break away from his father, from the object that had monopolized him since childhood. But here also was an unusual woman: she was comfortably married, and reputedly frigid. Harriet Taylor seems to have been perfect for Mill because she offered him fulfillment and threatened him at no major personality point. She seems to have given him a masculine identity on his own terms. Not all objects lend themselves so readily to idealization. They make us go beyond the old, comfortable rules into new performances that are threatening. Many a young schizophrenic enters a psychiatric hospital on the eve of marriage.

Sadism and Private Motives

It requires strength to people the world with objects that possess uniqueness and their own rules. In order to accept the object more for what it is than for what we want it to be, we require a sureness about our own identity. This is why it is often said that self-love is essential to mature object-love. One needs to be sure of himself in order not to feel threatened by uniqueness and a multiplicity of rules. The unique object gives our world richness, but it also does something else at the same time: The more there is for us to perceive, and the more things that are not reducible to the expected, the greater the element of purely "private" that enters the world. The more the object reveals to us facets that we cannot cope with behaviorally, the more threatening it becomes. The difference between love and hate resides specifically here. If we are strong enough to love, sure enough of ourselves, and able to trust ourselves to see the object, then we relish its difference. The very fact that it is not like any other, and does not fit neatly into any category, leads it to possess a certain privacy (cf. Scheler, 1954, pp. 71, 154 ff.). It is this very privacy that makes our world convincing. We saw in Chapter VI that we like the self to be thoroughly social, but at the same time it lacks conviction if it is. We want our social reality to be social *and* individual. And it can only be individual if people give the semblance of having private facets or private motives (Becker, 1962, pp. 184, 189, 190). If we think they have a uniqueness, a secret inner person separate from society, then our social drama is enriched; it includes social motives as well as private motives. The loved object strengthens us in two ways, then: It makes the social motives seem more real by willingly joining in the social drama with its own private motives. Thereby it consecrates the social drama: when we accept the private motives of the loved object it adds to our store of what is valid and sacred in the world. This is the great harvest of love–an abundance of meaning. Love is superbly counter-fictional.

Fromm calls love the "other path to knowing 'the secret.' . . . Love is the active penetration of the other person, in which my desire to know is stilled by union" (1956, p. 30). I should say, rather, that the desire to know the secret of the unique loved object is willingly deferred. We accept the unknowable and the integral. That is why the primary condition of love is self-love or self-acceptance. In self-love we affirm the sanctity of our own private motive, and believe in it. If we cannot do this, if the social motives constitute our whole self, then we cannot accept another's private motive (unless we efface ourselves). Further-more, we have to acknowledge the private motive in order not to be undermined by shame; we cannot love another shamelessly unless we grant their private motive.

The secret not only fascinates, then, it also offends and taunts. To those who are not strong it represents the threatening private motive in a social world. Fromm understands the sadist in these terms. The sadist roots out the secret by destroying the person.[6] Isaac Babel relates a story which conveys this directly: An officer in the Russian civil war has just finished stomping his former master to death, and explains: "With shooting—I'll put it this way—with shooting you only get rid of a chap. . . . With shooting you'll never get at the soul, to where it is in a fellow and how it shows itself. But I don't spare myself, and I've more than once trampled an enemy for over an hour. You see, I want to get to know what life really is . . ." (quoted in Fromm, 1956, p. 30). The sadist, literally, squeezes the private motive out of the other's hide and makes it public domain. The sadist seems to exaggerate the tendency we all have, to find out what others have inside. While we guard our own intimacy we seek to penetrate theirs (Nuttin, 1950). Some of us want our social world to have conviction, but cannot stand the private motives which impart this very conviction. For them the social must have primacy over the individual. In Tokugawa Japan a couple who committed adultery were hacked into pieces so small by an outraged community that they could no longer be easily cut. Thus, a communal sadism completely effaces the purely personal motive. The sanctity of the social is affirmed.[7] The sadist cannot tolerate the private motive, the existence of a world apart. Sartre thinks that it is the very impossibility of possession which leads to sadistic destruction (1953, pp. 137 ff.). But we could just as well say that it is the intolerance of the private. Hannah Arendt, for example, says that love "by its very nature, is unworldly," and that for this reason it is antipolitical (1958, p. 242). I think our discussion also shows something else: that love is indeed antipolitical because it grants the validity of the purely private truth. It transgresses the realm of shared meanings, and in this sense is counterfictional. For this reason sadism is so purely political: it denies the private truth, asserts the priority of the public, the communally verifiable and the socially tangible; it deals with the public body and not the private spirit.

Thus, we can see more fully why it is that only mature love has the power to forgive. When we respect the object, we lose, in a sense, our power over it. But we gain something in the loss: respect of the object relinquishes power over it only to gain the harvest of the object's privacy; that is, as we saw above, our world is enriched by the very uniqueness of the loved object. But the object gives us even more when we have the strength to forgive it and accept it on its terms. Forgiveness absolves the object from *any connection* from its own *past action*. This means that with forgiveness we harvest a potentially new object, in the form of a new spontaneity. It is just this spontaneity that the sadist fears and cannot stand. Hence the need for strength to love and forgive, because with them we liberate the object to a realm of indeterminacy which may be a threat to us.

Finally, then, we can see that the need to people the world with objects which carry with them their own indomitable conviction is a typical, creative human need. With all of our speculations on the incest taboo we have not to my knowledge considered this: that there is a positive accretion of meaning in peopling the immediate environment with free, unpossessable consciousnesses—and an offspring with whom one can mate is largely negated as a free self.

As for the sadist, it almost seems as though he is trying, in his torture of another's body, to ground the other's symbolic self in tangible flesh—to bring it into the world where it can be controlled and subdued (Sartre, 1956, p. 404). This is the nadir of human esthetics, to control the world and demonstrate power by reducing man's spirit to the corporeal. True esthetics, like true love, is something far removed from this moronic artistry. With them we enhance our powers by liberating the human spirit from the expected and approved. We educate ourselves to new harmonies and to new pluralities, to new tensions and to new experiences. For this man needs maturity, flexibility, self-confidence. Above all, he needs knowledge and continuing criticism of the old rules, of the stale designs that make people fearful and small. The post-psychiatric world, then, would be a world in which the fullest possible critical education is a dominant value —for only by this liberation can man truly create and truly love.

Notes

1. Thus there is nothing vitalistic or spiritually emergent about man's yearning for the esthetic. Rather, each animal strives for momentary integrations in virtue of the coping mechanisms placed at its disposal, that is, according to the particular types of adaptational problems presented to it.

2. The artist, therefore, has to be somewhat of a misfit in the culture. He must be alive to aspects of the existential object that others are blind to. He must, at the same time, be somewhat dis-

satisfied with traditional meanings, and be prepared to offer up versions of his own. He makes a private resolution of tensions to aspects of the world that others take for granted. For these reasons the artist—the original systematizer noted in Chapter VI—is usually recruited on the schizophrenic continuum, and may terminate his life at its extreme end—like Van Gogh, Nijinsky, Strindberg, and others.

3. Writers on esthetics have long stressed the fact that integration is a quickening of experience and yet a resolution of tensions; the esthetic object is possessed, yet a psychic distance is maintained—man holds himself off, freer, in a world that is richer. See especially Baldwin (1915) and Dewey (1934) for the elaboration of theoretical details on esthetic contemplation that I am forced here to treat casually and summarily. Cf. also Pepper (1955), and Mehlis (1961).

4. This may be one reason why some phallic-narcissists find the fiction so striking and so transparent. Deep down they cannot believe in their own creativity. The only way to overcome the fiction is by engagement in experience as creative matching of means and ends, which is why it has been observed that man "is forced to become dedicated."

5. I am not proposing a comprehensive theory of love here, but only delineating the similarity of its workings to esthetics; however, this does cover a considerable area.

6. The sadist finds a ready partner in the masochist who couldn't imagine having private motives, and who often may allow people to enter his life forcibly so he need not feel guilty about initiating action. Masochism is almost synonymous with "I have no private motive— nothing to oppose or to offer; but I recognize the validity of your private motive, and so submit to it." Compare a young female patient: "It is wonderful to be beaten up or killed because no one ever does that to you unless they really care and can be made very upset" (Hayward and Taylor, 1956, p. 218).

7. The same thread runs through mimicry and caricature. The purely individual is reduced to socially manageable proportions, or to no proportions at all: ". . . by singling out and reproducing an outstanding part of a personality, we destroy its unity, its individuality" (Kris and Gombrich, 1938, p. 321, note). For a further elaboration on masochism and sadism, see E. Becker, "Fetishism, Masochism, and Sadism: Dimensions of Human Experience," in *Essays Toward a Humanistic Psychology*, Henry Winthrop, Editor (forthcoming).

Bibliography

Adams, Donald K. (1953), "The Organs of Perception: Sentiments," *Journal of Personality*, Vol. 22, no. 1 (September), pp. 52-59.

Adler, Kurt A. (1961), "Depression in the Light of Individual Psychology," *Journal of Individual Psychology*, Vol. 17, pp. 57-67.

Alexander, Franz (1953), "Remarks About the Relation of Inferiority Feelings to Guilt Feelings," *International Journal of Psychoanalysis*, Vol. 34, pp. 41-49.

———— and French, Thomas M. (1946), *Psychoanalytic Therapy, Principles and Application* (New York: Ronald Press).

Allers, Rudolph (1961), *Existentialism and Psychiatry* (Springfield, Illinois: C. C Thomas).

Allport, Floyd H. (1955), *Theories of Perception and the Concept of Structure* (New York: Wiley).

254 BIBLIOGRAPHY

254 BIBLIOGRAPHY

254 BIBLIOGRAPHY

254 BIBLIOGRAPHY

Allport, Gordon W. (1935), "Attitudes," in A *Handbook of Social Psychology*, Carl Murchison (ed.) (Worcester, Massachusetts: Clark University Press), pp. 798-844.

—— (1937), *Personality: A Psychological Interpretation* (New York: Holt).

—— (1950), "A Psychological Approach to the Study of Love and Hate," in *Explorations in Altruistic Love and Behavior*, P. A. Sorokin (ed.) (Boston: Beacon Press), pp. 145-164.

—— (1952), "Prejudice: A Problem in Psychological and Social Causation," in *Toward a General Theory of Action*, Talcott Parsons and Edward A. Shils (eds.) (Cambridge: Harvard University Press), pp. 365-387.

—— (1954), "The Historical Background of Modern Psychology," in *Handbook of Social Psychology*, G. Lindzey (ed.), Vol. 1 (of 2 vols.) (Reading, Massachusetts: Addison Wesley).

—— (1955), *Becoming: Basic Considerations for a Psychology of Personality* (New Haven: Yale University Press).

—— (1961), *Pattern and Growth in Personality* (New York: Holt, Rinehart and Winston).

Angyal, Andras (1941), *Foundations for a Science of Personality* (New York: Commonwealth Fund).

Anonymous (1958), "A New Theory of Schizophrenia," *Journal of Abnormal and Social Psychology*, Vol. 57, pp. 226-236.

Arendt, Hannah (1958), *The Human Condition* (Chicago, Illinois: University of Chicago Press).

Arieti, Silvano (1961), "Volition and Value: A Study Based on Catatonic Schizophrenia," *Comprehensive Psychiatry*, Vol. 2, no. 2 (April), pp. 74-82.

—— (1962), "The Psychotherapy of Schizophrenia in Theory and Practice," paper delivered at Montreal (April).

Arnheim, Rudolf (1949), "The Gestalt Theory of Expression," *Psychological Review*, Vol. 56, no. 1 (January), pp. 156-171.

Arnold, Magda B. (1960), *Emotion and Personality*, Vol. 1 (of 2 vols.) (New York: Columbia University Press).

Asch, Solomon E. (1952), *Social Psychology* (Englewood Cliffs, New Jersey: Prentice-Hall).

Ausubel, David P. (1955), "Relationships Between Shame and Guilt in the Socializing Process," *Psychological Review*, Vol. 62, no. 5 (January), pp. 378-390.

Baldwin, James Mark (1895), *Mental Development in the Child and the Race* (New York: Macmillan).

—— (1899), *Social and Ethical Interpretations in Mental Development* (New York: Macmillan).

—— (1906), *Thought and Things*, Vol. 1, *Functional Logic, or Genetic Theory of Knowledge* (London: Swan Sonnenschein).

—— (1915), *Genetic Theory of Reality* (New York: Putnam's).

Barnes, Hazel E. (1959), *The Literature of Possibility: A Study in Humanistic Existentialism* (Lincoln: Nebraska University Press).

Barta, Frank R. (1952), *The Moral Theory of Behavior: A New Answer to the Enigma of Mental Illness* (Springfield, Illinois: C. C Thomas).

Bartlett, Frederic C. (1954), *Remembering: A Study in Experimental and Social Psychology* (London: Cambridge University Press).

Bateson, Gregory, *et al.* (1956), "Toward a Theory of Schizophrenia," *Behavioral Science*, Vol. 1, pp. 251-264.

Becker, E. (1961), *Zen: A Rational Critique* (New York: Norton).

———— (1962), *The Birth and Death of Meaning: A Perspective in Psychiatry and Anthropology* (New York: The Free Press of Glencoe).

Beers, Clifford W. (1960), *A Mind that Found Itself* (New York: Doubleday).

Benda, Clemens E. (1961), *The Image of Love: Modern Trends in Psychiatric Thinking* (New York: The Free Press of Glencoe).

Bentley, Arthur F. (1941), "The Behavioral Superfice," *Psychological Review*, Vol. 48, pp. 39-59.

———— (1954), *Inquiry into Inquiries: Essays in Social Theory*, Sidney Ratner (ed.) (Boston: Beacon Press).

Bergson, Henri (1910a), *Laughter: An Essay on the Meaning of the Comic* (London: Macmillan).

———— (1910b), *Time and Free Will* (New York: Macmillan).

———— (1959), *Matter and Memory* (first published 1896) (Garden City, New York: Doubleday Anchor Books).

Berne, Eric (1961), *Transactional Analysis in Psychotherapy: A Systematic Individual and Social Psychiatry* (New York: Grove Press).

Bexton, W. H., Heron, W., and Scott, T. H. (1954), "Effects of Decreased Variation in the Sensory Environment," *Canadian Journal of Psychology*, Vol. 8, pp. 70-76.

Bibring, Edward (1953), "The Mechanism of Depression," in *Affective Disorders*, Phyllis Greenacre (ed.) (New York: International Universities Press).

Binswanger, Ludwig (1958a), "The Existential Analysis School of Thought,"

———— (1958b), "The Case of Ellen West: An Anthropological-Clinical Study" (both) in *Existence: A New Dimension in Psychiatry and Psychology*, Rollo May, Ernest Angel, and Henri F. Ellenberger (eds.) (New York: Basic Books), pp. 191-213, 237-364.

Bliss, E. L., *et al.* (1959), "Studies in Sleep Deprivation—Relationship to Schizophrenia," *Archives of Neurology and Psychiatry*, Vol. 81, pp. 348-359.

Boisen, Anton T. (1960), *Out of the Depths* (New York: Harper).

Boring, E. G. (1950), *A History of Experimental Psychology* (New York: Appleton-Century-Crofts), 2nd edition.

Boverman, Maxwell (1953), "Some Notes on the Psychotherapy of Delusional Patients," *Psychiatry*, Vol. 16 (May), pp. 139-151.

Bowlby, John (1961), "Separation Anxiety: A Critical Review of the Literature," *Journal of Child Psychology and Psychiatry*, Vol. 1 (February), pp. 251-269.

Brewster, John M. (1936), "A Behavioristic Account of the Logical Function of Universals," *Journal of Philosophy*, Vol. 33: part 1, no. 19, pp. 505-514; part 2, no. 20, pp. 533-547.

Bridgman, Percy (1959), *The Way Things Are* (New York: Viking Books).

Bruch, Hilde (1962), "Falsification of Bodily Needs and Body Concept in Schizophrenia," *Archives of General Psychiatry*, Vol. 1, No. 6, pp. 18-24.

Bruner, J. S., *et al.* (1957), *Contemporary Approaches to Cognition* (Cambridge: Harvard University Press).

Buber, Martin (1957), "Distance and Relations," The William Alanson White Memorial Lectures, Fourth Series, *Psychiatry*, Vol. 20, pp. 97-104.

Buchler, Justus (1955), *Nature and Judgment* (New York: Columbia University Press).

Bull, Nina (1951), *The Attitude Theory of Emotion* (New York: Nervous and Mental Disease Monographs).

—— (1955), "The Mechanism of Goal Orientation and the Manner of its Disruption," *Journal of Nervous and Mental Disease*, Vol. 122, pp. 42-46.

—— (1957), "Emotion as Frustrational Behavior," *Journal of Nervous and Mental Disease*, Vol. 125, pp. 622-626.

Burke, Kenneth (1954), *Permanence and Change* (Los Altos, California: Hermes).

Burks, H. L. and Harrison, S. I. (1962), "Aggressive Behavior as a Means of Avoiding Depression," *American Journal of Orthopsychiatry*, Vol. 32, no. 3 (April), pp. 416-422.

Burnham, Donald L. (1956), "Misperception of Other Persons in Schizophrenia," *Psychiatry*, Vol. 19, pp. 283-303.

Burns, Tom (1958), "The Forms of Conduct," *American Journal of Sociology*, Vol. 64, pp. 137-151.

Burrow, Trigant (1949), *The Biology of Human Conflict* (New York: Harcourt-Brace).

Burtt, E. A. (1962), "The Value Presuppositions of Science," in *The New Scientist: Essays on the Methods and Values of Modern Science*, P. C. Obler and H. A. Estrin (eds.) (Garden City, New York: Doubleday Anchor).

Buytendijk, F. J. J. (1959), "The Function of the Parts within the Structure of the Whole: The Excitability of the Nerves as a Phenomenon of Life," *Journal of Individual Psychology*, Vol. 15, pp. 73-78.

Cantril, H., Ames, A. Jr., Hastorf, A. H., and Ittelson, W. H. (1949), "Psychology and Scientific Research," *Science*, Vol. 110: part 1, pp. 461-464; part 2, pp. 491-497; part 3, pp. 517-522.

Cassirer, Ernst (1953), *An Essay on Man* (Garden City, New York: Doubleday Anchor Books).

Chisholm, G. B. (1946), "The Reestablishment of Peace-time Society," *Psychiatry*, Vol. 9, pp. 3-20.

Cleveland, E. J. and Longaker, W. D. (1957), "Neurotic Patterns in the Family," in *Explorations in Social Psychiatry*, A. H. Leighton, J. Clausen, and R. N. Wilson (eds.) (New York: Basic Books).

Collingwood, R. G. (1960), *The Idea of Nature* (New York: Galaxy Books).

Cooley, Charles Horton (1909), *Human Nature and the Social Order* (New York: The Free Press of Glencoe), 1956 edition.

Coser, Lewis A. (1956), *The Functions of Social Conflict* (New York: The Free Press of Glencoe).

Coutu, Walter (1949), *Emergent Human Nature* (New York: Knopf).

Custance, John (1951), *Wisdom, Madness and Folly* (London: Gollancz).

David, H. P. and Brengelmann, J. C. (eds.) (1960), *Perspectives in Personality Research* (New York: Springer).

Davis, Kingsley (1948), *Human Society* (New York: Macmillan).

de Beauvoir, Simone (1953), *The Second Sex* (trans. and ed., H. M. Parshley (New York: Knopf).

Dewey, John (1896), "The Reflex Arc Concept in Psychology," *Psychological Review*, Vol. 3, pp. 357-370.

——— (1916), *Democracy and Education* (New York: Macmillan).

——— (1922), *Human Nature and Conduct* (New York: Holt).

——— (1934), *Art as Experience* (New York: Minton, Balch).

——— (1938), *Logic: The Theory of Inquiry* (New York: Holt).

——— (1958), *Experience and Nature* (first published 1925) (New York: Dover Books).

——— and Bentley, Arthur F. (1949), *Knowing and the Known* (Boston: Beacon Press).

Diamond, Stanley (1963), "The Search for the Primitive," in *Man's Image in Medicine and Anthropology*, Iago Galdston (ed.) (New York: International Universities Press), pp. 62-115.

Du Bois, Cora (1961), *The People of Alor* (New York: Harper Torchbooks) (2 vols).

Dunham, H. W. (1959), *Sociological Theory and Mental Disorder* (Detroit: Wayne State University Press).

Eissler, K. R. (1952), "Ego-Psychological Implications of the Psychoanalytic Treatment of Delinquents, in *The Psychoanalytic Study of the Child*, Ruth S. Eissler, Anna Freud, Heinz Hartmann, and Ernst Kris (eds.), Vol. 5 (New York: International Universities Press), pp. 97-121.

Ellenberger, Henri F. (1958), "A Clinical Introduction to Psychiatric Phenomenology and Existential Analysis," in *Existence: A New Dimension in Psychiatry and Psychology*, Rollo May, Ernest Angel, and Henri F. Ellenberger (eds.) (New York: Basic Books), pp. 92-124.

Erikson, Erik H. (1950), *Childhood and Society* (New York: Norton).

——— (1956), "Growth and Crises of the 'Healthy Personality,'" in *Personality in Nature, Society and Culture*, Clyde Kluckhohn, Henry A. Murray, and David M. Schneider (eds.) (New York: Knopf).

Faris, R. E. L. (1944), "Reflections of Social Disorganization in the Behavior of a Schizophrenic Patient," *American Journal of Sociology*, Vol. 50 (September), pp. 134-141.

Federn, Paul (1952), *Ego Psychology and the Psychoses* (New York: Basic Books).

Fenichel, Otto (1945), *Psychoanalytic Theory of Neurosis* (New York: Norton).

Field, M. J. (1960), *Search for Security: An Ethno-Psychiatric Study of Rural Ghana* (Evanston: Northwestern University Press).

Fite, W. (1903), "The Place of Pleasure and Pain in the Functional Psychology," *Psychological Review*, Vol. 10, pp. 633-644.

Frank, Lawrence K. (1938-1939), "Time Perspectives," *Journal of Social Philosophy*, Vol. 4, pp. 293-312.

Freeman, G. L. (1948), *The Energetics of Human Behavior* (Ithaca: Cornell University Press).

Freeman, T., Cameron, J. L., and McGhie, A. (1958), *Chronic Schizophrenia* (New York: International Universities Press).

Freud, Anna (1952), "The Role of Bodily Illness in the Mental Life of Children," in *The Psychoanalytic Study of the Child*, Vol. 7 (New York: International Universities Press), pp. 69 ff.

Freud, Sigmund (1917), "Mourning and Melancholia," *Collected Papers*, Vol. 4 (London: Hogarth Press, 1946).

——— (1920), *A General Introduction to Psychoanalysis* (New York: Liveright).

Fromm, Erich (1941), *Escape From Freedom* (New York: Rinehart).

——— (1956), *The Art of Loving* (New York: Harper).

——— (1959), *Sigmund Freud's Mission* (New York: Harper).

Gantt, W. Horsley (1960), "Pavlov and Darwin," in *The Evolution of Man: Mind, Culture and Society*, Sol Tax (ed.) (Chicago: University of Chicago Press).

Gendlin, Eugene (1961), "Experiencing: A Variable in the Process of Therapeutic Change," *American Journal of Psychotherapy*, Vol. 15, pp. 233-245.

Gerth, Hans and Mills, C. Wright (1953), *Character and Social Structure: The Psychology of Social Institutions* (New York: Harcourt Brace).

Goethe, Johann Wolfgang von (1829), "Maxims and Reflections 504," in *Goethe, Wisdom and Experience*, selection by Ludwig Curtius (trans. and ed., Hermann J. Weigand) (London: Routledge and Kegan Paul, 1949).

Goffman, Erving (1953), "Communication Conduct in an Island Community," unpublished Ph.D. dissertation, University of Chicago.

——— (1961), *Encounters* (Indianapolis: Bobbs-Merrill).

Goldfarb, William (1961), *Childhood Schizophrenia* (Cambridge, Massachusetts: The Commonwealth Fund).

Goldstein, Kurt (1939), *The Organism* (New York: American Book Company).

——— (1951), *Human Nature in the Light of Psychopathology* (Cambridge: Harvard University Press).

Graves, Alonzo (1942), *The Eclipse of a Mind* (New York: Medical Journal Press).

Greenacre, Phyllis (ed.) (1953), *Affective Disorders* (New York: International Universities Press).

Greenson, Ralph (1954), "The Struggle Against Identification," *Journal of the American Psychoanalytic Association*, Vol. 2, pp. 200 ff.

Grinker, R. R. Sr., *et al.* (1961), *The Phenomena of Depressions* (New York: Hoeber).

Hall, Calvin S. and Lindzey, Gardner (1957), *Theories of Personality* (New York: Wiley).

Hallowell, A. Irving (1955), *Culture and Experience* (Philadelphia: University of Pennsylvania Press).

Harlow, H. F. (1958), "The Nature of Love," *American Psychologist*, Vol. 13, pp. 673-685.

Hayek, F. A. (1951), *John Stuart Mill and Harriet Taylor, Their Correspondence and Subsequent Marriage* (Chicago: University of Chicago Press).

Hayward, M. L. and Taylor, J. E. (1956), "A Schizophrenic Patient Describes the Action of Intensive Psychotherapy," *Psychiatric Quarterly*, Vol. 30, pp. 211-248.

Hebb, D. O. (1949), *The Organization of Behavior* (New York: Wiley).

—— (1955), "Drives and the C.N.S. (Conceptual Nervous System)," *Psychological Review*, Vol. 62, no. 4 (July), pp. 243-254.

—— (1958), "The Motivation Effects of Exteroceptive Stimulation," *American Psychologist*, Vol. 13, pp. 109-113.

Hegel, G. W. F. (1910), *The Phenomenology of Mind* (J. B. Baillie, trans. with Introduction and Notes) (London: Swan Sonnenschein), 2 vols.

Heider, Fritz (1958), *The Psychology of Interpersonal Relations* (New York: Wiley).

Helson, H. (ed.), (1951), *Theoretical Foundations of Psychology* (Princeton, New Jersey: D. Van Nostrand).

Herman, S. N. (1961), "Explorations in the Social Psychology of Language Choice," *Human Relations*, Vol. 14, no. 2, pp. 149-164.

Heron, Woodburn (1957), "The Pathology of Boredom," *Scientific American* (January) pp. 52-57.

Hillman, James (1960), *Emotion: A Comprehensive Phenomenology of Theories and Their Meanings for Therapy* (London: Routledge and Kegan Paul).

Hocart, A. M. (1952), *The Life-Giving Myth and Other Essays* (London: Methuen).

Hoch, P. H. and Zubin, J. (eds.) (1954), *Depression* (New York: Grune and Stratton).

Hollingshead, August B. (1961), "Some Issues in the Epidemiology of Schizophrenia," *American Sociological Review*, Vol. 26, no. 1 (February), pp. 5-13.

Hughes, C. C., *et al.* (1960), *People of Cove and Woodlot* (Volume 2 of the Stirling County Study) (New York: Basic Books).

Hughes, H. Stuart (1961), *Consciousness and Society* (New York: Vintage Books).

Ittelson, William H. and Kutash, Samuel B. (eds.) (1961), *Perceptual Changes in Psychopathology* (New Brunswick, New Jersey: Rutgers University Press).

James, William (1890), *A Textbook of Psychology* (New York: Henry Holt).

—— (1892), *Psychology, The Briefer Course* (New York: Henry Holt). (Harper Torchbook Edition, 1961, edited with an Introduction by Gordon Allport.)

Jessor, Richard (1959), "Phenomenological Personality Theories and the Data Language of Psychology," in *The Phenomenological Problem*, Alfred E. Kuenzli (ed.) (New York: Harper), pp. 280-293.

Kafka, Franz (1948), *The Trial* (New York: Knopf).

Kapp, K. William (1961), *Toward a Science of Man in Society: A Positive Approach to the Integration of Social Knowledge* (The Hague: Nijhoff).

Kasanin, J. (1932), "Pavlov's Theory of Schizophrenia," *Archives of Neurology and Psychiatry*, Vol. 28, pp. 210-218.

Kattsoff, Louis O. (1953), *The Design of Human Behavior* (St. Louis: Educational Publishers).

Kelly, George A. (1955), *The Psychology of Personal Constructs* (New York: Norton), 2 vols.

Kety, S. S. (1959), "Biochemical Theories of Schizophrenia," *Science*, Vol. 129, part 1 (May 22), pp. 1528-1532; part 2 (June 12), pp. 1590-1596.

Klaf, F. S. and Hamilton, J. G. (1961), "Schizophrenia—A Hundred Years Ago and Today," *Journal of Mental Science*, Vol. 107 (September), pp. 819-827.

Kluckhohn, Clyde (1962), *Culture and Behavior* (New York: The Free Press of Glencoe).

Kuckhohn, Florence (1950), "Dominant and Substitute Profiles of Cultural Orientations: Their Significance for the Analysis of Social Stratification," *Social Forces*, Vol. 28, pp. 376-393.

Knight, Everett (1960), *The Objective Society* (New York: Braziller).

Koffka, Kurt (1935), *Principles of Gestalt Psychology* (New York: Harcourt-Brace).

Kris, E. and Gombrich, E. (1938), "The Principles of Caricature," *British Journal of Medical Psychology*, Vol. 17, pp. 319-342.

Kubie, Lawrence S. (1961), "Theoretical Aspects of Sensory Deprivation," in *Sensory Deprivation*, Philip Solomon, *et al.* (eds.) (Cambridge, Massachusetts: Harvard University Press), pp. 208-220.

Laing, R. D. (1960), *The Divided Self. A Study of Sanity and Madness* (Chicago: Quadrangle Books).

———— "Mystification, Confusion and Conflict," (unpublished paper).

Langfeldt, Gabriel (1951), "The Hypersensitive Mind," *Acta Psychiatrica and Neurologica Scandinavica*, Supp. 73 (Copenhagen).

Lasswell, Harold D. (1962), *Power and Personality* (New York: Compass Books).

Lecky, Prescott (1945), *Self-Consistency* (New York: Island Press).

Lee, Dorothy (1948), "Are Basic Needs Ultimate?" *Journal of Abnormal and Social Psychology*, Vol. 43, pp. 391-395.

Leighton, A. H., *et al.* (1959), *My Name is Legion* (Volume 1 of the Stirling County Study) (New York: Basic Books).

Leighton, Dorothea C. and Kluckhohn, Clyde (1947), *Children of the People* (Cambridge: Harvard University Press).

Levi, Albert W. (1959), *Philosophy and the Modern World* (Bloomington, Indiana: Indiana University Press).

Lewes, G. H. (1853), *Comte's Philosophy of the Sciences* (London: Bell and Sons, 1897 edition).

Lewis, Aubrey (1961), "Current Field Studies in Mental Disorders in Britain," in *Comparative Epidemiology of Mental Disorders*, P. H. Hoch and J. Zubin (eds.) (New York: Grune and Stratton), pp. 207-234.

Lovejoy, Arthur O. (1961), *Reflections on Human Nature* (Baltimore: The John Hopkins Press).

Luchins, Abraham S. and Luchins, Edith H. (1959), *Rigidity of Behavior* (Eugene, Oregon: University of Oregon Press).

Lynd, Helen Merrell (1958), *On Shame and the Search for Identity* (New York: Harcourt-Brace).

Lynd, Robert S. (1939), *Knowledge for What?* (Princeton: Princeton University Press).

Macalpine, Ida and Hunter, Richard A. (1955) (trans., ed., with Introduction, Notes, and Discussion), *Daniel Paul Schreber: Memoirs of My Nervous Illness* (London: Dawson).

―――― (1956), *Schizophrenia in 1677* (London: Dawson).

McClelland, David C. (1956), "Personality: An Integrative View," in *Psychology of Personality, Six Approaches*, J. D. McCary (ed.) (New York: Logos Press), pp. 322-365.

McCord, William, Porta, Judith, and McCord, Joan (1962), "The Familial Genesis of Psychoses: A Study of the Childhood Backgrounds of Twelve Psychotics," *Psychiatry: Journal for the Study of Interpersonal Processes*, Vol. 25, no. 1 (February), pp. 60-71.

McDougall, William (1923), *Outline of Psychology* (New York: Scribner's).

―――― (1960), *An Introduction to Social Psychology* (London: Methuen).

McGill, V. J. (1941-1942), "Scheler's Theory of Sympathy and Love," *Philosophy and Phenomenological Research*, Vol. 2 (September-June), pp. 273-291.

―――― (1949), "A Psychological Approach to Personality," in *Philosophy for the Future*, R. W. Sellars, V. J. McGill, and M. Farber (eds.) (New York: Macmillan).

―――― (1956-1957), "Some Issues in Current Psychological Literature," *Philosophy and Phenomenological Research*, Vol. 17, pp. 89-104.

―――― and Welch, Livingston (1945-1946), "A Behaviorist Analysis of Emotions," *Philosophy of Science*, Vol. 12-13, pp. 100-122.

MacKinnon, D. W. (1954), "A Topological Analysis of Anxiety," in *The Study of Personality*, H. Brand (ed.) (New York: Wiley), pp. 135-147.

Macleod, Robert B. (1949), "Perceptual Constancy and the Problem of Motivation," *Canadian Journal of Psychology*, Vol. 3, no. 2 (June), pp. 57-66.

Malamud, William, Sands, S. L., and Malamud, Irene T. (1941), "The Involutional Psychoses: A Socio-Psychiatric Study," *Psychosomatic Medicine*, Vol. 3 (October), pp. 410-426.

Mannheim, Karl (1953), *Essays on Sociology and Social Psychology*, edited by Paul Kecskemeti (London: Routledge and Kegan Paul).

Maslow, Abraham H. (1954), *Motivation and Personality* (New York: Harper).

―――― (1961), "Existential Psychology—What's in it for Us?" in *Existential Psychology*, Rollo May (ed.) (New York: Random House), pp. 52-60.

―――― (1962), *Toward a Psychology of Being* (Princeton, New Jersey: Van Nostrand).

May, Rollo (1958), "Contributions of Existential Psychotherapy," in *Existence: A New Dimension in Psychiatry and Psychology*, Rollo May, Ernest Angel, and Henri F. Ellenberger (eds.) (New York: Basic Books), pp. 37-91.

Mead, George H. (1936), *Movements of Thought in the 19th Century* (Chicago: University of Chicago Press).

Meerloo, Joost A. M. (1954), *The Two Faces of Man: Two Studies on the Sense of Time and on Ambivalence* (New York: International Universities Press).

Mehlis, Georg (1961), "The Aesthetic Problem of Distance," in *Reflections on Art*, Susanne K. Langer (ed.) (New York: Galaxy Books), pp. 79-90.

Mendelson, Myer (1960), *Psychoanalytic Concepts of Depression* (Springfield, Illinois: C. C. Thomas).

Menninger, K. (1945), "Present Trends in Psychoanalytic Theory and Practice," in *Yearbook of Psychoanalysis*, S. Lorand (ed.), Vol. 1 (New York: International Universities Press), pp. 89-93.

Miller, Daniel R. (1961), "Personality and Social Interaction," in *Studying Personality Cross-Culturally*, Bert Kaplan (ed.) (Elmsford, New York: Row, Peterson), pp. 271-298.

Mills, C. Wright (1940), "Situated Actions and Vocabularies of Motive," *American Sociological Review*, Vol. 5, pp. 904-913.

Minkowski, Eugene (1929), "Jalousie Pathologique sur un Fond D'Automatisme Mental," *Ann. Med. Psychol.*, Vol. 87, part 2.

―――― (1958), "Findings in a Case of Schizophrenic Depression," in *Existence: A New Dimension in Psychiatry and Psychology*, Rollo May, Ernest Angel, and Henri F. Ellenberger (eds.) (New York: Basic Books), pp. 127-138.

Moulyn, Adrian C. (1947), "Mechanisms and Mental Phenomena," *Philosophy of Science*, Vol. 14, pp. 242-253.

———— (1952), "Reflections on the Problem of Time in Relation to Neurophysiology and Psychology," *Philosophy of Science*, Vol. 19, pp. 33-49.

Murphy, Gardner (1947), *Personality: A Bio-Social Approach to Origins and Structure* (New York: Harper).

Murray, Henry A. (1952), "Toward a Classification of Interactions," in *Toward a General Theory of Action*, T. Parsons and E. A. Shils (eds.) (Cambridge: Harvard University Press), pp. 434-464.

Northway, Mary L. (1939-1940), "The Concept of the 'Schema,'" *British Journal of Psychology*, Vol. 30, pp. 316-325.

Nuttin, Josef (1950), "Intimacy and Shame in the Dynamic Structure of Personality," in *Feelings and Emotions*, M. L. Reymert (ed.) (New York: McGraw-Hill), pp. 343-352.

Oldfield, R. C. and Zangwill, O. L. (1941-1942, 1942-1943), "Head's Concept of the Schema and its Application in Contemporary British Psychology," *British Journal of Psychology*, Vol. 32, part 1, pp. 267-286; Vol. 33, parts 2, 3, 4, pp. 58-64, 113-129, 143-149.

Orbach, Charles and Bieber, Irving (1957), "Depressive and Paranoid Reactions," *Archives of Neurology and Psychiatry*, Vol. 78, no. 3 (September), pp. 301-311.

Ovesey, Lionel (1955), "Pseudohomosexuality, the Paranoid Mechanism, and Paranoia," *Psychiatry*, Vol. 18, pp. 163-173.

Parker, Seymour (1962), "Eskimo Psychopathology in the Context of Eskimo Personality and Culture," *American Anthropologist*, Vol. 64 (February), pp. 76-96.

Parsons, Talcott and Bales, Robert F. (1955), *Family, Socialization and Interaction Process* (New York: The Free Press of Glencoe).

———— and Shils, Edward A. (eds.) (1952), *Toward a General Theory of Action* (Cambridge: Harvard University Press).

Pasch, Alan (1958), *Experience and the Analytic, a Reconsideration of Empiricism* (Chicago, Illinois: University of Chicago Press).

Pepper, Stephen C. (1955), *The Work of Art* (Bloomington: Indiana University Press).

Perry, Ralph Barton (1935), *The Thought and Character of William James* (Boston: Little, Brown), 2 vols.

Piaget, Jean (1932), *The Moral Judgment of the Child* (trans., Marjorie Gabain) (New York: The Free Press of Glencoe).

Pickford, R. W. (1950), "Aspects of the Psychology of Meaning," *Journal of Genetic Psychology*, Vol. 77, pp. 231-255.

Piers, Gerhard and Singer, Milton B. (1953), *Shame and Guilt* (Springfield, Illinois: C. C. Thomas).

Polanyi, Michael (1959), *The Study of Man* (Chicago: University of Chicago Press).

Prange, Arthur J. Jr. and Vitols, M. M. (1962), "Cultural Aspects of the Relatively Low Incidence of Depression in Southern Negroes," *International Journal of Social Psychiatry*, Vol. 8, no. 2 (Spring), pp. 104-112.

Radin, Paul (1957), *Primitive Religion* (New York: Dover Books).

Rado, Sandor (1951), "Psychodynamics of Depression from the Etiologic Point of View," *Psychosomatic Medicine*, Vol. 13, pp. 51-55.

———— (1961), "The Automatic Motivation System of Depressive Behavior," *Comprehensive Psychiatry* (October), pp. 248-260.

Ribot, Théodule (1895), *The Diseases of Personality*, 2nd revised edition (Chicago: Open Court Publishing Co.).

Riezler, Kurt (1942-1943), "Comment on the Social Psychology of Shame," *American Journal of Sociology*, Vol. 48, pp. 457-465.

———— (1960), "The Social Psychology of Fear," in *Identity and Anxiety: Survival of the Person in Mass Society*, Maurice R. Stein, Arthur J. Vidich and David M. White (eds.) (New York: The Free Press of Glencoe), pp. 144-157.

Rioch, David McK. (1959), "Problems of 'Perception' and 'Communication' in Mental Illness," *Archives of General Psychiatry*, Vol. 1, no. 1 (July), pp. 81-92.

Robbins, Bernard S. (1955), "The Myth of Latent Emotion," *Psychotherapy*, Vol. 1, pp. 3-29.

———— (1957), "Schizophrenic Consciousness and Practice," in *Schizophrenia in Psychoanalytic Office Practice*, Alfred H. Rifkin (ed.) (New York: Grune and Stratton), pp. 17-21 (discussion, pp. 22-29).

Rodnick, H. and Garmezy, N. (1957), "An Experimental Approach to the Study of Motivation in Schizophrenia," in *Nebraska Symposium on Motivation*, M. R. Jones (ed.) (Lincoln: University of Nebraska Press), pp. 109-184.

Rogers, Carl R. (1951), *Client-Centered Therapy* (Boston: Houghton-Mifflin).

———— (1959), "A Theory of Therapy, Personality and Interpersonal Relationships, as Developed in the Client-Centered Framework," in *Psychology: A Study of a Science*, Sigmund Koch (ed.), Vol. 3 (New York: McGraw-Hill), pp. 184-256.

———— (1962), "Toward Becoming a Fully Functioning Person," in *Perceiving, Behaving, Becoming: A New Focus for Education*, Arthur W. Combs (ed.) (Washington, D. C.: Association for Supervision and Curriculum Development, National Education Association), Chap. 3.

Rogler, Lloyd H. and Hollingshead, August B. (1961), "Class and Disordered Speech in the Mentally Ill," *Journal of Health and Human Behavior*, Vol. 2 (Fall), pp. 178-185.

Rose, Arnold M. (1962), "A Social-Psychological Theory of Neurosis," in *Human Behavior and Social Process: An Interactionist Approach*, A. M. Rose (ed.) (Boston: Houghton-Mifflin), pp. 537-549.

Rosenbaum, G., MacKavey, W. R., and Grisell, J. S. (1957), "Effects of Biological and Social Motivation on Schizophrenic Reaction Time," *Journal of Abnormal and Social Psychology*, Vol. 54, pp. 364-368.

Rosenzweig, Norman (1959-1960), "Sensory Deprivation and Schizophrenia: Some Clinical and Theoretical Similarities," *American Journal of Psychiatry*, Vol. 116, pp. 326-329.

Ruesch, Jurgen (1948), "The Infantile Personality: The Core Problem of Psychosomatic Medicine," *Psychosomatic Medicine*, Vol. 10, pp. 134-144.

Russell, Bertrand (1960), *A History of Western Philosophy* (New York: Simon and Schuster).

Russell, Claire and Russell, W. M. S. (1961), *Human Behavior: A New Approach* (Boston: Little, Brown).

Ryle, Gilbert (1949), *The Concept of Mind* (London: Hutchinson).

Salzman, Leon (1961), "Guilt, Responsibility and the Unconscious," *Comprehensive Psychiatry*, Vol. 2, no. 4 (August), pp. 179-187.

Sartre, Jean-Paul (1948), *The Emotions: Outline of a Theory* (New York: Philosophical Library).

——— (1953), *Existential Psychoanalysis*, Introduction by Hazel E. Barnes (New York: Philosophical Library).

——— (1956), *Being and Nothingness: An Essay On Phenomenological Ontology*, (trans., Hazel E. Barnes) (New York: Philosophical Library).

——— (1961), *The Psychology of Imagination* (New York: The Citadel Press).

Schachtel, Ernest (1959), *Metamorphosis* (New York: Basic Books).

Scheler, Max (1954), *The Nature of Sympathy*, translated by Peter Heath, with an Introduction by Werner Stark (London· Routledge and Kegan Paul).

Schilder, Paul (1936), "Psychopathology of Time," *Journal of Nervous and Mental Disease*, Vol. 83, pp. 530-546.

——— (1942), *Mind: Perception and Thought in Their Constructive Aspects* (New York: Columbia University Press).

Schiller, Friedrich (1954), *On the Aesthetic Education of Man* (first published 1795) (Reginald Snell, trans. with Introduction) (London: Routledge and Kegan Paul).

Schmideberg, Melitta (1956), "Multiple Origins and Functions of Guilt," *Psychiatric Quarterly*, Vol. 30, pp. 471-477.

Schneirla, T. C. and Rosenblatt, J. S. (1961), "Behavioral Organization and Genesis of the Social Bond in Insects and Mammals," *American Journal of Orthopsychiatry*, Vol. 31, no. 2 (April), pp. 223-253.

Schwartz, D. A. (1961), "The Agitated Depression," *Psychiatric Quarterly*, Vol. 34, no. 4 (October), pp. 758-776.

Searles, Harold F. (1956), "The Psychodynamics of Vengefulness," *Psychiatry*, Vol. 19, pp. 31-39.

——— (1961a), "Anxiety Concerning Change, as Seen in Psychotherapy of Schizophrenic Patients—With Particular Reference to the Sense of Personal Identity," *International Journal of Psychoanalysis*, Vol. 42, pp. 74-85.

——— (1961b), "Schizophrenia and the Inevitability of Death," *Psychiatric Quarterly*, Vol. 35, no. 4, pp. 631-665.

Sechehaye, Marguerite A. (ed.) (1951), *Autobiography of a Schizophrenic Girl* (New York: Grune and Stratton).

Shakow, David (1962), "Segmental Set: A Theory of the Formal Psychological Deficit in Schizophrenia," *Archives of General Psychiatry*, Vol. 6, no. 1 (January), pp. 1-17.

Shand, Alexander F. (1920), *The Foundations of Character* (London: Macmillan), 2nd edition.

Sheldon, W. H. (1950), "The Absolute Truth of Hedonism," *Journal of Philosophy*, Vol. 47, pp. 285-304.

Shepherd, Michael (1961), "Morbid Jealousy: Some Clinical and Social Aspects of a Psychiatric Syndrome," *Journal of Mental Science*, Vol. 107, no. 449 (July), pp. 687-704.

Sherrington, Sir Charles (1955), *Man on His Nature* (Garden City, New York: Doubleday Anchor Books).

Shibutani, Tamotsu (1961), *Society and Personality* (Englewood Cliffs, New Jersey: Prentice-Hall).

Slotkin, J. S. (1942), "The Nature and Effects of Social Interaction in Schizophrenia," *Journal of Abnormal and Social Psychology*, Vol. 37 (June), pp. 345-368.

Snygg, Donald and Combs, Arthur W. (1949), *Individual Behavior* (New York: Harper).

Solomon, Philip, et al. (eds.) (1961), *Sensory Deprivation* (Cambridge, Massachusetts: Harvard University Press).

Sperry, R. W. (1952), "Neurology and the Mind-Brain Problem," *American Scientist*, Vol. 40, no. 2 (April), pp. 291-312.

Spiegel, Leo A. (1959), "The Self, The Sense of Self, and Perception," in *The Psychoanalytic Study of the Child*, Vol. 14 (New York: International Universities Press), pp. 81-109.

Spiro, Melford E. (1961), "Social Systems, Personality, and Functional Analysis," in *Studying Personality Cross-Culturally*, Bert Kaplan (ed.) (Elmsford, New York: Row, Peterson), Chap. 2.

Stagner, Ross (1951), "Homeostasis as a Unifying Concept in Personality Theory," *Psychological Review*, Vol. 58, pp. 5-18.

Stanton, Alfred H. and Schwartz, Morris S. (1954), *The Mental Hospital* (New York: Basic Books).

Storr, Anthony (1961), *The Integrity of the Personality* (New York: Atheneum).

Straus, Erwin W. (1962), "On Memory Traces," *Tijdschrift voor Filosofie*, Vol. 24, no. 1 (March), pp. 1-32.

Strauss, Anselm (1959), *Mirrors and Masks, The Search for Identity* (New York: The Free Press of Glencoe).

Strawson, P. F. (1959), *Individuals: An Essay in Descriptive Metaphysics* (London: Methuen).

Stuntz, Edgar C. (1959), "The Beard as an Expression of Bodily Feelings in a Schizophrenic," *Psychosomatic Medicine*, Vol. 21, pp. 28-33.

Sullivan, Harry Stack (1956), *Clinical Studies in Psychiatry* (New York: Norton).

Szasz, Thomas S. (1957a), "A Contribution to the Psychology of Schizophrenia," *Archives of Neurology and Psychiatry*, Vol. 77 (April), pp. 420-436.

―――― (1957b), *Pain and Pleasure* (New York: Basic Books).

―――― (1960), "The Ethics of Birth Control," *The Humanist*, Vol. 20, no. 6 pp. 332-336.

―――― (1961), *The Myth of Mental Illness: Foundations of a Theory of Personal Conduct* (New York: Hoeber-Harper).

Tiggelaar, J. (1956), "Pathological Jealousy and Jealousy Delusions," *Fol. Psychiatr. Neerl.*, Vol. 59, pp. 522-541.

Tillich, Paul (1944), "Existential Philosophy," *Journal of the History of Ideas*, Vol. 5, no. 1, pp. 44-70.

Tiryakian, Edward A. (1962), *Sociologism and Existentialism: Two Perspectives on the Individual and Society* (Englewood Cliffs, New Jersey: Prentice-Hall).

Toch, Hans H. and Hastorf, Albert H. (1955), "Homeostasis in Psychology, A Review and Critique," *Psychiatry*, Vol. 18, pp. 81-91.

van den Berg, J. H. (1955), *The Phenomenological Approach to Psychiatry: An Introduction to Recent Phenomenological Psychopathology* (Springfield, Illinois: C. C. Thomas).

―――― (1962), "The Human Body and the Significance of Human Movement," in *Psychoanalysis and Existential Philosophy*, Hendrik M. Ruitenbeek (ed.) (New York: Dutton), pp. 90-129.

Veblen, Thorstein (1932), "Some Neglected Points in the Theory of Socialism," *The Place of Science in Modern Civilization and Other Essays* (New York: Viking Press).

Volkart, Edmund (1957), "Bereavement and Mental Health," in *Explorations in Social Psychiatry*, A. H. Leighton, J. A. Clausen, and R. N. Wilson (eds.) (New York: Basic Books), pp. 281-307.

von Bertalanffy, Ludwig (1952), *Problems of Life* (New York: Wiley).

von Uexküll, Jacob (1957), "A Stroll Through the Worlds of Animals and Men; A Picture Book of Invisible Worlds," in *Instinctive Behavior* (C. H. Schiller ed. and trans.) (New York: International Universities Press), Part 1.

White, Winston (1961), *Beyond Conformity* (New York: The Free Press of Glencoe).

Wild, John (1959-1960), "Contemporary Phenomenology and the Problem of Existence," *Philosophy and Phenomenological Research*, Vol. 20 (September-June), pp. 166-180.

Williams, Gardner (1950), "Hedonism, Conflict, and Cruelty," *Journal of Philosophy*, Vol. 47, pp. 649-656.

Williams, Richard H. (1941-1942), "Scheler's Contributions to the Sociology of Affective Action with Special Attention to the Problem of Shame," *Philosophy and Phenomenological Research*, Vol. 2, pp. 349-358.

Wolters, A. W. (1933-1934), "On Conceptual Thinking," *British Journal of Psychology*, Vol. 24, pp. 133-143.

Zilboorg, Gregory (1953), "The Emotional Problem and the Therapeutic Role of Insight," in *Yearbook of Psychoanalysis*, Vol. 9 (New York: International Universities Press), pp. 199-219.

Author Index

271

Subject Index

274